Northwestern University

STUDIES IN *Phenomenology &*

Existential Philosophy

GENERAL EDITOR
John Wild

ASSOCIATE EDITOR
James M. Edie

CONSULTING EDITORS
Hubert L. Dreyfus
William Earle
Dagfinn Føllesdal
Aron Gurwitsch
Emmanuel Levinás
Alphonso Lingis
Maurice Natanson
Paul Ricoeur
George Schrader
Calvin O. Schrag
Herbert Spiegelberg
Charles Taylor

Hermeneutic
Phenomenology

Don Ihde

Foreword by Paul Ricoeur

Hermeneutic
Phenomenology
The Philosophy
of Paul Ricoeur

Northwestern University Press

Evanston   1 9 7 1

Copyright © 1971 by Northwestern University Press
Library of Congress Catalog Card Number: 71–138922
Printed in the United States of America
All rights reserved
ISBN 0–8101–0347–8

Don Ihde is associate professor of philosophy at the
State University of New York at Stony Brook.

Material from the following books has been
quoted with the permission of the publishers:
Paul Ricoeur, *The Symbolism of Evil,* trans.
Emerson Buchanan, Harper & Row, New York,
1967. Paul Ricoeur, *Freud and Philosophy: An
Essay on Interpretation,* trans. Denis Savage,
Yale University Press, New Haven, Conn., 1970.

For Carolyn

Contents

Foreword

IT IS WITH GRATITUDE that I have accepted the invitation to write a short foreword for the work which Don Ihde has devoted to my writings, for it gives me an opportunity to say how highly I regard his presentation. He does not limit himself to describing and summarizing works which appeared in the course of more than twenty years; he tests the unity of my work and the consistency of the methods I have used. In this undertaking he proves himself both vigorously exacting and deeply sympathetic. I feel even more indebted to him for the first of these qualities than for the second.

It is indeed a formidable test for an author to be placed under an inquiry of this type; each of his books has answered limited questions and has responded to different situations and challenges. Suddenly they are placed under a single perspective which encompasses them as a whole. A new question is addressed to them: What are they saying, not only separately, but all together? Do they say something which is, if not unique, at least consistent?

In this regard I am grateful to Don Ihde for having respected both the evident change of perspective and the underlying continuity between, on the one hand, the eidetic or structural phenomenology of *Freedom and Nature* and, on the other hand, the hermeneutic phenomenology of my latest works.

The change of perspective is clear. To begin with, it is the result of a difference of times and a shifting of philosophical "fronts." Earlier I situated myself in relation to Sartre and Merleau-Ponty, and I sought to integrate the influences of Gabriel Marcel and of Jaspers to that of Husserl. I further had to face the human sciences, represented principally by psychology. I next felt the need to root myself again in the soil of traditional philosophy, principally the reflective tradition. That was the period of *Fallible Man,* when I confronted classical philosophy rather than the human sciences. Today the philosophical landscape has changed: the semiological sciences have taken the place of the natural sciences in the confrontation of philosophy with its other. What is more, the "end of metaphysics" is being proclaimed by the thinkers of the Hegelian left and even more by those inspired by Nietzsche. The task of recovering meaning can no longer, then, be separated from that of evaluating the hermeneutics of suspicion. So in an initial sense—still external, to be sure—it is the difference in landscape which determines the difference of problematics.

But more important internal reasons, perfectly perceived by Don Ihde, also determine the shift in perspective. At first I was absorbed by the question: What is will? I took it as equivalent to the question undertaken by Merleau-Ponty: What is perception? It was thus that the relation voluntary-involuntary became the center of gravity for all other questions. Today the relationship between speech and action (or saying-doing) seems to me to be more encompassing. The question of language is thus no longer simply a milieu in which a discourse on action can be articulated; it is a mode of being, a pole of existence as fundamental as action itself. A new equilibrium between saying and doing must be sought, but it has not yet been found. It will give the future "Poetics of the Will" an entirely different aspect from the one which was initially foreseen.

It is through this displacement of problematics that Don Ihde has sought a continuity once again combining generosity with a suspicious vigilance.

He justifies this continuity first by all the anticipations of hermeneutic phenomenology which he discovers in *Freedom and Nature* and *Fallible Man.*

He finds an anticipation of hermeneutic method in the use made, in *Freedom and Nature,* of the "diagnostic" relation between the human sciences on the one hand and phenomenology on the other. I admit today that he is even more correct because, reflecting on the conditions of a discourse on action, I have become very attentive to the contribution of ordinary language analysis, emanating from Wittgenstein, Austin, and Strawson, for the philosophy of action. I would now be inclined to return to the theme of the "diagnostic" of phenomenological experience in relation to objective data with the resources of an analysis that is both linguistic and phenomenological. The conjunction would be as beneficial for linguistic analysis as for phenomenological analysis: the latter would be guarded against the danger of immediacy, the former from the absence of a transcendental justification. A single example will illustrate this: The debate between cause and motive and its importance during recent years in the linguistic analytic school is familiar. A better correlation between the analysis of ordinary language, the description of lived experience [*vécu*], and the data of scientific observation would, without a doubt, permit this problem to be pulled out of the impasse in which it is imprisoned by a theory of language games lacking sufficient phenomenological support.

Don Ihde sees a second index of continuity between the structural phenomenology of the earlier works and the hermeneutic phenomenology of recent writings in my permanent mistrust of the pretensions of the subject in posing itself as the foundation of its own meaning. The reflective philosophy to which I appeal is at the outset opposed to any philosophy of the Cartesian type based on the transparency of the ego to itself, and to all philosophy of the Fichtean type based on the self-positing of that ego. Today this mistrust is reinforced by the conviction that the understanding of the self is always indirect and proceeds from the interpretation of signs given outside me in culture and history and from the appropriation of the meaning of these signs. I would now dare to say that, in the coming to understanding of signs inscribed in texts, the meaning rules and gives me a self. In short, the self of self-understanding is a gift of understanding itself and of the invitation from the meaning inscribed in the text. Don Ihde has well seen that this dispossession of immediacy, of which the extreme form is the reading of texts, is already sketched in what I formerly called the transcendental "naïveté," which superseded the naturalistic "naïveté." I called for a second "Copernican revolution" which would deliver me from the second "naïveté." I understand better today that if this second Copernican revolution must be the result of a "Poetics of the Will," it must begin with the discovery that this poetics is first of all an understood and appropriated mythic word and that meaning comes to the ego through the power of the word.

Consequently, everything in my first writings which points to an indirect interpretation, applied first to the indices of external objectivities, anticipates the subsequent role of the text as the place for the decentering and dispossession of immediacy. The idea of a reading of signs, as Don Ihde detects very early (for example in the interpretation of birth in *Freedom and Nature*), is found to be the most fundamental anticipation of a hermeneutic rule for phenomenology.

I would even permit myself to note, in this context, that the hermeneutics which is anticipated is latently broader than that which was actually expressed in *The Symbolism of Evil* and *Freud and Philosophy*, where the idea of interpretation is still posed in a limited sense—too limited, I would say today—insofar as it is bound to the notion of symbol, of double meaning. If one takes the widest notion of a text as a guide on the hermeneutic level, instead of simply the notion of the signification of a double meaning, then one can say that the "dialectic of the diagnostic" directly anticipates this hermeneutics of a text—which is to say hermeneutics in the broad sense.

It is in relation to this strategy of the whole that Don Ihde interprets *Fallible Man*. Certainly the extremely Kantian tone of this work does not appear to be favorable for a hermeneutic reflection. Yet the place held by the idea of limit (and of limit concept) has some relevance for the forging of a hermeneutic phenomenology. First, the "disproportion" at the heart of human reality and the avoidance of the "third term," both of which serve as the leitmotiv for three chapters of this book, belong to the same enterprise of self-criticism of Husserlian phenomenology as does the end of *Freedom and Nature*. In both places I recognized the impotence of the Cogito to posit its own foundation and to be self-contained. The deciphering of signs is the counterpart of the limits of self-knowledge. In this sense I would say today that all hermeneutics are Kantian to the degree that the powerlessness of self-knowledge is the negative counterpart of the necessity to decipher signs given in me and outside me. It is the limited character of self-knowledge which imposes the indirect strategy of interpretation.

In relation to this general thesis, the theory of symbol, and the application made of it in *The Symbolism of Evil*, clearly appears to be a very partial realization of this project. It gives the impression that there is only a hermeneutics of symbols. I readily grant today that the interpretation of symbols is not the whole of hermeneutics, but I continue to hold that it is the condensation point and, if I may say so, the place of greatest density, because it is in the symbol that language is revealed in its strongest force and with its greatest fullness. It says something independently of me, and it says more than I can understand. The symbol is surely the privileged place of the experience of the surplus of meaning. That is why that which is gained from a limited example—from symbols, or, more precisely, from the symbols of evil—has direct universal value: First, the signs with which hermeneutic phenomenology struggles are given by the entire culture and not simply by the psychological nature of man. Second, the symbols invite an interpretation, as can be seen in myth, which is already a symbolism of the second degree with an explicative pretension. Finally, the "self" which is the intended goal of interpretation is not the narrow and narcissistic "I" of immediate consciousness but is the subject founded by understanding itself.

It is thus that a general theory of text is anticipated which will be at the heart of the "Poetics of the Will."

Lastly, Don Ihde has well demonstrated that the "conflict of hermeneutics," illustrated by the battle between the hermeneutics of suspicion of the Freudian type and the restoration of symbols, is a possibility inscribed at the beginning of phenomenology insofar as it is always in conflict with another naïveté in addition to its own naïveté. A critical project is thus inevitably bound to the poetic project.

I am grateful to Don Ihde for having given me the courage to continue by indicating the vectors which call for further development.

PAUL RICOEUR

Preface

Two PURPOSES are served in this book. The first is to provide an overdue introduction to the philosophy of Paul Ricoeur. The translation of his books and many of his articles has stimulated interest in this philosopher who has already achieved major stature in Europe. But I wish to address myself not so much to the content of Ricoeur's work as to the development and intricacies of his methods, which are admittedly often puzzling due to the indirect paths he takes toward his goals.

Secondly, in the light of the vast interest in the problems of language in this country, and more recently in France, Ricoeur evokes a special interest. His turn to the problems of language results in a distinctive *hermeneutic phenomenology* which gives and promises to give new perspectives to the philosophy of language. This linguistically oriented phenomenology arises not only from the suite of problems posed by language but also from the dialectical way in which Ricoeur addresses himself to often opposing methods. Ricoeur succeeds in keeping the door open to the genuine knowledge often offered by "objectivist" sciences and the philosophies often dismissed by other phenomenological thinkers.

I realize that scholarly hazards are posed by taking up an interpretation of a philosopher so clearly in the middle of his career. And the proliferation of books on Sartre and Heidegger offers only mild encouragement. But corrections or supplements to this interpretation are warmly welcomed. It has been necessary to underplay the current of religious questions and concerns which make Ricoeur important on the theological front as well as in philosophy. I have focused on the main line of the development of hermeneutic phenomenology. Hopefully, however, there will be compensation if the theme of method and language emerges in brevity and clarity.

There is one matter of procedure which will also be open to question: the question of translations. Ricoeur, perhaps more than others, has suffered the fate of multiple translators—there have been, for example, a different translator and publisher for each of the three parts of the *Philosophy of the Will!* Obviously this means that terms will often be translated differently from book to book and from article to article. Yet I have chosen to utilize extant translations wherever possible rather than add to the muddle already existing. I attempt in footnotes to settle the largest particles to the bottom, and elsewhere the context should make the issue clear.

Finally, I wish to acknowledge the debts which have made this book possible. To the Franco-American Commission (Fulbright) for a research fellowship and to Southern Illinois University for summer research grants which made possible a year in France, 1967–68, I offer my thanks. To Paul Ricoeur I am especially grateful for his gentlemanly, open, and hospitable help, particularly for the supererogatory act which allowed me access to his study. I am also indebted to André Schuwer for a long discussion on Ricoeur interpretation and to Denis Savage, Charles Kelbley, James Edie, and Herbert Spiegelberg for criticisms and clues. And to John Lavely and Erazim Kohák, who some years ago guided me through my first study on Ricoeur, I give credit for much of the present work. Finally, to my wife for her patience and support I also owe a cheerful debt.

D. I.

List of Abbreviations

Full citations for the following works by Ricoeur will be found in the bibliography.

FM	*Fallible Man*
FN	*Freedom and Nature*
HT	*History and Truth*
INT	*Freud and Philosophy: An Essay on Interpretation*
SE	*The Symbolism of Evil*

Hermeneutic
Phenomenology

1 / Introduction

INTERPRETERS OF PHENOMENOLOGY frequently distinguish between two related but distinct developments of that philosophy. At its inception phenomenology may be seen to stand in the long tradition of Continental thought which gives primacy to questions concerning the thinking subject and which runs at least from Descartes through Kant and Hegel. Edmund Husserl's *transcendental* phenomenology in its most extreme form, "transcendental idealism," continues this emphasis with a series of concepts such as "egology," "intentionality," and "structures of consciousness." The thinking subject retains centrality.

Later, and most particularly in France, Husserlian methods were adapted by philosophers whose main interests were directed to the whole of concrete human existence. The paradigmatic problem of the body, seen in Gabriel Marcel's idea of "incarnate existence" and extended in the highly developed theories of Maurice Merleau-Ponty's "lived body" (*corps vécu*), utilized in varying degrees a phenomenology become *existential*.

There remain with both Husserlian and existential versions of phenomenology a unique emphasis upon the concrete experience of the subject and an epistemology closely linked to a philosophy of perception.[1] Husserl's demand that the philosopher turn "to the things themselves" became in substance the elaboration of a theory of evidence which weights perception over abstract theory construction. Later, Merleau-Ponty's "primacy" of

---

1. I shall use the term *perception* in a broad sense. Ricoeur often calls it a "theory of representation," which would include both perceptual and imaginative functions.

perception elaborated a phenomenological theory of perception as the basis for the whole range of human activity. In this sense both Husserlian and existential phenomenologies are "perceptualist" philosophies.

Today there has appeared upon the horizon yet another French thinker who begins by calling into question some important aspects of both extant versions of phenomenology and who seeks to formulate a third direction, a *hermeneutic* phenomenology.[2] Paul Ricoeur, by raising in a specific way the issue of language, opens the way for a questioning of the perceptualist emphasis by moving phenomenology toward a linguistic focus. Ricoeur's divergence may be located in a preliminary way through his indirect criticisms of existential phenomenology and his direct criticisms of Husserlian phenomenology.

While all phenomenologists give credit in varying degrees to the pioneer work of Husserl, it was perhaps Merleau-Ponty's interpretation of Husserl which served to set the pattern for the existential version of phenomenology. For Merleau-Ponty it was the "late" Husserl who was of most interest, particularly in the elaboration of the notion of the *Lebenswelt*. In effect Merleau-Ponty saw in this concept the possibility for elaborating a series of existential significations out of the world of perceptual experience itself. This interpretation made Husserl the anticipator of an existential phenomenology.

Ricoeur, in contrast, argues that:

> The fruitfulness of the noetico-noematic analysis of the period of the *Ideas* has probably been underestimated by the generation of phenomenologists which went immediately to the writings of the period of the *Crisis*. That school of phenomenologists has sought inspiration in a theory of the *Lebenswelt* for a description which is

2. I am not unaware of the fact that Martin Heidegger formulated what might be called a hermeneutic phenomenology even prior to Ricoeur. In some ways Heidegger's hermeneutics may be more radical than Ricoeur's. But I believe the strength of Ricoeur's approach lies in an area which is always indirect in the Heideggerian context. Ricoeur confronts directly and more thoroughly the various countermethods of linguistics, linguistic analysis, and other forms of contemporary language theory. And if in this process Ricoeur finds himself more openly influenced by the countermethod, he also is able to express himself in a way which allows a debate, with some mutual understanding, between Anglo-American and European philosophies.

too quickly synthetic for my liking. . . . In the early stages at least, phenomenology must be structural.[3]

On the surface this might appear to be merely the assertion of preference for the "middle" Husserl over the "late" Husserl. This point is partly supportable if the lack of extensive references to the *Crisis* in Ricoeur's own publications is noted.

But while it is true that Ricoeur emphasizes the transcendental aspects of Husserl's phenomenology and claims that insofar as phenomenology is phenomenology at all it must be transcendental,[4] the argument is made on behalf of his own program which develops in a different direction. This is evidenced in the more direct attacks he makes upon the "transcendental idealism" of Husserl. "Has the doctrine of transcendental idealism value only within the limits of a theory of representation, of the spectator consciousness?"[5]

This general question, answered affirmatively in Ricoeur's concepts, raises a question for the general models of phenomenology. It ultimately can be directed at the perceptualist basis which weights phenomenology in one direction. To this weighting Ricoeur applies a series of limits—but within a retained preference for a phenomenological starting point. On one side Ricoeur wishes to extend or stretch phenomenology, "even in the course of the blood stream."[6] But on the other side there is to be a progressive application of limits, generally symbolized by what Ricoeur characterizes as *Kantian* limit concepts. This means from the beginning that phenomenology does not carry the significance of universal method for Ricoeur that it did for Husserl.

If Ricoeur's phenomenology is to be bound by a set of limits in which countermethods cannot be totally subsumed into a monistic approach, the result is one of a *dialectic* of methods. Out of a sympathetic and careful reading of counterpositions there is to be found in Ricoeur's thought a constantly reappearing

3. Paul Ricoeur, *Husserl: An Analysis of His Phenomenology*, trans. Edward G. Ballard and Lester E. Embree (Evanston, Ill.: Northwestern University Press, 1967), pp. 214–15. (Hereafter cited as *Husserl*.) Whenever possible references are taken from existing English translations of Ricoeur's writings.

4. *Ibid.*, p. 203. Cf. "New Developments in Phenomenology in France: The Phenomenology of Language," *Social Research*, XXXIV, no. 1 (Spring, 1967), 3.

5. *Husserl*, p. 221.

6. *Ibid.*, p. 216.

inquiry into "naturalist" or objectivist methods. Missing are the often stringently negative responses to empiricism or scientifically oriented positions found in the critiques of Jean-Paul Sartre and Merleau-Ponty. Ricoeur's reading, from behaviorism to biology, displays an almost "Hegelian" appetite for that suggestive idea which may inform the central direction of *reflective philosophy*. In the encounter and re-evaluation of objectivist theories Ricoeur claims that "A good implicit phenomenology is often concealed in the most objectivistic sciences and sometimes comes to the fore through the 'naturalistic' concepts of psychology." [7]

If phenomenology is internally limited by its central model and externally limited by other methods, it nevertheless remains basic to Ricoeur's development. The "hermeneutic turn" remains within the tradition which is concerned with the concrete human subject of phenomenological inquiry. The "Socratic" question of self-knowledge underlies Ricoeur's inquiries, and much of his work to date is broadly a philosophical anthropology. The way in which this "hermeneutic turn" emerges and reorients phenomenology toward language is a key to Ricoeur's development in a "hermeneutic philosophy of existence" [8] and to wider implications for phenomenology generally.

Hermeneutics, however, is not a well-defined field. In its broadest sense hermeneutics means interpretation and generally suggests the idea of a text as that which is interpreted—but there is no unified or agreed upon criteria for interpretation. Even in its historical uses the broadness of its meanings are suggestive. Aristotle's *Peri Hermeneias* is "interpretation" as logic; Plato's *technē hermeneia* is an art of making obscure expressions clear; and classical biblical exegesis was the elaboration of four levels of meaning to be found in a sacred text. Ricoeur utilizes all these meanings in varying ways, but the question of interpretation is precisely that which must be worked out in an understanding of Ricoeur's philosophy.

What can be said at the outset by way of generalization is that Ricoeur's application of phenomenology to language or his transformation of phenomenology into hermeneutics finds its justification in a need to elaborate concepts *indirectly* and *dialectically*

---

7. *Ibid.*, p. 219.
8. "A Conversation," *The Bulletin of Philosophy*, I, no. 1 (January, 1966), 2. This terminology begins to appear from about 1965 on.

rather than directly and univocally. Out of the whole range of possible expressions and out of a wide range of linguistic "sciences," Ricoeur chooses to address himself to a certain set of symbolic expressions (and myths) by which man may better understand himself. This indirect route via symbol and through interpretation constitutes the opening to a hermeneutic phenomenology.

For Ricoeur it is impossible that man may know himself directly or introspectively. It is only by a series of detours that he learns about the fullness and complexity of his own being and of his relationship to Being. This emphasis upon indirectness pervades the whole of Ricoeur's methodology from the early structural phenomenology to the more recent hermeneutic phenomenology. In its structural form, phenomenology is indirect insofar as it arrives at the eidetic structures of consciousness by a reflective procedure. Hermeneutics refocuses this indirectness by developing a parallel set of reflections upon the expressions of equivocal symbols. It is here that the major thesis which animates this exposition may be entered: *If existential phenomenology broke the bounds of Husserl's transcendental idealism in its application of phenomenological procedures to the problems of the lived body, intersubjectivity, and human freedom, Ricoeur's phenomenology opens the way for a second breaking of the bounds under the sign of hermeneutics. Ricoeur begins the shift from a perceptualist phenomenological model to a linguistic phenomenology.*

With the indirectness required in the "reading" of symbols, a level of application for a phenomenologically based philosophy is reached which has as its unique problem questions regarding the philosophy of culture and history. In a sense this, too, is a return to an aspect of the *Lebenswelt* insofar as that world is a world of language—but it is a return which takes the indirect route of interpretation.

Indirectness as a vehicle attempts to avoid some of the problems which a philosophy of subjectivity can easily fall into in the temptation of consciousness to be self-deceived. The fascination with subjective certainty can be as deceptive as the fascination with the world of the object found in prephenomenological philosophies. If, as Ricoeur argues, the "first Copernican revolution" in philosophy was the turn to the subject made by transcendental philosophy, there is an equal need to create a "second Copernican revolution" which breaks the bonds the subject makes with itself. But the question is how to do this without returning to the naïve objectivism which transcendental philosophy overthrows. It is this path which Ricoeur attempts to follow.

BACKGROUND TO RICOEUR'S PHILOSOPHY

IT IS EASY to become too involved in an intellectual biography; thus a capsule survey of what Ricoeur admits in his philosophical confession will serve to set the stage for the analysis to follow.

1. Credit for one major influence on Ricoeur goes to Gabriel Marcel, his professor from 1935 through the graduate years. Ricoeur's first individually published book was *Gabriel Marcel and Karl Jaspers*, and early articles openly reflect some of Marcel's questions. Of these, three show Marcel's lasting influence on Ricoeur's thought. With Marcel, Ricoeur holds a profound respect for the *mystery* of being. Here a deep distrust for any simple reductive explanation of man or culture remains constant. Ricoeur's modification of this Marcellian theme is one which complements the respect for mystery with an appreciation of the complexity of method required to make any enigma comprehensible.

Ricoeur early followed the Marcellian teaching concerning *incarnate existence*—I am my body—but diverged from it to a degree in that he considered it a premature solution to the philosophical problem of the body. *Freedom and Nature* clearly reflects the Marcellian uses of a body-subject and a body-object and is, in a sense, a revised commentary upon incarnation.

Ricoeur accepted and still maintains the basic conviction that philosophy is recuperative and unifying in its aim. There are secret or hidden unities which lie at the base and which remain the source for philosophical struggle. The ultimate aim of philosophy is a "reconciled ontology."

The doctrinal element in Marcel's thought, however, is not what Ricoeur cites as most important. Rather, it was the "Socratic" method of teaching discovered in the seminars held in Marcel's apartment. The guiding rule was that all students were to speak first from experience—prior to citing texts or making commentaries. It was this turn to experience which provided the basis for philosophizing. Readers of Marcel will here recognize the style of the *Metaphysical Diary* and the concept of the "second reflection," which attempts a return to a unified and primitive first-person experience of the world.

Ricoeur's greatest divergence from Marcel, supported by Ricoeur's Germanic persistence, was in a dissatisfaction with the inexactness of Marcel's method. While studying with Marcel, Ricoeur was working upon Husserl's philosophy. What was needed, he felt, was more a systematic and rigorous approach than a philosophical diary.

2. The time to study Husserl in detail was afforded Ricoeur under rather trying circumstances. At the outset of World War II, Ricoeur, an officer in the French army, was captured, sent to a series of POW camps, met Mikel Dufrenne, and spent the war reading German philosophy. With Dufrenne, Ricoeur later published *Karl Jaspers et la philosophie de l'existence*.

But it was Ricoeur's translation and commentary upon Husserl's *Ideen I* which was the major work of this period. The translation and exposition, still considered a major work on Husserl, established Ricoeur as one of France's foremost Husserl experts.[9] It is conjecture, though not unevidenced, that it was during this time that Ricoeur developed his strong respect for the pre-*Crisis* Husserl. In the *Ideas* Ricoeur found the strictness of method he had earlier sought and from which, he still maintains, any phenomenology going beyond Husserl must begin.

3. The third influence is broad in contrast to the specific nature of the impact on Ricoeur of Marcel and Husserl. Ricoeur cites the ten years spent as a teacher of the history of philosophy at the University of Strasbourg as important for his appreciation of the whole philosophical tradition. In this context it is not difficult to understand one of Ricoeur's earliest intellectual shifts. While he began his career with an open and friendly attitude toward the existentialist philosophies, during ten years of teaching he found his general sympathies tempered by more traditional emphases which eventually moved him further from existentialism.

A mixed attitude is apparent in 1949 in an article, "Le Renouvellement du problème de la philosophie chrétienne par les philosophies de l'existence." [10] In general Ricoeur is positive. With the philosophies of existence Ricoeur rejects any "inexistential" or "pure" philosophy as pretentious. There is no "timeless" philosophy, not only because philosophy has its roots in the

9. Herbert Spiegelberg, *The Phenomenological Movement* (The Hague: Martinus Nijhoff, 1960), II, 536.
10. Paul Ricoeur, "Le Renouvellement du problème de la philosophie chrétienne par les philosophies de l'existence," *Le Problème de la philosophie chrétienne* (Paris: P.U.F., 1949).

specific history of ancient Greece and in the work of a specific tradition, but because the claim of timelessness hides a *hubris*. With existentialism Ricoeur is ready to criticize *"homo philosophicus* [who] has cut the umbilical cord which joins the existant to his body, to his historical moment, to others . . ."[11] With existentialism Ricoeur is ready to say that the question of human existence itself is raised by the question of freedom and all pretended objectivities or neutralities are dissolved—even those which hold a pretended neutrality by claiming to be merely descriptive.[12] With existentialism Ricoeur wishes to join the effort to formulate a concrete philosophy of human existence.

But in the midst of this evaluation Ricoeur brings forth a respect for certain traditional problems in philosophy. For him the inner *telos* of all philosophy is *rationality*. If "there is a *philosophia perennis* it is not because a philosophical system has the privilege of intemporality; it is because the concern to understand rationally—even the irrational—is the permanent concern of all philosophy—even the existential."[13] Thus, even if the philosophies of existence do not recognize it, their main contribution lies in the discovery of a new dimension of rational universality. "A new universality [which is] more subtle than that promoted by science . . . this is their hidden rationality that can be recovered from the questions and problems of existential philosophies."[14] This emphasis upon rationality is reaffirmed much later (1962): "For my part, I do not in the least abandon the tradition of rationality that has animated philosophy since the Greeks."[15]

It was also during this period that a second traditional problem—the problem of necessity—was being reappraised. Ricoeur recounts that he became more and more impressed with necessity as an aspect of existence through his reading of Spinoza. If the existentialist turn to human freedom closed off certain pretensions concerning neutrality and timelessness, a second limitation may be posed in relation to freedom itself. For Ricoeur the problem of freedom remains linked, as in earlier traditions, to necessity. A plausible reading of *Freedom and Nature* may thus be

11. *Ibid.*, p. 47.
12. *Ibid.*, p. 49.
13. *Ibid.*, p. 55.
14. *Ibid.*, pp. 56–57.
15. Paul Ricoeur, "The Hermeneutics of Symbols and Philosophical Reflection," trans. Denis Savage, *International Philosophical Quarterly*, II, no. 2 (May, 1962), 200.

made in terms of a friendly critique of existentialist theories of freedom. In its final cycle, *Freedom and Nature* returns to the reciprocity of freedom and necessity.

RICOEUR'S CONCEPT OF PHILOSOPHICAL AIMS

THE GUIDING COMMITMENT, made in varying ways throughout his career, is to what Ricoeur calls *reflective philosophy*. In its broadest sense reflective philosophy stands in the Socratic tradition of seeking to understand oneself in understanding man. In speaking of the philosophical use of history— for which any discipline related to man as a subject could be substituted—Ricoeur holds:

> The philosopher has a specific way of fulfilling in himself the historian's work. This consists in making his *own* "self-discovery" coincide with a "recovery" of history.
> I do not hide the fact that this reflection does not agree with all conceptions of philosophy. Yet I think it applies to the whole group of philosophies which we may broadly call reflective, whether they take their starting point from Socrates, Descartes, Kant, or Husserl. All these philosophies are in search of the *authentic* subjectivity, of the *authentic* act of consciousness.[16]

Philosophy is reflection upon existence and upon all those means by which that existence is to be understood.

Such a concept of philosophy holds the possibility for a series of encounters between philosophy and other disciplines concerning man. The aim is a rational ontology of human existence. The concept of reflective philosophy affirmed by Ricoeur is one which sees the inner *telos* of philosophy as a search for unity—a unity which defines Reason itself.[17] In explicating his own understanding of the demands for a unified or "reconciled" ontology, Ricoeur manifests a habitual practice of setting up a polar tension. Internally, philosophic rationality must balance itself between two needs, *clarity* and *depth*. There are "two requirements of philosophical thought—clarity and depth, a sense for distinctions and a sense for covert bonds—[which] must constantly con-

16. Paul Ricoeur, *History and Truth*, trans. Charles A. Kelbley (Evanston, Ill.: Northwestern University Press, 1965), p. 32. (Hereafter cited as *HT*.)
17. *HT*, p. 10.

front each other." [18] A clarity without depth is empty so far as it is capable of shedding any ultimate light upon the mystery of human existence; but a suggestion of depth without rational clarity is merely "effuse romanticism."

This internal set of polarities is matched by an opposition between philosophy and prephilosophy. A reflective philosophy takes as its field of inquiry the prereflective. This introduces a set of tensions between *source* and *method*. ". . . Philosophy seems to be guarded against itself by nonphilosophy. . . . It seems that in order to be independent in the elaboration of its problems, methods, and statements, philosophy must be dependent with respect to its sources and its profound motivation. This act cannot fail to be disquieting." [19] This situation implies that from the outset there are always some limits to be recognized in relation to philosophic autonomy.

The internal demands of clarity and depth and the external demand for reflection to be thought directed upon the prephilosophical meet in a summary interpretation:

> [Philosophic interpretation] is not a question of giving in to some kind of imaginative intuition, but rather of thinking, that is to say, of elaborating concepts that comprehend and make one comprehend concepts woven together, if not in a closed system, at least in a *systematic* order. But at the same time it is a question of transmitting, by means of this rational elaboration, a richness of signification that was already there, that has preceded rational elaboration. [20]

This double set of tensions carries with it the question of the very possibility of the philosophic enterprise and poses a set of temptations for the thinker. If prephilosophic life always precedes and in a sense exceeds the powers of reflection, then philosophy remains short of the "last word." Yet the venture is undertaken, and this very shortcoming may be elaborated in a *limit concept*. In a meditation upon philosophic unity (Reason) Ricoeur introduces one of his earlier uses of a myth to suggest a directive idea for philosophy.

The specific problem in which the myth of the "Last Day" is inserted is a dilemma which arises over the history of philosophy.

18. Paul Ricoeur, *Freedom and Nature: The Voluntary and the Involuntary*, trans. Erazim Kohák (Evanston, Ill.: Northwestern University Press, 1966), p. 15. (Hereafter cited as *FN*.)
19. *HT*, p. 14.
20. Ricoeur, "The Hermeneutics of Symbols," p. 200.

Is there a sense in which all philosophies stand in the same truth? Ricoeur defines the problem by noting extreme values which oppose one another. At one extreme lies the demand of philosophy itself for unity—this is its rationality, but hidden in this demand is a possible dogmatism, the temptation to a philosophical *hubris*. If one philosophy is "true," then all others must be "false." On the other extreme lies the alternative of an irreducible plurality of warring philosophies with a temptation to skepticism in which all unity is abandoned or merely imposed by fiat.

Ricoeur wishes to find a third way between these extremes in the form of a *limit idea*. A philosophic *hope* is in effect the *postponing of a synthesis* by purposely limiting philosophy itself. In its first form the idea of hope is spoken of as a guiding or directive feeling concerning the continuity of truth in the history of philosophy.

> Within the bounds of truth: This relation of belonging, of inclusion . . . is accessible only to a regulative feeling capable of purifying historical skepticism, a feeling which is reason but not knowledge—the feeling that all philosophies are ultimately within the same truth of being. This feeling I call "hope". . .[21]

But hope as a feeling needs further interpretation. It is at this point that Ricoeur introduces what he admits is an "incurably mythical" notion—the myth of the "Last Day." Philosophy may "listen" to the non-philosophical myth even if there remains a wide gap between myth and the philosophical consciousness of truth.[22]

In its own context the "Last Day" is a symbol of religious hope for perfect justice. Since perfect justice does not occur in history, the reference of the myth is always to the "not yet." But at the same time the myth promises that justice will be rendered, and signs in the present refer to a "from now on . . ." Ricoeur converts the mythological notion into a limit idea for philosophy itself:

> From one point of view, the concept of "Last Day" works as a *limiting concept* in the Kantian sense, that is, as an active limitation of phenomenal history by a total meaning which is "thought" but not known. . . . I am always short of the Last Judgment. By setting up the limit of the Last Day, I thereby step down from my seat as final judge. The last word therefore is not uttered any-

21. *HT*, p. 6.
22. *HT*, p. 7.

where . . . the limiting concept of an end to history protects the "discontinuity" of unique visions of the world. . . .

But the philosophical impact of hope for the Last Day is not limited to this dethronement of our rational supremacy. In the very midst of this sort of agnosticism in the philosophy of history, it is the source of affirmation. . . .

This recuperative reflection is certainly the philosophical impact of hope, no longer merely in the category of the "not yet" but in that of the "from now on." [23]

The end result of taking the myth as a limit concept is to accept a "living tension" for philosophy. The tension preserves a recognition of limits on one side and a desire, as hope, to probe as fully as possible towards unity on the other. There is to be no premature synthesis, but the drive for unity is to remain the animating *telos*. The limit idea of a postponed synthesis becomes a functional rule designed to protect thought against both *hubris* and skepticism.

PROBLEMS OF METHOD

THE GENERAL STRATEGY of opposing two sides of a polarity leading to a limit concept becomes a major tactic of Ricoeur's thought. This characteristic, dialectical in its outline, is one which has three main features:

1. At its lowest level of operation Ricoeur's dialectic uses a *weighted focus*, a favored method, against which all opposing or counterfoci are to be played. In its weighting some version of phenomenology as analysis is central. But Ricoeur uses phenomenology in at least three recognizable senses. In its first and strictest sense phenomenology is Husserlian. The use of an intentional (noetico-noematic) description stresses a systematic, clear, and structural approach to the problem at hand. Structural characteristics must precede existential significations and variations. Thus, in his main project to date, a philosophy of the will, Ricoeur begins with what he calls an *eidetic* of the will. But even so late as *Freud and Philosophy: An Essay on Interpretation* a basically Husserlian analysis is used as a counter to psychoanalysis.[24]

23. *HT*, pp. 12–13.
24. Paul Ricoeur, *Freud and Philosophy: An Essay on Interpretation*, trans. Denis Savage (New Haven, Conn.: Yale University Press, 1970). (Hereafter cited as *INT*. The translation inverts the

In a broader sense Ricoeur sees phenomenology as a historical development beginning, implicitly at least, in Kant and proceeding through Hegel to Husserl. Ricoeur does not hesitate to apply "phenomenology" to each philosopher in a different way. Although Kant is understood to have anticipated phenomenology in the *Critiques*, his philosophy is oriented by specific epistemological questions and is weighted toward a "phenomenology" of judgment rather than toward Husserlian representationalism. Ricoeur seems to use a Kantian "phenomenology" to limit Husserlian phenomenology.

Hegel's phenomenology, too, plays an increasingly important role in Ricoeur's thought. In a general way Ricoeur's dialectic of opposing values moving toward a third term suggests the Hegelian dialectic—but in a much more specific sense it is the Hegelian development of a genetic or developmental phenomenology which is utilized by Ricoeur. Both the movement from consciousness to self-consciousness and the notion that the "truth" of one moment is revealed only in the moment which follows are important in Ricoeur's broad understanding of phenomenology.

Finally, in the widest sense reflective philosophy, as a part of the transcendental tradition, is a type of "phenomenology" as well. In this sense any philosophy which takes as its guiding theme the existent subject and which begins under the sign of the "first Copernican revolution" is open to "phenomenology." The distinctive problematization of the given as the reflective first move away from the naïve, a demand used in various ways by transcendental philosophies, plays a recurring role in Ricoeur's method.

This series of centrally valued "phenomenologies" provides the weighted focus for all subsequent movement of the dialectic. What provokes that dialectic, however, are the limitations which keep the "phenomenologies" from gaining an exclusive position. In Ricoeur's working habits all methods are dialectically limited and are *founded* through the discovery of limits. "There is a chance that in discovering what limits a method one also discovers what justifies and founds a method." [25] And to discover

French title *De l'interprétation: Essai sur Freud* [Paris: Editions du Seuil, 1965]. I have chosen the abbreviation *INT* to reflect Ricoeur's primary emphasis on interpretation.)

25. Paul Ricoeur, "Sympathie et respect: Phénoménologie et éthique de la seconde personne," *Revue de métaphysique et de morale*, LIX (1954), 380.

the limit of a method also opens the possibility of exceeding that method.

2. The opposition of methods provides the second level of operation in Ricoeur's dialectic. To recognize limits to a single focus is to implicitly grant that a counterfocus is possible. In principle such an operation remains within the spirit, if not the letter, of Husserlian philosophy. Husserl called not only for the development of a transcendental phenomenology but also for a thoroughly philosophical criticism of that phenomenology. Ricoeur substitutes a dialectical play of countermethods to locate limits rather than an ascent to a higher-level interpretation of phenomenological psychology.

In its first appearance Ricoeur's dialectic is double-focused, suggesting the use of a geometrical metaphor. From two fixed points at least two figures are possible. The first is a set of partly overlapping circles; the second an ellipse. In the case of *Freedom and Nature* one point or focus is clearly weighted centrally as an eidetic phenomenology. But against this focus are played a series of counterfoci all of which have in common a type of objectivism (empirical psychology, psychoanalysis, and biology among them).

In the play and counterplay of phenomenology and counter-phenomenology Ricoeur seeks to isolate latent phenomenologies from their objectivist contexts and to provide a critique which destroys the naïveté of the objectivist attitude toward the subject. But in the same play and counterplay a set of limits ultimately shows that the countermethods may not be taken up into a centrally weighted focus. The dialectic remains one of only partly overlapped circles.

3. It is in and through the dialectic that Ricoeur evolves the use of a third term which functions as an operational unity binding it together. *Freedom and Nature* does not explicitly evolve such a term but is left with the recognition of two partly overlapped circles of theory. There is implicit in the very recognition of limits for the countermethods and in the concept of the *index* a beginning movement toward a third term. In *Fallible Man* the third term is explicitly introduced as a limit idea. The dialectic of oppositions, limited in a third term, remains a hallmark of Ricoeur's method. *The third term, the struggle with a postponed synthesis, and the origin of the problem of hermeneutics are all one and the same problem.*

If these problems were merely internal to Ricoeur's philosophy, they might be less interesting as a way of posing questions concerning the development of phenomenological philosophy. But the problems which are caught up in Ricoeur's philosophical net are of lasting import for wider inquiry. One such problem is the continuing confrontation between phenomenologically based philosophies and the persistent advance made by objectivist thought. On its side phenomenology as a theory is a series of methods and concepts which take as their central value the primacy of concrete experience.[26] And in a narrower sense within the whole range of experience the final weight is placed upon immediacy. The Husserlian theory of evidence in which the aim is "to the things themselves" always finds its verification only when that which is under investigation is "bodily" present. In this sense the so-called "subjectivism" of phenomenology is an inversion of all objectivist positions which contrarily weight their theories of evidence in a theory of explanation (positing that which presumably lies *behind* experience).

If phenomenology has shown a new philosophical strength, it is precisely in its ability to uncover and expose to thought just those phenomena of experience which tend to be overlooked or discounted by objectivism. It is with justifiable right that the phenomenologist accuses empiricism of a naïveté regarding human experience. But at this metatheoretical level another question must be raised, since it seems at least unlikely that a phenomenological overthrow will be completed. Might there not be a corresponding naïveté within phenomenology itself? What phenomena, for example, are overlooked or underrated in phenomenology itself? A suggestive answer may be found in just those phenomena which today go by the term *"scientific fact"* for which there remain no clear correlate in human experience. These "facts" include a whole series of phenomena quite familiar to the sciences which deal with man. Or, put otherwise, is it entirely accidental that we have today a phenomenological psychology but no phenomenological neurology?

There are, of course, some responses which may be given by the defender of phenomenology. Perhaps the most likely is that phenomenology is itself prescientific. Its task, at most, remains to remind the sciences that they relate back to the lifeworld whether or not they are aware of it. But this reduction of phenomenology is in effect a limitation of its epistemology to one

26. I shall use *experience* in a broad sense, roughly synonymous with what later phenomenologists call "subjectivity," rather than in Husserl's sense of *Erfahrung*.

area and in no way accounts for the obviously successful development of objectivism in our day.

Ricoeur's philosophy opens another possibility. He leads one to suspect that phenomenology itself contains a naïveté in relation to methods which function *indirectly* (and in spite of their naïveté) and which find their justification precisely in given types of indirectness. The "third way" which Ricoeur seeks is not to be a return to a prephenomenological objectivism—although these methods are re-evaluated through Ricoeur's inquiries—it is to be a radicalization of phenomenology itself, an uncovering of the naïveté of transcendentalism itself, a "second Copernican revolution":

> The constitutive character of consciousness is a conquest of criticism over naturalistic (or mundane) naïveté. But the transcendental level thus won conceals a second-level naïveté—the naïveté of criticism which consists in considering the "transcendental," the "constitutive," as the absolutely irreducible. . . . It is as if a second naïveté were involved in it, a transcendental naïveté which takes the place of the naturalistic one. The transcendental reflection creates the illusion that philosophy could be a reflection without a spiritual discipline (*ascèse*), without a purification of its own seeing.[27]

In this way, within the dialectic, the re-evaluation of objectivism leads to a second act, the reduction of the transcendental naïveté or of phenomenology itself.

The major movement of Ricoeur's series of "readings" of the will becomes a progressive "demythologization" of the two illusions which correspond to transcendental and objectivist presuppositions. Beginning with transcendental thought, the illusion which is first to be excised is precisely that which lay open in a "natural attitude," the possibility for the subject to be "lost" in the world. The naïveté of the natural attitude is presubjective.

> Initially I am lost and forgotten in the world, lost in the things, lost in the ideas, lost in the plants and the animals, lost in others, lost in mathematics. Presence . . . is the occasion of temptation; in seeing there is a trap, the trap of my alienation; there I am external, diverted. Now it is evident how naturalism is the lowest stage of the natural attitude . . . For if I lose myself in the world, I am then ready to treat myself as a thing of the world. The thesis of the world is a sort of blindness in the very heart of seeing. What

27. *Husserl*, pp. 228, 232.

I call living is hiding myself as naïve consciousness within the existence of all things . . . [contrarily] phenomenology is a true
conversion of the sense of intentionality, which is first the for-
getting of consciousness, and then its discovery of itself as given.[28]

Once the phenomenological turn, which reflexively reveals the
subject, is made, the illusion is no longer possible in its naïve
sense, "the point of view of transcendental constitution
triumph[s] over the naïveté of natural man." [29]

Subjectivity, now isolated and extricated from being an object among objects, becomes a theme to be investigated for its
own sake. But in becoming a theme a second illusion occurs in
which the subject, "tends to posit itself. . . . The self becomes
detached and exiles itself into what the Stoics have already called
the circularity of the soul . . . the circle which I form with myself." [30] This second illusion, arising in transcendental thought
itself, is a naïveté even more difficult to deal with than the first:

> This naiveté may be more difficult to overcome than that of
> the "natural" attitude. If the ego loses itself easily in its world and
> understands itself willingly in terms of the things that surround it,
> an even more tenacious illusion imprisons it in the very matrix of
> its own subjectivity. . . . The "vanity" of the ego is stretched like
> a veil over the very being of its own existence.[31]

The question is how to dispel this second illusion without returning to the reign of the object and its naïveté.

Ricoeur's promise is to do this by a final reading of the will
in a *poetics* which would displace the subject from its self-made
circle. "In relation to this first Copernican revolution, the poetics
of the will ought to appear as a second Copernican revolution
which displaces being from the center, without however returning to the rule of the object." [32] This poetics, hermeneutic in its
mode of indirectness, has not yet been formulated—but its demands have been clarified in *Freud and Philosophy* and anticipated from the outset of Ricoeur's project.

> The Ego must more radically renounce the covert claim of all con-
> sciousness, must abandon its wish to posit itself, so that it can re-

28. *Ibid.*, p. 20.
29. *Ibid.*, p. 24.
30. *FN*, p. 14.
31. *Husserl*, p. 232.
32. *FN*, p. 32.

ceive the nourishing and inspiring spontaneity which breaks the
sterile circle of the self's constant return to itself.[33]

This new "reduction" is a reduction of transcendental thought
itself. It is the methodological goal implied in Ricoeur's attempt
to radicalize phenomenology.

PHILOSOPHICAL ANTHROPOLOGY

THE DEVELOPMENT of Ricoeur's philosophy falls into
two broad divisions. The first division is a *structural* phenomenology developed primarily in *Freedom and Nature* and continued in *Fallible Man*. The leading questions concerning the
subject in the structural phase remain strictly limited to what
Ricoeur calls *fundamental possibilities*. These "structures" of the
will are open to rational philosophy without the necessity of symbol or myth. Structural phenomenology, however, "brackets out"
what Ricoeur terms the Fault (*la faute*). Only when the realm of
experienced evil and suffering is reintroduced can there be a fully
existential development of philosophical anthropology.

The second phase of phenomenology is properly hermeneutic, and its major outlines occur in *The Symbolism of Evil* and
Freud and Philosophy. Here the turn is made from the structures
of experience to the concrete expressions in symbol and myth
that man makes concerning his existence.

The major content of Ricoeur's philosophy revolves around
the will and the question of freedom. "With freedom, the existential and the ontological become synonymous. The being of man
consists in existing . . ."[34] But all freedom, all human existence, stands under the sign of the Fault. For Ricoeur man is a
faulted being.

The Fault suggests a double metaphor (in both French and
English). In a geological context a fault is a discontinuity in a
given layer or stratum of the earth's structure. Due to some dis-
turbance deep in the earth, a crack may occur in such a way that
a given layer becomes discontinuous (though not necessarily totally) with itself. This metaphor, expressed with particular clarity in *Fallible Man*, is used in Ricoeur's contention that man
carries a noncoincidence within himself. But the structural aspect of fault is not Fault in the full sense.

33. *FN*, p. 14.
34. *Husserl*, p. 210.

The other sense of Fault is roughly moral; in ordinary usage to say, "It is my (or his) fault," is to impute some type of blame usually connected with a consciously undertaken act. Ricoeur expands this usage to cover the whole dimension of evil suffered and enacted. The imputation of guilt lies within this aspect of Fault.

The discontinuity between the two metaphorical senses of the Fault is purposely maintained. Ricoeur sees in the philosophical treatment of Fault a tendency to treat all of existence structurally.

> Philosophy tends to reduce the event of guilt to a structure homogenous with other structures of the voluntary and the involuntary. In this respect the philosophies of existence, which have done so much to reintroduce error (*faute*) into philosophical reflection, proceed no differently than Plotinus and Spinoza: for them also finitude is the ultimate philosophical alibi for guilt . . .[35]

To the structural treatment of will must be added a hermeneutics of Fault which must reveal both the dramatic aspect of guilt which escapes a structural analysis and the limits which are inherent in philosophy in its structural guise.

The general division between a structural and a hermeneutic phenomenology is further specified by a series of "readings" of the will. Beginning from an analysis of consciousness in the will, Ricoeur first performs what he calls an *eidetic*. Eidetic repeats the Husserlian dictum that any factual science must first be preceded by an eidetic or essential science. Possibilities or ideal limits precede the actual variations of the facts. Thus Ricoeur demands "a description . . . capable of revealing man's structures or *fundamental possibilities* . . . [an] abstraction . . . in some respects akin to what Husserl calls eidetic reduction, that is, bracketing of the fact and elaborating the idea or meaning."[36] Bracketed out are the questions of Fault, as the experience of guilt, and Transcendence, as the ultimate source of the subject itself. Only what is characterized as a *neutral* realm of pure possibilities is to be described. "We sketched the neutral sphere of man's most fundamental possibilities, or as it were, the undifferentiated keyboard upon which the guilty as well as the innocent man might play."[37]

35. *Ibid.*, p. 230.
36. *FN*, pp. 3–4.
37. Paul Ricoeur, *Fallible Man*, trans. Charles Kelbley (Chicago: Henry Regnery Co., 1966), p. xvi. (Hereafter cited as *FM*.)

Eidetic is a first move away from the lifeworld of Fault, a deliberate attempt to remove the sense of immediacy found in prereflective life in order to make that life thematizable. Such a reduction restricts itself to a description which eschews all "explanation" and remains short of the full range of actual experience.

The second "reading" of the will consists of a removal of these brackets, a movement toward what Ricoeur calls an *empirics* of the will. But the second reading stops short of the existential and interprets the totality of the structures of the will as *fallible*. At its utmost structural limits, the will is seen to be open to the possibility, but not the necessity, of the experience and enactment of evil.

The abstract atmosphere of *Freedom and Nature* and the removal of brackets in *Fallible Man* yield to a third reading of the will in what Ricoeur terms in *The Symbolism of Evil* a *mythics*. Here is a partial methodological discontinuity which parallels the distinction between the structural and moral senses of Fault. Ricoeur "leaps" to an examination of the concrete expressions of man's experiences of evil and suffering in a move which is both tactical and indirect.

The move from the structures of possible experience to the facticity of actual expressions is the move from possibilities to an already formulated language. Ricoeur chooses the religious confessions of evil as his field of inquiry and makes *The Symbolism of Evil* a first exercise in explicit hermeneutics. Underlying this shift of strategy is the presupposition that symbols and myths have a certain power to reveal in and through indirect expressions. The mythics pose the problem of how philosophic thought may be "informed by" symbol and myth without either falsely reducing the symbolic or being taken into the myth in uncritical fashion. Employing "sympathetic imagination" in the reading of texts, the first hermeneutic exercise seeks to recover the donation of symbolic significance for thought.

The symbolic, however, hides and dissembles as well as reveals. Its indirectness is not only a wealth, but an opacity and equivocity as well. *Freud and Philosophy* encounters another possibility in the development of hermeneutics. The sympathetic imagination of a first reading is here chastized by a hermeneutics which "suspects" the symbolic. In a decisive confrontation between phenomenology and psychoanalysis, between a hermeneutics of restoration and a hermeneutics of suspicion, Ricoeur reaches a critical point in the development of hermeneutic phenomenology. The question of language, beginning with the symbolic, becomes the new center for such a phenomenology.

LANGUAGE AND "WORD"

THE NEED TO UNDERSTAND symbolic expressions is the theme for Ricoeur's entry into language in the "hermeneutic turn." But underlying this privilege of hermeneutics are several broad motivating concerns.

1. *Man is language*, Ricoeur says today, and the problem of language remains a problem of the human subject. But the problem which situates man as language revolves around what may be termed a crisis of language at a certain state of civilization. In one of his first published papers Ricoeur claims, *"I belong to my civilization as I am bound to my body. I am situated-in-civilization and it no more depends upon me to have a different history than to have a different body. I am implicated in a particular adventure, in a particular complex history . . ."* [38]

That civilization, as Ricoeur understands it, is marked by the rise of critical thought. If it is through language that man expresses his self-understanding, it is just those expressions which mediate this understanding which are called into question by critical thought. Historically, the language of symbol and myth provided a means for understanding man's situation and possibilities. But critical thought destroys all "first naïveté" concerning belief in myth and successfully separates myth from empirical history. This is not to say that Ricoeur belongs to that group of modern philosophers who would romantically and nostalgically hint at a return to some age of prephilosophical innocence. For Ricoeur all myth is already "fallen" and no age of innocence ever existed. Myth and symbol are imaginative variations which intend without necessarily fulfilling an intention. But they are also the means by which human possibilities are made concrete in imaginative form. The crisis of critical thought is one which again raises the question of the "fullness" of language.

> The historical moment of the philosophy of symbol is both the moment of forgetting and the moment of restoring . . . In the very age in which our language is becoming more precise, more univocal, more technical, better suited to those integral formaliza-

38. Paul Ricoeur, "Le Chrétien et la civilisation occidentale," *Christianisme social* (October–December, 1946), p. 424.

tions that are called precisely "symbolic" logic . . . —it is in this age of discourse that we wish to recharge language. . . . But this too is a gift from "modernity." For we moderns are men of philosophy, of exegesis, of the phenomenology of religion, of the psychoanalysis of language. The same age develops the possibility of emptying language and the possibility of filling it anew. It is therefore no yearning for a sunken Atlantis that urges us on, but the hope of a re-creation of language. Beyond the wastelands of critical thought we seek to be challenged again.[39]

Language, in the symbolic, the mythological, is a function of self-understanding. It portrays a directive image of man through which he portrays his possibilities. In the symbol is a "word."

2. The role of language as "word" which reveals, which brings into the open for reflection, is echoed in several ways in Ricoeur's thought. Ricoeur understands himself as a man of language: "What do I do when I teach? I speak. I have no other means of livelihood and I have no other dignity; I have no other means of transforming the world and no other influence upon men. The word is my work; the word is my kingdom." [40] Later, in another statement of vocational role, Ricoeur again relates "word" as the philosophical vocation:

As a university professor, I believe in the efficacity of instructive speech; in teaching the history of philosophy, I believe in the enlightening power, even for a system of politics, of speaking devoted to elaborating our philosophical memory. As a member of the team of *Esprit*, I believe in the efficacity of speech which thoughtfully elucidates the generating themes of an advancing civilization. As a listener to the Christian message, I believe that words may change the "heart," that is, the refulgent core of our preferences and the positions which we embrace.[41]

3. Given a growing preoccupation with "word," with language, and a project Ricoeur today terms the "hermeneutical philosophy of human existence," the door gradually opens for the philosophy of language itself. The way into this question is one which sees the linguistic sciences and philosophies as themselves having a certain development.

Linguistics itself developed at first in terms of smaller unities of language, phonology, lexical units, simple syntax, but all exegesis

39. Ricoeur, "The Hermeneutics of Symbols," pp. 192–93.
40. Paul Ricoeur, "La Parole est mon royaume," *Esprit*, XXIII (February, 1955), p. 192.
41. *HT*, p. 5.

has to confront greater wholes of language—a myth, a dream . . .
We are still waiting to see what are all the consequences of transforming linguistics into a hermeneutical science.[42]

But what Ricoeur does is to invert the history of linguistic sciences and begin (phenomenologically) with the whole or the
most complex—with what he calls the fullness of language.

Ricoeur distinguishes between thinking *in* a language and
thinking *about* language. To begin with the fullness of language
is to begin with language at its most perplexing moment, from
the equivocity of the symbol. This is an attempt to rethink language *with* and *in* its presuppositions. But there is also the need
to meet and understand the theories about language, and to these
Ricoeur increasingly turns.

> I am especially interested in the problem of language—a cross-
> roads, a confrontation of all the schools. Language is a problem
> for phenomenology as well as for linguistic analysis. It has an im-
> portant role to play in theological exegesis, psychoanalysis, and
> other fields . . . In particular I would like to examine the passage
> from thought, nourished by symbols, especially mythical symbols,
> to speculation. I am very much interested in the transition from
> symbols to reflection and that is why I am working on language.[43]

In language, in the symbol, cross all the concerns of method, of
the subject, and of the opening to a philosophy of culture which
motivate Ricoeur's thought.

42. Ricoeur, "A Conversation," p. 1.
43. *Ibid.*, p. 2.

2 / Structural Phenomenology: The Latent Hermeneutics of *Freedom and Nature*

AN EXPOSITION OF *Freedom and Nature* as an anticipation of hermeneutics places severe limits upon the range of relevant material to be dealt with. In its own context the eidetic reading of the will is primarily an adaptation of Husserlian phenomenology to the complex activities of the will. Moving through three cycles of description beginning with *decision*, extending to *action* or bodily motion, and culminating in *consent* to necessity, Ricoeur carefully employs the models of transcendental phenomenology.

An *epochē* or suspension of all beliefs regarding both ordinary and causal theories of what may lie behind or "explain" the will is imposed. "The first principle which guided our description is the methodological contrast between description and explanation" (*FN*, p. 4). The aim is to display experience to the limits of phenomenological possibility. "The task of describing the voluntary and the involuntary is in effect one of becoming receptive to [the] Cogito's *complete* experience, including even its most diffuse affective margins" (*FN*, p. 8).

Through *epochē*, *willing-as-consciousness* becomes thematic. And although an important reservation must be added, it is the voluntary aspect of willing which centralizes consciousness in its first appearance. "This descriptive study will always begin with a description of the voluntary aspect, after which we shall consider what involuntary structures are needed to make that act or that aspect of the will intelligible" (*FN*, p. 5).[1] In each cycle

---

1. The same principle holds that one must begin with normal, as against pathological, behaviors in relation to will.

the first task is to thematize consciousness—though with a difficulty, the difficulty of applying the perceptual model implicit in phenomenology to nonrepresentational behavior.

The descriptions are further recognizable as *intentional* (noematic-noetic) *analyses*. In Husserlian fashion this is to begin with the "appearance" of the object-correlate of experience. The formula "all consciousness is consciousness of _____" applies to the will, and the description begins when the blank is filled in. The experienc*ed* precedes the understanding of experienc*ing*. Thus in each cycle a description of the aim or reference of the experience comes prior to the specific reflection upon the subject. To decide has as its object the formation of a *project* in the world; to act is to undertake a *pragma* in the world; and to consent is to acquiesce to *necessity* against which the will is impotent in the world.

The subject becomes strictly thematic only reflectively or noetically. It is this movement of intentional analysis which separates it from ordinary introspection. The reflective turn finds one of its justifications genetically. Self-awareness arises secondarily in will as in other dimensions of experience. And in the case of *Freedom and Nature* a special caveat may be entered—the reflective turn to the subject may, and often does, arise when the first intentional moment is interrupted or broken in its aim (i.e., involuntarily). Again in each cycle the reflective turn thematizes a field for description: reflectively the project is *motivated;* the pragma is possible only by means of the *organ* of motion which capacitates movement; and consent reaches an absolute limit in the *invincible.*

It is in a special consideration within the reflective turn that Ricoeur introduces an innovation which brings into play a "latent" hermeneutics. This innovation arises in relation to what is called the *involuntary,* and the latent hermeneutics is the concept of the *diagnostic.* Basic to the entire notion of willing is what Ricoeur takes as a primitive reciprocity: "The initial situation revealed by description is *the reciprocity of the involuntary and the voluntary*" (*FN*, p. 4). Voluntary willing meets and is limited by capacities which are involuntary. It is the involuntary side of this reciprocity which poses the need for a second type of indirectness which is already latently hermeneutic.

In the beginning Ricoeur weights the voluntary side of the reciprocity—a weighting which is both psychological and phenomenological:

Not only does the involuntary have no meaning of its own, but understanding proceeds from the top down, and not from the bottom up. Far from the voluntary being derivable from the involuntary, it is, on the contrary, the understanding of the voluntary which comes first in man. I understand myself in the first place as he who says, "I will." The involuntary refers to the will as that which gives it its motives and capacities, its foundations and even its limits (*FN*, p. 5).

The question becomes one of how to deal with the involuntary which limits and founds the voluntary.

Were Ricoeur's approach an *existential* phenomenology in the full sense, the involuntary would be dealt with in a fashion similar to that of the voluntary, strictly within the limits of experience. A converted noematic-noetic analysis of the involuntary would turn first to the "appearance" of the involuntary in the world and then reflect upon what is found within the subject. In this case the first description might be one which opens the area of "situated freedom" which contrasts facticity as the situation in which the voluntary finds itself; reflectively the problem would be to describe the limits of experience as those of bodily existence in a "lived body."

Such a movement is not entirely foreign to *Freedom and Nature*. The echoes of the Marcellian theme of *incarnation* and the concept of a *personal body* (*corps propre*) [2] place much of Ricoeur's eidetic of the involuntary in sympathy with existential thought. But two modifications prevent a direct movement toward existential significations. The first appears symptomatically in an emphasis upon the reflective side of puzzles concerning the involuntary. The "external" limits of the world are recognized, thus situating the will, but these limits are used throughout as indicators for limits within the subject. It is precisely these limits which are enigmatic for a reflective philosophy.

This symptomatic emphasis upon the reflective involuntary is most apparent in the crucial discussion of consent. In that cycle of the will Ricoeur specifically underplays a consideration of absolute limits in the world and steps back from any cosmological implications involved, concentrating instead almost exclusively upon the limits of the subject as character, unconscious,

2. I shall use Ricoeur's *corps propre* variously as the personal body (Kohák's translation) and as the I-body. This term in the general literature is often translated as the "owned body" or the "lived body." Ricoeur's use is close to that of Merleau-Ponty's *corps vécu*.

and biological life.[3] The goal is to "[exhibit] the mutual rooted-
ness of freedom and nature up to the most unmistakable forms
of necessity, at the level of the indistinct awareness of being
alive" (*Husserl*, p. 225). The nature spoken of in this case is the
nature of the subject.

The second modification emerges as *two different readings
of the involuntary*. The first reading of the involuntary is functionally parallel with existential phenomenology. In each instance of dealing with the body—which will become in this
exposition the paradigmatic example to the exclusion of other important aspects of *Freedom and Nature*—Ricoeur undertakes a
first reading which discloses the body as the body of an experiencing subject. But these descriptions do not stand alone.

Ricoeur recognizes a whole range of studies which also deal
with the involuntary. These studies, though in method the inverse of a phenomenological thematization of the body, range
from behavioral psychology to genetic biology, sciences that also
deal with the body. Ricoeur, when he grants them a counter-
weighting with uncharacteristic phenomenological charity, goes
beyond the limits of a strictly eidetic reading of the will. In relation to the paradigmatic examples in question Ricoeur grants:
"The body is better known as an empirical object elaborated by
experimental sciences. We have a biology, endowed with an objectivity . . . for knowing the objectivity of facts within a nature encompassed by *laws* of an inductive kind" (*FN*, p. 8). The
door is opened to a dialectic between phenomenological and objective universes of discourse, and in the conflict of these separate
theories the latent hermeneutics of *Freedom and Nature* emerges.

The involuntary is "read" first phenomenologically, but then
diagnostically. The special role played by objectivist studies is
only indirectly used in the second diagnostic interpretation, however. Ricoeur is neither a scientist nor a psychologist and does
not pretend to be one. Objective studies are used as counterfoci
which *limit* phenomenology and which provide a series of *indices*
for a recovery of vague or likely-to-be-hidden areas of experience.
The expanded but to-be-limited phenomenology of *Freedom and
Nature* is in part made possible by objectivism.

The diagnostic of Ricoeur's invention relies upon a reversed
medical metaphor. The doctor in his training learns to relate the
subjective discourse of the patient to what he knows concerning

3. Here one glimpses an anticipation of what is to become the
problem of the "archeology of the subject."

the objective characteristics of a disease. Ricoeur reverses this process and proposes the diagnostic as a way to take objective characteristics as *signs* for obscure or border experiences in relation to the involuntary. "This relation is not at all *apriori*, but is gradually formed in a sign-learning process. Such an analysis of symptoms, which we are here using with respect to the Cogito, is used by a doctor in the service of empirical knowledge, an experience indicating a functioning or a functional disorder of the object body" (*FN*, p. 13). The task is to take the objective indicator as a sign for an experience of the Cogito in order to locate obscure areas within experience and to limit in more definite fashion the borders of experience. But at the same time this indirectness shifts the center of Ricoeur's method from a purely reflective examination of the Cogito to a second order reading of signs.

> Philosophy of man appears to us as a living tension between an objectivity elaborated by a phenomenology to do justice to the Cogito (itself recovered from naturalism) and the sense of my incarnate existence. The latter constantly overflows the objectivity which in appearance respects it most but which by its very nature tends to eschew it. That is why the concepts we use . . . are *indications* of a living experience in which we are submerged more than signs of mastery which our intelligence exercises over our human condition. But in turn it is the task of philosophy to clarify existence by the use of concepts (*FN*, p. 17).

In dialectic between objectivism and phenomenology proper, the mediation of the diagnostic functions as the second reading of the involuntary.

A more detailed outline of the method in *Freedom and Nature* is now possible: (a) Beginning within the limits of a more strictly Husserlian model, the first step is to describe the fundamental structure of the will. Within each cycle of decision, action, and consent, an analysis of the world-directed aim of experience is analyzed. This first noematic movement, described acutely and with respect for complexity, outlines each form of transcending behavior in the will. (b) The reflective return to the subject, again within the limits of a Husserlian pattern, situates the references of experiences back into relation with the life of the Cogito. The final reflective terminus of the noetic movement is the personal body (*corps propre*), the subject as incarnate. (c) But the body is precisely what is obscure for reflection itself. The "mystery" of incarnate existence is opaque even for phenomenology. At these margins of experience, open only in degree to a phenomenology as the discovery of an obscurity area, a second reading of bodily existence (as involuntary) is introduced by (d) the diagnostic. By detouring into the realm of objective studies, Ricoeur proposes to extract from their universes of discourse an "alienated phenomenology." In practice the diagnostic develops several of its own methodological steps. The first use of the diagnostic is critical. By playing the findings of phenomenology off against the counterweights of objective studies, the diagnostic is a "demythologization" of the naturalism of those sciences. The gain, indirectly, is a better understanding of the movement from existence to objectivity in which the subject becomes alienated from the full sense of its experience. But since the dialectic involved in the diagnostic occurs at the borders of experience, in the vague and obscure, a second process involves the locating and mapping of these borders. This serves to limit the universes of discourse at borders which overlap only in an ambivalence. Finally, the location of limits extends to a philosophy of consciousness itself. Through the diagnostic a phenomenology of the will as consciousness is itself limited. Although in *Freedom and Nature* these steps often tend to merge, the gain in understanding the functioning of universes of discourse may be shown by utilizing only a very restricted set of examples.

The use of the diagnostic is not without problematic effect. Two complications arise out of this dialectical version of phenomenology. Ricoeur poses as his main aim in the eidetic reading of the will a display of the *fundamental possibilities* of the will, the limits within which all possible willing occurs. These ideal limits, however, manifest two quite different characteristics, each of which corresponds to two different meanings of limit. On one side the fundamental possibility is an *ideality*, the highest possible notion of a will within the structural limits of being human; on the other side the limit is that of a border in which the reciprocity of the voluntary and involuntary is located as a margin between subjective and objective universes of discourse. The first meaning, which opens the way to overtly mythological themes as "dreams of innocence," stands in contrast to the second, which relates to existential obscurity. The generation of this problem is to be found in the double use of Husserlian and diagnostic methods.

The second problem centers more directly in the use of the diagnostic itself, which Ricoeur uses in both a *weak* and a *strong* sense. In its weak sense, objective studies are used merely to provide *indices* which help uncover otherwise obscured experiences. But in the strong sense Ricoeur claims that where no overlap or equivalent between objective and subjective universes of discourse may be discovered one must revert to an *interiorization* of the significance of objectivity. The untenability of the strong use of the diagnostic results from the temptation of phenomenology to employ a movement which falls into the same errors as its counterpart, the movement from existence to objectivity, does from the opposite direction.

THE BODY AS PARADIGMATIC PROBLEM

TWO QUITE DIFFERENT WAYS of dealing with the body have already been indicated. One, the "objective," deals with the body as one object among others in a series. The other, the "subjective," deals with the body as personal. The objective reading, from the phenomenologist's point of view, allows experience to be gradually excluded from its primacy. Empirical treatments of the body are counter to all that is proper to phenomenology in the reduction of experience to *facts*.

> Conceiving of the body as an object . . . tends to divorce knowledge of the involuntary from the Cogito and bit by bit makes all psychology fall on the side of the natural sciences. . . . In becoming a fact, the experience of consciousness becomes degraded and loses its two distinctive characteristics: its intentionality and its reference to an "I" which lives in its experience. . . . [This alienation occurs] by contamination from the object-body which alone has the privilege of being exposed among objects (*FN*, pp. 8–9).

The final result is the dissipation of the (conscious) voluntary altogether in the subsequent reduction of the subject into object. The involuntary "explains" the voluntary.

This counterphenomenological "reduction" is itself a total reading of the body couched in suppositions quite different from and contrary to those of phenomenology. And because empiricism claims to be a total reading (as does Husserlian phenomenology) the superficial rendering of one reading as external, the other as internal, is not what is at stake.

> What in effect characterizes empirical psychology is not in the first instance its preference for external knowledge, but its reduction of *acts* (with their intentionality and their reference to an

Ego) to *facts*. Could we say that *acts* are better known from the "inside" and *facts* from the "outside"? That is only partly true. For introspection can itself be degraded to a knowledge of *facts* if it omits the mental as intentional act and as someone's act. . . . Introspection can be interpreted in a naturalistic sense if it translates acts into the language of anonymous facts, homogenous with other natural facts, that "there are" sensations as "there are" atoms. Empiricism is a discourse in the mode of "there is." Inversely, knowledge of subjectivity cannot be reduced to introspection . . . Its essence is to respect the originality of the Cogito as a cluster of the subject's intentional acts. But the subject is myself *and* yourself (*FN*, p. 10).

These are two different "languages" concerning the subject. The one "reads" the subject as homogenous with all anonymous facts; the other "reads" all subjects as intending subjects. Thus are constituted two different universes of discourse.

This is not the last word, however, because each universe of discourse has a certain drift which situates it at one or the other pole of the voluntary-involuntary reciprocity being described. The reduction of experience to facts and its subsequent alienation have a functional result—objectivity gains a privilege in relation to the involuntary.

We cannot pretend that we are unaware of the fact that the involuntary is often better known *empirically*, in its form, albeit degraded, of a natural event. . . .

It is too easy to say that the body appears twice, once as a subject, then as an object, or more exactly the first time as the body of a subject, the second time as an anonymous empirical object. It would be vain to suppose that we can elegantly resolve the problem of dualism by substituting a dualism of viewpoints for a dualism of substances. The body of a subject and the body as anonymous empirical object do not coincide (*FN*, pp. 11–12).

But the non-coincidence of the two universes of discourse is not total. Between them lies what may be termed an *ambivalence border* which allows the movement from existence to objectivity to occur (and which allows Ricoeur to speak implicitly of a "subjectivization" of empirical notions). Both refer to *the* body.

Does that mean that there is no relation between the body as mine or yours and the body as an object among the objects of science? There ought to be one, because it is the same body. But this correlation is not one of coincidence but of a *diagnostic* . . . [in which] any moment of the Cogito can serve as an indication of the object body . . . and each moment of the object body is an indication of a moment of the body belonging to a subject (*FN*, pp. 12–13).

At the borders of the two universes of discourse, non-coincidental by their respective drifts to opposite poles of the voluntary and involuntary, the diagnostic comes into play in both its weak and strong senses. Its weak use is to recover the subjective equivalent of what normally is dealt with objectively in a "translation" into the language of the Cogito. But in its strong sense, when no equivalence may be found, only a subjectivization is to be used.

> The two points of view are not cumulative; they are not even parallel. The use of the descriptive method shows that the lessons of biology or of empirical psychology are a *normal* path for discovering the subjective equivalent which is often quite ambiguous. . . . Description of the Cogito will frequently recover from empirical psychology the vestiges of a phenomenology which it discovers there in an objectified and in some way alienated form. But with equal frequency a phenomenological concept will be no more than a subjectivization of a concept far better known along an empirical path (*FN*, p. 13).

Within the limits of the development of the diagnostic as latent hermeneutics, only one example of its use from each cycle of the will (with special reference to consent as the most illuminating case) need be followed. In each case the paradigmatic problem of the body focuses the issues.

1. *Decision: The Body as Source of Motives*

The general movement of the three cycles of the will is one which begins with the most obviously conscious aspects of the will and moves through a series of adumbrations toward its less representable aspects. Decision, in this context, is the aspect of the will which begins from the center of conscious deliberations. A general movement from "top" to "bottom" applies within the cycle under consideration. Thus, in Ricoeur's definition of decision:

> To decide means first of all to project a practical possibility of an action which depends upon me, secondly to impute myself as the author responsible for the project, and finally to motivate my project by reasons and variables which "historialize" values capable of justifying them (*FN*, p. 84).

The movement of the definition repeats the basic eidetic pattern of intentional analysis.

Consciousness is first a reference toward the world, a transcending behavior. The *project* as the possibility of an action in the world is the direction of decision. It is only reflectively that the "I" is thematized. To decide is at one and the same time to project a possibility and reflectively to "make up my mind." The intricacies of the more obvious conscious will must yield here to an exclusive consideration of the reflective terminus which finds its center of interest in the third part of the definition, the motivation of decision.

Implied in the projection of the possibility in the world undertaken by a subject is a reflective reference to "reasons" for the decision. The ultimate movement of reflection ends in the body which constitutes a partial source of motives. "The circular relation of motive to project demands that I recognize my body as body-for-my-willing and my willing as project-based-(in part)-on my body. The involuntary is *for* the will, and the will is *by reason* of the involuntary" (*FN*, pp. 85–86).

Although Ricoeur restricts the theme of the body in this cycle to the *relative involuntary*, the body retains its enigmatic feature as ultimate reflex pole of the eidetic. As a source of motives the body does not constitute the entire field, since it is possible to decide a project "because of" some other set of values (motives may be read as values), for example, cultural or aesthetic ones. And in extreme cases one may even decide against one's body, as in instances of self-sacrifice.

What gives the body its privileged position as a source of motives is the need to finally identify the body with the subject— and this also poses the enigma for the diagnostic. "All other values assume a serious, dramatic significance . . . through my body. It is my body which introduces this existential note; it is the initial existent, underivable, *involuntary*" (*FN*, p. 85).

But the body as source of motives is itself *obscure*. A double reason for this obscurity may be given. In the first place the body, in the process of decision, ordinarily remains unthematized. The project is decided upon the world, not upon the body. This is true even in the case of the direct bodily need of hunger, as example will indicate. In an ordinary or normal decision the "I" who decides does not even explicitly consider the body. To "live" one's body is not yet to give it a clear conceptual meaning.

But if and when the reflective turn is made and the phenomenological theme of "I am my body" is revealed, a second type of obscurity appears. The very experiencing of bodily existence is opaque and obscure. Among the range of motives clearly supplied within bodily existence, the area of needs indicates this obscurity. "Now our needs are opaque not only to reasoning which would deduce them from the ability to think, but even to the light of reflection. To experience is always more than to understand" (*FN*, p. 86).

Bodily needs (hunger, thirst, sexual urges, etc.) are experienced. To be understood, an eidetic must uncover these needs. Needs further present themselves as possible motives for decision (I must eat, drink, make love, etc.), as involuntary "givens." Needs are involuntary "givens" in which the double reading, first strictly phenomenological, then diagnostic, may occur.

> Description of need will be an excellent opportunity to test the usual schemas and to substitute for them the diagnostic relation between objective knowledge of the body and the living experience of [the] incarnate Cogito . . . I do not know need from the outside, as a natural event, but from within, as a lived need and, when needed, through empathy as yours; but I have an objective symptom of it in the deterioration of blood and tissue, and in the nervous or glandular reaction to such deterioration (*FN*, p. 87).

Needs are first "lived" and thus constitute an aspect of first-person experience. Ricoeur locates need as an aspect of thought —necessary if the analysis is to be limited to the Cogito—as "the adherence of affectivity to thought itself" (*FN*, p. 88). Felt needs are experienced, but the experience is obscure, at least in the sense that a felt need is prerepresentational. The objectifying aim (perception, imagination) which internally limits the basic Husserlian model is made difficult here by the lack of objectification in a felt need. The reflective movement toward bodily significations presents a certain ambiguity. Ricoeur converts this ambiguity into an indication of the ultimate reference of reflection. "To feel is still to think, though feeling no longer represents objectivity, but rather reveals existence" (*FN*, p. 86).

The obscurity is not total, and the adherence of need to consciousness opens it to a description of intentional type. The case of appetite or hunger suffices to demonstrate the intentionality of felt need.

> Appetite presents itself as an indigence and an exigence, an experienced lack of . . . and an impulse directed towards. . . .
> . . . [There is an] other directedness which is an essential aspect of need and which testifies that, as all acts of the Cogito, it

is a consciousness of . . . and an impetus towards. . . . Even
without an image of bread, my hunger would still carry me beyond
myself (*FN*, pp. 89, 90).

In this sense even felt needs are transcending behaviors which
direct themselves toward the world in a definite pattern which is
intentional in its reference.

> In this retrogression towards purely organic functioning we
> can sense a lack and an urge which are not yet a perceived,
> imagined, or conceptualized intention. Yet it is not an indefinite
> lack, an indefinite urge, but a specific lack, a directed urge. . . .
> The lack from which I suffer, the lack I suffer, has a form (*FN*,
> p. 89).

To a degree phenomenology may penetrate and conceptualize felt
need in its backward reference toward bodily functions.

But at the same time that the obscurity of need is recognized
the double reason for movement from existence to objectivity
may begin. The very reference of the vague experience of need
toward the world (I search for food, for drink) overreaches the
body. Simultaneously, the prerepresentational urge remains
ambiguous to the degree that the body becomes open to a double
possibility. It is here that the first encounter between a phenomenologically employed diagnostic and objectivity may enter. From
the obscurity of affectivity Ricoeur notes that there is "[an] inevitable objectification of the body [which] infects all experience
of the self. The central, primitive fact of incarnation is simultaneously the first hallmark of all existence and the first invitation
to treason" (*FN*, p. 87).

The ambiguity within existence is the border which opens
the way for the alienation of the self from its body. The experiencing of need leads to its false objectification.

> This opaqueness of affectivity leads us to seek the light which
> the Cogito refuses to itself in the objectification of need and of
> bodily existence. Everything invites us to treat involuntary organic
> life as an object, in the same way as stones, plants, and animals.
> The very fact that the will feels besieged by need and at times op-
> poses it violently as if to eject it from consciousness places need
> midway between consciousness and foreign objects (*FN*, pp.
> 86–87).

The movement from existence to objectivity is begun. Need,
originally "felt" by the Cogito as opaque or even opposed to the
voluntary, becomes the occasion for its displacement to the bor-

derline between consciousness and objects. At this border it becomes possible to interpret felt need either dualistically (consciousness versus body) or in such a way that the subject's own understanding of himself as incarnate is alienated. Consciousness, once separated from existence, may then be interpreted as epiphenomenal or dispensed with altogether.

The movement from existence to objectivity establishes the possibility for two theoretical approaches to the body. Ricoeur continues to reject a metaphysical dualism but admits to a functional dualism of the two universes of discourse:

> . . . The problem presents itself not in terms of the relation of two realities, consciousness and the body, but of the relation of two universes of discourse, two points of view of the same body, considered alternately as a personal body inherent in its Cogito and as object-body, presented among other objects. The diagnostic relation expresses this encounter of two universes of discourse.
>
> This, then, is our task: to attempt to *clarify* the experience of the corporeal involuntary within the *limits* of eidetic analysis of motivation and in *tension* with objective, empirical treatment of the body (*FN*, p. 88).

The eidetic analysis has already been referred to in its function of description of felt need as an intentional behavior. Its limits, however, have not yet been established, nor has the tension between the objective treatment of the body and the eidetic been clarified.

The tension between objective and phenomenological insights performs this double task of the denaturalizing of objectivist models and the establishing of limits for eidetics. Put in its briefest form, the eidetic first calls into question the models of felt needs employed by objectivism. Needs are neither inner sensations nor stimulus-response patterns. The objectification of the body with its subsequent reduction of both external and internal experience to facts in the mode of "there is" overlooks the intentional pattern of even so vague an experience as bodily need.

> . . . Need is not an *inner sensation*. First of all, the expression "inner" does not account for the other-directedness which is an essential aspect of need and which testifies that, as all acts of the Cogito, it is a consciousness of. . . . It is because the impetus of need is not an automatic reflex that it can become a motive which inclines without compelling and that there are men who prefer to die of hunger rather than betray their friends (*FN*, pp. 90–93).

The diagnostic attempts to "demythologize" any such mechanical models which overlook the referential or transcending behavior of conscious acts.

Yet bodily needs are involuntary. The transcending act has a lower limit which it cannot coerce and which in the end presents a limit to consciousness itself. In the case of hunger, "while the impetus can be mastered by the will, the lack always remains uncoercible—I can refrain from eating, but I cannot help being hungry" (*FN*, p. 91). Such lower limits vary from case to case, and the efforts of the (conscious) voluntary are not in every case masterable. In what Ricoeur classifies as a hindered reflex such a limit to the voluntary is indicated:

> The case of respiration is the most remarkable. Air is obviously an object of an assimilatory need. Since there is air all around us, this pseudo-need is continually being satisfied without a previous lack; furthermore this assimilation is governed by a reflex which in the last instance is not coercible (man can go on a hunger strike, but not on a breathing strike). It is not a conduct governed at the same time by perceived signs and by an organic lack. Yet inhibited respiration presents itself as a need (*FN*, p. 113).

In both cases a lower limit is reached beyond which the voluntary may not go and which remains obscure to consciousness.

At this borderline the reciprocity of voluntary and involuntary is located and characterized by opacity. Only the relation of a secondary indirectness, the *index*, can equate what is known objectively with what is experienced. The language of "reflex," of "contractions," is symptomatically locatable from experience but remains outside experience. All the use of objective language remains, "the objective, empirical symptoms of an affective experience which belongs to thought, that is, to the Cogito itself" (*FN*, p. 91).

The diagnostic, in this weak use, correlates but does not internalize these symptoms, and the language of the Cogito (as phenomenology) only borders upon such symptoms.

> A need of . . . does not reveal my body to me but through my body reveals that which is not here and which I lack. I do not sense contractions and secretions—I am aware of the I-body as a whole lacking. . . . Neither organic difficulties nor movement are *that of which* I am aware; they are objective, empirical symptoms of an affective experience which belongs to thought, that is, to Cogito itself. This affective experience, as all *cogitatio,* has an intentional

object. The I-body is implicated in it only as the subject-pole of the affect (*FN*, p. 91).

The diagnostic sharpens, rather than dulls, the duality of points of view but recognizes the ambiguity which makes the two readings possible.

A projection from this recognition of limits is possible regarding the confusion of "languages" involved. In Ricoeur's terms, to say "I feel secretions of gastric juices" would be to mix or confuse universes of discourse. Nor is such a statement equatable with "I am hungry." There are secretions of gastric juices, however, and through the sign learning process they may be regarded as *indices* of "I am hungry." The location and description of the area of confusion which may arise, however, has been achieved through the location of an ambivalence border within experience.

The location and continued affirmation of the opacity of that border of ambivalence constitutes the one meaning of limit within the concept of fundamental possibilities of the will. Need as a source of motivation in the paradigmatic problem presents decision with an unresolvable obscurity at the lower limits of reflection. It is by contrast, one might almost say by reaction, that the other meaning of limit arises. The "normal" case of motivated will passes over the body, and if no difficulties are encountered the will is able to fulfill its needs with a certain simplicity. All decision is motivated, but motivation has a top and bottom to its limits. At the bottom motivation is opaque and confused; at the top—particularly as an ideality—motivation is relatively transparent. Out of this highest possibility arises the concept of the wish for a will which is *perfectly* transparent. In contrast to the possible confusions of motivation a "dream of innocence" is born within the variations upon motivated will.

2. Action: The Body as Organ of Movement

The second cycle of the will is action. As an adumbration, voluntary motion moves even closer to the body as a limit. The body in relation to voluntary motion is considered as the *organ* of the will. The theme of the body, however, remains a reflective theme, second in the order of description. The will as action is in its conscious aspects primarily directed toward the world. The pragma (the action concept which corresponds to the project in the cycle of decision) is an action undertaken in the world. Consciousness is first directed toward what it wishes to accomplish, and the doing of something ordinarily "exhausts" the attention.

Here again it is evident that the body remains unthematized in normal action and is unreflectively passed over. "When I act I am not concerned with my body. I say rather that the action 'traverses' my body" (*FN*, p. 210). This ordering of the role of body in acting serves a negative conceptual role in warning against any taking of the body as the terminus of will. "[The body] is not the terminus of action but rather a usually unnoticed stage in my relation to things and to the world. It is in an ebbing of attention that I notice my body and constitute its original meaning: *the body is not the object of action but its organ*" (*FN*, p. 212).

The first reason for bodily obscurity in reflective thought is complicated by the fact that a phenomenological reflection, if it is to be efficacious, must be able to describe action as a species of "consciousness of. . . ." But the body, in the case of action as in the case of need, presents itself non-representationally. "It is a non-representative consciousness, no longer even a practical representation, as a project. It is a consciousness which is an action, a consciousness which presents itself as matter, a change in the world through a change in my body" (*FN*, p. 209). Nevertheless, Ricoeur applies the intentional mode to action. "Acting seems to us for several reasons an aspect of intentional thought in a broader sense. Thought as a whole, including bodily existence, is not only light, but also force. The power of producing events in the world is a kind of intentional relation to things and the world" (*FN*, p. 207). Action as a non-representational force is a "lived" meaning, which is to say that it is an experience which is immediate without a corresponding conceptual clarity. "I experience—rather than know by a direct inspection of meaning of words—what 'being able to' and 'moving' mean. . . . I grasp it in a single example" (*FN*, p. 219).

The case of *effort* provides an instance for Ricoeur's subsequent double reading of the will. In this instance the generation of the upper limit of a fundamental possibility may be noted immediately. In ordinary cases of carrying out actions in the world the conscious side of the will may not note effort to any considerable degree. At the same time, so long as effort is minimal, the body does not become a problem either. Action which "traverses" the body with little effort has as its ideality the notion of an effortless or at least graceful action. All acting is in terms of its organ (body), but bodily docility and relative effortlessness are the normative possibility for the acting human will. The docility of body as the top limit of action capacitated by the body becomes, for Ricoeur, the primary eidetic form from which all subsequent variations may be understood.

> Genuinely voluntary motion is one which passes unnoticed because it expresses *the docility of a yielding body*. Docility is transparent, resistance opaque. . . .
> Yet it is the docility of the body, though most difficult to *describe*, which enables us to *understand* the body as an organ of willing. What is first and initially intelligible is not the opposition of effort and a resistance, but the actual deployment of the imperium in the docile organ. Resistance is a crisis in the unity of the self with itself (*FN*, pp. 309–10).

Here also, the ideality of this fundamental possibility rises from eidetic description. The "dream of innocence" of a completely graceful and effortless will in action becomes the mythical anticipation for a later explicitly hermeneutic expansion.

Effort, however, complicates the ideality of the will as the will meets a resistance. "Resistance can be understood only as a complication of the very docility of the body, which, from another viewpoint, corresponds to willing" (*FN*, p. 215). The complication of a resistance interrupts the transcending behavior which is first directed toward the doing of something in the world. A type of shock opens the way to a reflective problematization of action.

> Action as a whole encounters *obstacles*, resistances which ceaselessly require a readjustment of movement. In a general way, it is the body's resistance which makes me conscious of its mediating function. This situation, which is propitious to reflection on the body, is what we ordinarily call effort. Effort is moving itself, made more complex by an awareness of resistance (*FN*, p. 214).

Once the reflective turn is made the body as organ of willing may be thematized.

In Ricoeur's double reading of this thematization the first move is within the limits of the eidetic. Action is described as the movement originating in the Cogito and directing itself, through a series of adjustments, to the world.

> In effect voluntary motion as it is "acted" presents itself as an application, as a continuous change of plans, as if willing grew from a non-dimensional point to a volume lived as mine, a personal volume, having extension in the flesh in first person. Thus it would

move without interruption from a non-spatial simplicity to the level of multiplicity and organization. Bodily application of the I will is that by which I *become* actively extended and composed, by which the "I *become*" is a lived interval which is my body (*FN*, p. 220).

Such "lived" intentionalities retain a certain obscurity. The body as organ remains opaque and becomes the theme which invites a second reading.

> Notions which are too close to the body actually lack a clarity of their own. Concepts such as . . . moving serve more as indices, as "signa" of a situation which the mind never perfectly masters. . . . The "essences" here are extremely inexact and "indicate" a mystery which understanding inevitably transposes into an insoluble problem. . . . Phenomenology must go beyond an eidetics which is all too clear, and go on to elaborate the "indices" of the mystery of incarnation (*FN*, p. 219).

The eidetic reaches a lower limit in "lived meanings" which are non-representative. This opacity provides the occasion for the movement from existence to objectivity.

It is once again from a border of ambivalence that the temptation to make the body solely an object emerges. Here a dualism of points of view finds its justification. Returning to the problem of effort, the double movement is located at this obscure border of reflective experience.

> But while effort is what makes the organ-body available to reflection, it is at the same time effort which can falsify this reflection: it tempts us to reduce the description of moving to one of its forms, namely, to the relation between effort and organic resistance. Here dualism finds further justification: we no longer see anything but the opposition of body and willing (*FN*, p. 214).

The phenomenologically essential notion of a movement from the Cogito to the world "traversing" the body intersects with action as it is interpreted objectively.

Beginning from the "non-spatial" Cogito, which becomes an action in the world, effort "is the application of myself, who am not an object, to my body which is still myself but which is also an object" (*FN*, p. 217). But once it has become an object or placed in a field of objects, "The 'naturalization' of this voluntary force seems inevitable because of the objective character of the movement which this force produces and in some sense ex-poses among objects" (*FN*, p. 209). The "subjective" and "objective" universes border upon each other at precisely that point which is most obscure from the phenomenological point of view.

The "hermeneutic" function of the diagnostic is brought into play. And in the case of motion its use becomes more clearly that of a mapping of the universes of discourse. The ambivalence at the borders of these universes is recognized linguistically in the double use which is possible for the word *action:*

> This duplicity of the word "action" can be easily explained: human agent, considered as an object among objects, is the cause of change. Empirical causality is the objective indicator of corporeal motion. In virtue of the diagnostic relation which we have recognized between personal body and the object-body, a certain correspondence is established between voluntary action and objective relations of causality. This correspondence . . . explains the terminological ambivalence. But this ambivalence has become a confusion. Words like action, efficaciousness, force, dynamism are now also loaded with ambiguity. The realm of subjectivity and the realm of objectivity infect each other. In this way physics becomes loaded with anthropomorphisms and forces of nature are conceived as types of human energy. At the same time psychology becomes loaded with physics: corporeal force of willing is conceived as a cause whose effect is movement (*FN,* pp. 207–8).

However, what underlies the linguistic confusion is the possibility of reading action from two different directions. The movement from voluntary to world may also be reversed. The series is constituted from the eidetic description in the direction will-organ-tool-work. The transcending behavior of consciousness reads this series as follows:

> In effect on the one hand the customary use of a tool in some sense incorporates the tool into the organ: the worker acts at the end of his tool as a blind man extends his touch to the end of his cane. From the point of view of the man who acts, tool in hand, the action passes through a single organic mediator. Attention is focused primarily in the pragma, secondarily in the indivisible pair of organ and tool seen as an extension of the organ (*FN,* p. 213).

But the direction of will to pragma, as that which is performed in the world, borders on what objective discourse takes as its field. The series may be read in a reverse direction.

> In this respect the series will-organ-tool-work is rather ambiguous because it can be read in two directions: starting with the will —and thus from the point of view of phenomenology—or starting

with the work—and thus from the point of view of physics (*FN*, p. 213).

Once work is situated as an effect in the world it may become part of the series which deals only with the thematization of objective relations. The role of consciousness is absorbed. "The physical, industrial character of the relation of the tool to the work [objective] absorbs the organic character of man to the tool [phenomenological]" (*FN*, p. 213). Thus is completed the alienation of experience in the field of objects and their relations.

The possibility of the absorption of the will by rethematizing it in the objective universe of discourse is the "externalizing" of what begins in the "I." Ricoeur does not, however, note that the confusion which alienates experience into objectivity has a counterconfusion in the possibility of "internalizing" a set of objective concepts. He remains content in this case with locating the borders of the two universes of discourse and noting the non-correspondence which allows only an indirect relation by means of indices.

Now this mystery of the application of effort cannot be strictly compared with knowledge of the object-body. While the personal body presents itself as a body-moved-by-a-willing, that is, as the terminus of a movement which *comes down* from the "I" to its mass, the object-body is conceived as simply body, as first of all and only space. . . . The idea which grows from the non-spatial to spatiality has no objective meaning. This impossibility, which clings to the constitution of the world of objects itself, is more basic than the law of conservation of energy of which we can always say that it only applies to the structure of a scientific universe and that it is a postulate limited in its applicability. Consequently the application of effort has no objective correspondent which would be exactly parallel to it (*FN*, p. 220).

The will as action, like the will as decision, is left with a certain sense of irresolution. Only the reciprocity of the voluntary and the involuntary is described, thus leaving intact the dualism of points of view.

3. *Consent: The Body as Invincible Limit*

More careful attention is necessary in the examination of the diagnostic in the cycle of consent. Consent not only completes the possible movements of the will but also raises a series of problems which complicate a phenomenology of the will. Consent displays a certain asymmetry with the cycles of decision and action. In the face of absolute necessity the question of a voluntary correlate itself is problematic. The only movement of the voluntary is that of acquiescence, but in what sense is such a movement voluntary?

Ricoeur argues that "wise men have always construed the recognition of necessity as a moment of freedom" (*FN*, p. 344). But how can phenomenology treat necessity as an element of experience? An immediate application of an intentional analysis would seem to call for the description of necessity in the world against which the will finds an impossibility of movement. Yet in *Freedom and Nature* the reflective turn is introduced almost immediately, and discussion centers upon the noetic pole. This reflective move proves the importance of the theme of the body as the paradigmatic example for the elaboration of the involuntary. The "world" in this case is introduced in a reverse fashion: "It is to the extent to which the entire world is a vast extension of our body as pure fact that it is itself the terminus of our consent" (*FN*, p. 343). *Bodily necessity* as absolute limit is the dominant theme of the will as consent. Experience here reaches its lowest limit, and the encounters of the phenomenological and objective universes of discourse become the most crucial for the diagnostic.

With bodily necessity in an invincible form, the involuntary and the absolute conditions of will are identified. Here the final obscurity of experience is reached, and with it the final set of questions concerning the limits of an eidetic phenomenology of (conscious) will are posed. Eidetically, the need is to find absolute necessity *within* the experience of the Cogito.

> Existence is imposed on us in different ways: only necessity experienced within ourselves can be matched with the freedom of consent, for only an internal experience can be partial with respect to freedom and call forth an act of the will which it completes (*FN*, p. 351).

"Lived" necessity is the most opaque of all the regions investigated to this point. Its experiential correlates are of the vaguest type:

> Necessity seems to demand that the mind should place it outside of itself in order to consider it and reduce it through explanation since it is unable to subdue it through action.

Man's condition, insofar as it is irrevocable, is principally knowable from without; intimate experience of what I call character, the unconscious, and biological life is crude, fleeting, or even null (*FN*, p. 348).

The most concrete example of necessity is posed in relation to the case of birth as the beginning of a subject. Birth, classified under the most opaque stratum of experience, is correlated with biological life. It is the case in which the use of the diagnostic is seen as methodologically necessary.

The detour through objective knowledge is necessary; at its limit we begin to sense necessity for us and in us. It is always a definite objective knowledge which lends its inadequate language to Cogito's experience. We shall thus be led to retain the language of causality as an index of that investment of freedom by necessity subjectively experienced (*FN*, pp. 351–52).

The phenomenology of birth is the instance which is made possible by the indices of objectivity. The detour by way of objective accounts and the "language of causality" is a reversal of the usual order in which the eidetic description may precede the diagnostic. In this case the opacity of experience, when compared to the type of clarity and range of knowledge available empirically, is almost impenetrable. "Unfortunately the reflection for which [birth] calls is almost impossible: the word birth evokes a collection of confused ideas none of which correspond to a subjective experience and which seem susceptible only to a scientific elucidation" (*FN*, p. 433).

The detour by means of concepts originally foreign to a phenomenology of birth begins from regions which are primarily objective and which, by a series of approximations, approach a place of contact with experience itself. Birth means: (a) to inherit a *capital of heredity*—one's body is "inherited" from others and the language of "caused by" seems inevitable; (b) to have a parent (*filiation*) in such a way that the subject not only comes from a source other than himself but is dependent upon others; and (c) to have a *beginning*, but a beginning which is closed to experience or which at least always precedes experience. In each case the language of causality seems inevitable in relation to consciousness. In all cases the primacy of consciousness, and with it the primacy of a phenomenological beginning, is called into question.

The dialectic of the diagnostic consists first in a "demythologizing" of objectivity so as to purge it of its tendency to absorb and alienate the subject. Ricoeur asks, is there an *objective equivalent* of *my birth*? Moving from genetic biology, the discipline most distant from phenomenology, the enigma of objectivity in relation to subjectivity is posed.

Biology as a strict empirical discipline begins with a point of view inverse to the whole phenomenological point of view. The transcendental perspective of the subject is reversed, and the explanatory perspective of an observer "outside" the series is presupposed. "Biology only clarifies this feeling [of beginning with myself as absolute perspective] by reversing the perspective: the center of perspective is the ancestor; I explain my filiation not as *my* ancestry, but as my ancestor's posterity" (*FN*, p. 435). The *other* "explains" the subject in this universe of discourse.

In a yet stricter sense not only is the point of view of the subject reversed, but the individual in a system of empirical laws assumes secondary importance. "The individual no longer comes into consideration except as the bearer of seed, itself coming from a parental seed. Thus a new posture develops a consistency, the posture of the species. Through it the individual is basically servant of the species" (*FN*, p. 436). The "my" of my birth is not only "explained" by the other but also is subsumed under the generality of the species.

Finally, the movement of objectivity reduces the incident of birth itself to a merely arbitrary occurrence of the series:

> For biology . . . birth is only an incident between the intra-uterine and external life of the same individual, while conception is only a union of two cells which themselves continue the life of germination. There is in no sense here a beginning in the radical sense in which "I" begin to be (*FN*, p. 435).

The whole direction of objectivity is one which moves away from consciousness and alienates any connection with experience in the first person. There is no objective equivalent to *my* birth.

Yet the temptation to read the subject into even this most alien form of objectivity seems impossible to resist. The overlap or bordering of the object-body with the I-body poses an ambiguity which allows the objective universe of discourse to be read (wrongly) as a self-interpretation:

> I appear to myself as an effect of chance. . . . I am fascinated by the immense combination in which determinism takes the form of statistical determinism, alien to me since it places me in a causal

sequence. . . . At the end of these considerations I myself shall appear as a possible combination out of a considerable number of combinations which did not come about. The spell of objectivity has become the spell of combinations. . . . Absurdity follows me into the very confines of genetic rigor. . . . This is the alienation I inflict on myself in genetics (*FN*, pp. 435–36).

This confusion of universes of discourse which have no clear equivalent presupposes a change in level and function. The "I" is equated with the description of combination, and, without recognizing this change of level and subjectivity, chance becomes "absorbed" into the interpretation proffered by objectivity.

The facile lyricism which follows from this is familiar enough: the flow of the species rolls on beneath me and I am only its fleeting manifestation on the surface. Yet such false pathos expresses well enough the type of spell which this change of level brings about. On this new level of necessity a self-sufficient reading of man becomes possible. It is possible to stay on this level once we have chosen it and follow out a limitless explanation . . . " (*FN*, p. 436).

From the suppositions of the diagnostic such a *mixing* of levels and universes of discourse should not be possible in a direct way. There is no objective equivalent of *my* birth—but Ricoeur argues that there must be some relation between objective and subjective universes of discourse.

This relation is that of the index. Genetics locates my birth even if there is no experience of my birth. "Biology, without the compensation of an apperception of the Cogito, alienates me. And yet the study of genetics must become a guide in my consideration of myself. . . . I must at the same time break through the nascent dogmatism which follows from genetics and convert genetics philosophically into an index of my birth" (*FN*, p. 437). In the case of heredity, experience would seem to be null. There is no experience which can yield, "I feel my genes." This confuses universes of discourse and mistakes objectivity for existence.

The use of an index, however, proposes a relation through an indirect interpretation. From within the perspective of the Cogito a conjunction is made with the idea of heredity as a capital given to the subject:

The geneticist in me says that existence is capital received from the other and that this capital is a collection of genetic properties inscribed in a chromosomic structure; thus this capital is a diversity which, while possessing some functional unity, remains fundamentally multiple. The philosopher in me *translates* this: this multiple capital is the indivisible unity of my life, of my sheer existence; this capital received from the other is not the burden of an external nature, it is my self given to myself (*FN*, p. 438; italics added).

The indivisible unity my life, the vague feeling of being alive, is conjoined to genetic biological structure. But the diagnostic which originally sharpens and separates the universes of discourse cannot rejoin them. The index which "translates" biology into phenomenology remains a very rough translation.

But left to itself the weak use of the diagnostic reading of signs might retain a certain useful suggestiveness. However, the strong use of the diagnostic, in perhaps its most obviously questionable instance, is employed in an attempt to reduce the distances between the two universes of discourse. Ricoeur calls for an interiorization of the idea of heredity: "I have first of all to conceive of heredity as in me, and I have to conceive of it as the idea of my character. . . . I must constantly repeat that my heredity is only my character externalized, that is, the finite mode of my freedom alienated in the ancestor" (*FN*, p. 438).

This excess of the strong use of the diagnostic is in effect the counterpart to the confusion which entices one to use a science as a lyrical self-interpretation in a direct rather than hermeneutic fashion. If the movement from existence to objectivity falsifies experience, it should equally be the case that the movement from objectivity back to existence is a falsification. What is lacking at this point of the latent hermeneutics is a two-way limiting of universes of discourse. The first movement of a critique or "demythologization" of objective studies which portrays how and why the subject is alienated in objectivity is not counterbalanced by an equal "demythologization" of the favored phenomenological focus.

The dialectic of the diagnostic is thus weighted, and the whole direction of the reading is one which remains within the general limits of transcendental or Husserlian thought.

If it remains impossible to reduce biology as an objective discipline to the language of the Cogito and if the conjunction of biology and "being alive" remains tenuous, a second possibility for interpretation arises with birth as filiation. With filiation the ancestor, who is another subject, is introduced into the series. The ancestor as other subject opens the way between a reflective discipline and an indirectness which allows for more than the tenuous conjunction of experience and a system of empirical laws.

Unfortunately, there remains an ambiguity within Ricoeur's treatment of the ancestor which does not separate as clearly as possible the differences between what may be called the "ancestor's account" of my birth and the account of birth given scientifically in biology. The ambiguity, however, goes further back than Ricoeur's use of the eidetic, which presupposes *epoché*. In Husserlian phenomenology the suspension of the "natural attitude" includes a suspension of both mundane and scientific attitudes or presuppositions. When both universes of discourse are placed in a single grouping, the distinctive differences between ordinary discourse and scientific discourse are blurred. These differences have, particularly since Husserl's times, become sharper with the development of science as a self-consciously functional system.

What Ricoeur does recognize, from the Husserlian perspective which locates all sciences in relation to the originary life-world, could probably be accepted by today's biologist as well: "Even as geometry is born through the abstraction of the center of perspective from the body, so genetics adopts a point of departure and follows the series of growth by starting from what is an arbitrary starting point" (*FN*, p. 439). This is to say that with the maturation of contemporary epistemologies of science a concept of objectification as a deliberate abstraction and even as a deliberate counterbracketing and suspension is possible.

The overlapping of mundane and scientific accounts within *epoché* can be repeated in relation to the ancestor and his "account." The ancestor as a human being may be "read" in two ways, as an instance of an individual in an abstract series (empirically) or as another experiencing subject (phenomenologically). In this case the conflict between the two universes of discourse would lead to variations of the difficulties involved in the accounts of consciousness and objectivity but in terms of indirectness.

But a second possibility arises with the ancestor as subject. As another subject the ancestor is no longer merely a member of a system of laws but belongs to the same intersubjective world as the subject himself. This possibility introduces a subtle change into the problem of "objectivity." The series ancestor-progeny may be read in two ways, but in both cases the series is one of experiencing subjects. From the point of view of the subject the ancestor's "account" still displays the general structure of the language of "caused by . . . ," but only in the general sense of being indirect. The ancestor's account is a history which belongs to the history of subjects, and thus from the point of view of the subject the account may be reversed and read as "coming from. . . ." The ancestor's account, from the point of view of the subject, is a prehistory but nevertheless a history which deals with human experience. "Thus it is that every history sums up a prehistory. But this prehistory is the very seat of the Cogito, concealed from its apperception. Thus heredity adds to the sense of *my*-life-*in*-me, the unease of *the*-life-*behind*-me-clinging-to-me" (*FN*, p. 440). Ricoeur argues that in such a case it is possible to locate within experience itself an ambivalent sense of being suspended from the ancestor and that to all adult experience there clings a vestige of the child consciousness.[4] The language of "caused by . . ." as history, placed in conjunction with experience, serves as an *index* which helps one

> . . . discover that this foggy consciousness of being suspended from other beings and of owing my being to them, this consciousness of my attachments is not entirely overcome by the act which institutes the autonomy of consciousness. There sleeps within me an umbilical consciousness which biology can reveal at the cost of its own effacement and of the inversion of its rule of thought. It is in my child-soul that I retain the mark of this dependence and quasi-corporeal adherence (*FN*, p. 439).

Here, since there is an overlap between the ancestor's account and the subject's experienced history, the index serves very well to locate and correlate experience with the indirect account.

In this connection biology is invoked, but by the back door. It can only be invoked by inverting its own "*epochē*," and sub-

4. In an interesting anticipation of his later exploration of the fringes of experience as indicators of obscurity, Ricoeur adds, concerning the child-self:

> Freud is rather interesting in this respect when he shows, in our dreams and in our attitudes as waking men, something like a desire to return to the womb. This does not mean that the sleeping man or the unconscious have a better memory or remain children longer, but the unconscious, which bears the mark of the oldest impression, gives matter to our thought so that the waking man can free himself from its heavy unformed nostalgia only by formulating, with the help of a decipherer of dreams, the idea of a return to the womb (*FN*, p. 440).

sequently its "caused by . . ." becomes absorbed in the "account" of the ancestor, which is also a type of indirect recounting of *my* birth. Ricoeur does not make precise the movement which seems to be in operation at this point. In fact the original confusion of an ordinary "history" and a scientific "explanation" is continued in this transition.

It is with the meaning of birth as *beginning* that a connection is finally made with an experience specific enough to merit an eidetic description which locates absolute limits within experience. Birth as beginning is indicated and located indirectly, but the indirect accounts point to the temporal and finally structural limits within the Cogito itself.

> Two converging ways aim at this limit. It is indicated on the one hand as the terminus of a half-successful effort to apply to myself the objective event of my birth: it is the particular instance of a biological law and object of my neighbor's remembrances. In applying to myself the objective law and the memories of others— neither of which are a testimony to the beginning of an "I" but simply a change in the state of my parent's life—my attention is turned towards a point which is not an event for me, but which is designated by a certain essential characteristic of my memory (*FN*, p. 442).

Within memory and thus within consciousness itself a lower limit is indicated. Although such a limit theoretically could be found within the variations of consciousness without the indirect accounts, it is unlikely that it would be clearly recognized as an absolute limit. In the case of birth the indices of the diagnostic pose and make possible the locations of the invincible involuntary. The eidetic account correlates with the objective account.

> At first sight it seems that I have to give up hope of finding in consciousness the least testimony to its birth. Even the most obscure consciousness finds me already alive. And yet this flight from my birth which escapes the hold of my memory is precisely the most characteristic trait of my experience—if we can call this lack of experience experience. . . . I notice in effect that the regression to the womb of my own memories is not endless. My past, while not exactly delimited and not showing a precise beginning, forces its way into a crepuscular consciousness or into the dark memory and becomes extinguished: certainly my oldest memory is still my childhood, but I have at least a feeling of losing my own tracks (*FN*, pp. 441–42).

This phenomenological reading of a beginning within experience does not, of course, resolve the dualism of subjective and objective views. In fact, the lack of overlap here—memory does not reach back to the "objective" event—is, if anything, more strongly pointed up.

The weak use of the diagnostic, however, is justified insofar as the beginning thus located is recognized as a limit. The vague and obscure nature of the experience itself is used to indicate this limit.

> The silence of my memory at the end of more and more enigmatic and intermittent memories is, undoubtedly, not the equivalent of an experience of my birth. An absence of memory is not the memory of a beginning; but this silence nonetheless has something specific about it. This silence beneath the shadows of earliest childhood attests negatively that the flight of my origin is not endless. My birth is the terminus which I sense as limit by the spacing of the last points of memory in its direction. . . . It remains the case that my birth is never reached by my consciousness as an experienced event. However, this obstacle is not purely negative: it reveals the lower limit of the Cogito (FN, p. 442).

This limit to the experience of the Cogito is then interpreted as the experience of invincible necessity in a horizon for consciousness itself.

> My birth in the first person is not an experience but the necessary presupposition of all experience. This necessity of being born in order to exist remains a horizon of consciousness but it is demanded as a horizon by consciousness itself. The Cogito implies the anteriority of its beginning apart from its own perception (FN, p. 437).

Unhappily, at the end of Ricoeur's analysis of birth as heredity, filiation, and beginning, there is once again a use of the diagnostic in its strong sense as interiorization. "A limit can only be integrated into consciousness in consent" (FN, p. 442).

But in this last instance the integration into consciousness by consent brings into play a new theme, which is the *movement* of the will faced with invincible necessity. Consent is acquiescence to necessity—but acquiescence may take more than one form and hence is a genuine movement of the will. These movements, however, are all interpretative of the whole of the human condition. Four such possibilites are described in *Freedom and Nature*. Faced with absolute necessity, the will may *refuse* its condition in rebellion; may seek to identify itself with its condition in a lyric romanticism; may divorce itself from its condition in a dualism; or may consent with reservation to an "eschatology." Each of these movements is, however, already hermeneutic and mythological in the full sense. *The strong use of the diagnostic in this case identifies the movement of the will in necessity as an already hermeneutic movement.* By this stroke the universe of discourse proper to the pure eidetic is exceeded.

The methodological dialectic of the diagnostic which anticipates hermeneutics is only the first place in which hermeneutics is anticipated in *Freedom and Nature.* The very concepts which lie at the base of fundamental possibilities cross the specifically hermeneutic field of myth and symbolic language. At both extremes of fundamental possibility, as ideality and as border limit, variations become possible as mythological themes.

FUNDAMENTAL (STRUCTURAL) POSSIBILITIES

THE STRUCTURAL PHENOMENOLOGY of *Freedom and Nature* anticipates Ricoeur's subsequent hermeneutics in a twofold way. The diagnostic is the methodological anticipation of a general dialectic which animates all of Ricoeur's thought. It is the technique which after a series of transformations and refinements eventuates in a radicalizing of reflective philosophy. But its use in *Freedom and Nature* is one which remains limited to a clarifying role. At the end of the series of encounters between phenomenology and objective studies the duality of points of view remains:

> I must give up harmonizing the subjective experience of willing and the objective knowledge of structuring in a coherent knowledge. I have to give up harmonizing in a single universe of discourse the concepts of the Cogito and those of biology which belong to two incommensurate universes of discourse (*FN*, pp. 420–21).

But the dualism of perspectives is also a crisis for the understanding of the subject. *How is it possible that man may take two such perspectives upon himself?* This question contains within it an implication for a second step in a structural phenomenology, a step which must resolve both epistemological and ontological issues.

The answer to the question, from the ontological side, is a reaffirmation of Ricoeur's anthropology of man as faulted creature.

> Why is the dualism of soul and body the doctrine of understand-
> ing? Why is this dualism, in the virulent form of dualism of
> freedom and necessity, seemingly invincible? . . . Why? if not
> because the rent lies not only in the weakness of the intellect in
> grasping the mystery of the union of soul and body, but also up to
> a certain point is a lesion in being itself (FN, p. 444).

The answer to the question, from the methodological side, is
found in a new formulation which raises the duality of perspectives to a different level.

There is and has been under the whole dynamics of subjectivity and objectivity a silent third question which may be
posed epistemologically in relation to Ricoeur: What perspective
does a study which deals with both subjectivity and objectivity
take? Ricoeur's aphorism concerning ontology—"A paradoxical
ontology is possible only if it is covertly reconciled" (FN, p. 19)
—applies to method as well. The answer becomes the leading
question of *Fallible Man*. It is possible for man to take two divergent and non-reconcilable perspectives upon himself because
within man there is a non-coincidence which is that of the *finite*
and *infinite*.

> The duality of the voluntary and the involuntary is brought back
> into a much vaster dialectic dominated by the ideas of man's dis-
> proportion, the polarity within him of the finite and the infinite,
> and his activity of intermediation or mediation (FM, p. xx).

In summary, Ricoeur's conclusions in relation to the fundamental possibilities of the will are parallel to those of much existential phenomenology. All will is conditioned or situated—in
Ricoeur's somewhat stronger use, all will is *bound*. "Freedom is
not a pure act, it is, in each of its moments, activity and receptivity. It constitutes itself in receiving what it does not produce:
values, capacities, and sheer nature" (FM, p. 484). In terms of
the three cycles of the will (a) all decision is conditioned by
motives. *All human freedom is motivated freedom.* (b) The will
in action is always limited by the relative involuntary of capacities which are bodily. *All human freedom receives capacities
for motion.* And, finally, (c) a human freedom is one which is
absolutely limited by a nature of character. *All human freedom
is bound by a nature.*

Each of these limits, in Ricoeur's use, has an upper and a
lower meaning. Within the limits described an ideality is a possibility. Each cycle has a possible "dream of innocence": (a)

the "dream" for a motivated freedom which had a complete transparency of motive would be a *perfectly enlightened freedom;* (b) the "dream" for a capacity of motion which has a body completely docile and an effortlessness action is the wish for a *perfectly gracious freedom;* and (c) the idea of a freedom in which its nature was perfectly unlimited implies an *unbound freedom.*

Each of these "dreams of innocence"—which have mythological equivalents—contrasts with the second meaning of limit as obscure border. At its lower limit the fundamental possibility is revealed as an existential opacity of motive, capacity, and nature. At the lowest limit the movement of the will is consent to necessity. But consent is a movement which holds only interpretative possibilities, and once again mythological equivalents appear. A "Promethean" refusal, an "Orphic" identification of freedom and nature, a "Stoic" duality, or an "eschatological" hope are the themes which consent allows.

The conclusion of *Freedom and Nature* is a paradox: What can human freedom mean when it is *a freedom bound by nature?* The need for the paradox is revealed when the upper and lower meanings of fundamental possibilities are exceeded. When the "dreams of innocence" at the top and the refusal of condition at the bottom exceed the paradox of bound freedom, the result is not a human but a divine freedom, a limit of limits.

> The idea of God as a Kantian idea is a limit degree of a freedom which is not creative. Freedom is, so to speak, on the side of God by its independence from objects, by its simultaneous character of indetermination and self-determination. But we have in mind a freedom which would be no longer receptive with respect to motives in general (of capacities and of a nature). . . . such a freedom would no longer be a *motivated freedom,* in the human sense of a freedom receptive to values and finally dependent on a body, it would no longer be an *incarnate* freedom, it would no longer be a *contingent* freedom (*FM,* p. 484).

To exceed this limit is to pass beyond the fundamental human possibilities—it is the limit idea which limits the whole.

But, if these conclusions are not unsympathetic to existentially derived conclusions, Ricoeur remains reluctant to claim structural characteristics as a fundamental ontology. Only after the Fault is fully explicated can an ontology be claimed. But, "the fault is not an element of fundamental ontology homogeneous with other factors discovered by pure description . . .

fault remains an alien body in the essential structure of man" (*FM*, p. 24). Fault can only be dealt with poetically, says Ricoeur, and this hermeneutic turn is both a turn to expression and the movement which initiates the second Copernican revolution away from the subject. "The passage from transcendental phenomenology to ontological phenomenology is . . . a sort of conversion which removes the ego from the center of ontological concern" (*Husserl*, pp. 232–33).

Phenomenology within
"Kantian" Limits:
Fallible Man

THE FUNDAMENTAL POSSIBILITIES OF *Freedom and Nature* were seen to have both upper and lower limits, the first in an ideality and the second in a border of obscurity. But these structural limits were given an interpretation "in a Kantian sense." *Fallible Man* begins from this Kantian sense of limits as it elevates the problem of structural phenomenology to a higher level. Kant becomes the symbol for Ricoeur's self-imposed limitation of phenomenology. This appeal to a Kantian idea as a limit concept is symptomatic of Ricoeur's use of Kant to cut off transcendental pretensions which Ricoeur holds are inherent to the Husserlian version of phenomenology.

Fallible Man continues to employ the Husserlian meaning of phenomenology for description and analysis—but throughout this meaning is cast in a Kantian interpretative outline. Kant becomes the limit which is to prevent the Cogito from making a circle with itself, the limit which stops transcendental philosophy from becoming fully "idealistic."

Ricoeur argues that in Husserl's use of phenomenological reduction, "a methodological conversion and a metaphysical decision cross each other." [1] The methodological conversion is necessary and in varying ways is common to all transcendental reflection. It is the conversion which "causes the 'for me' of every ontic position to arise." [2] But the metaphysical decision which concludes that the Cogito is accorded an absolute position

1. Paul Ricoeur, "Kant and Husserl," *Philosophy Today*, X (1966), 148.
2. *Ibid.*

is precisely that which creates the second illusion Ricoeur wishes to avoid.

To stop short of this "idealism," Ricoeur *inserts* his version of a Kantian limitation at the intersection of method and metaphysics. All Husserlian phenomenology henceforth is to be interpreted through a Kantian philosophy of limits. But this imposition of limits is where Ricoeur makes his own decision between methodological conversion and metaphysical commitment.

> It is the glory of phenomenology to have raised to the dignity of science, by the "reduction," the investigation of appearance. But the glory of Kantianism is to have known how to co-ordinate the investigation of the appearance with the limiting function of the in-itself and to the practical determination of the in-itself as freedom and all persons.
> Husserl does phenomenology. But Kant limits and grounds it.[3]

The key to the Kantian foundation and limit is provided in Ricoeur's case by a return to a distinction between intention and intuition, which in the Kantian framework allows the in-itself to surpass its appearances.

> The key to the problem is the distinction, fundamental in Kant but totally unknown in Husserl, between *intention* and *intuition*. Kant radically dissociates the relation to something _____ and the vision of something. The *Etwas* = X is an intention without intuition . . . It is *because* the relation to the object = X is an intention without intuition that he returns to objectivity as unification of a manifold.[4]

Translating this limitation back into Husserlian terms is to say that an intention need not be fulfilled (empty intentions, for example). Ricoeur's claim, however, is stronger and in effect means that *all* intentions stop short of total fulfillment.[5]

This insertion of a Kantian distinction would seem to break apart precisely what is united in Husserlian phenomenology. Ricoeur recognizes that in the Husserlian context "the empty act of signifying is nothing other than intentionality" (*Husserl,*

3. *Ibid.*, p. 167.
4. *Ibid.*, p. 158.
5. This claim is in keeping with most of Husserl's followers, who dissent from his presumed "idealism." Cf. Merleau-Ponty's claim in his *Phenomenology of Perception* that the greatest lesson of the reduction is the impossibility of its completion.

p. 6). Moreover, sense and presence are united in intentionality. "Phenomenology itself is possible because intentionality goes to the sense. This is the sense which determines presence, just as much as presence fulfills the sense" (*Husserl*, p. 7). But, once given the distinction between sense and presence, it is possible to speak of intentionality as double. "Consciousness is doubly intentional, in the first instance by virtue of being a signification and in the second instance by virtue of being an intuitive fulfilling. In short, in the first works, consciousness is at once speech (*la parole*) and perception" (*Husserl*, p. 204).

The Kantian distinctions which separate two aspects of intentionality make possible the dialectic which dominates *Fallible Man*. To create a dialectic of finite and infinite as a disproportion within man, Ricoeur has to go *behind* Husserlian phenomenology. The idea of a paired or cointentional consciousness is a reintroduction of the Kantian problem of understanding and sensibility. Thus, in the transcendental synthesis which becomes the paradigmatic case for each of the following areas of investigation, the Kantian problem of understanding and sensibility appears as the need to pair speech and perception.

> One should not begin . . . with the simple, for example, perception, but with the couple, perception and word; not from the limited but with the antinomy of limit and unlimited. From this vantage point it becomes possible to detect something of the originally dialectical structure of human reality which is position, negation of finitude, limitation. [6]

The *finite* focus of the dialectic becomes perspective and calls for a phenomenology of perceptual perspective; the *infinite* focus of the dialectic is potentially language and calls for a phenomenology of signification. Both sides of the duality converge in the object, and *knowledge* is both to perceive and to judge.

> This dialectic of signifying and perceiving, of saying and seeing, indeed seems absolutely primal, and the project of a phenomenology of perception wherein the moment of saying is postponed and the reciprocity of saying and seeing destroyed is ultimately untenable (*FM*, p. 10).

6. Paul Ricoeur, "The Antinomy of Human Reality and the Problem of Philosophical Anthropology," in *Readings in Existential Phenomenology*, ed. N. Lawrence and D. O'Connor (Englewood Cliffs, N. J.: Prentice-Hall, Inc., 1967), p. 391.

But a dialectic of finite and infinite is also the separation of the problem of a phenomenology of perception from the problem of a phenomenology of language. The use of Kant becomes an anticipation of Ricoeur's movement toward the privileged position of language as the transcendental pole of the dialectic.

It is to be expected that the phenomenology of Kant should be primarily a phenomenology of judging. Such a phenomenology is most apt to offer a propaedeutic to epistemology. On the other hand, it is to be expected that Husserl's phenomenology should be, preferably, a phenomenology of perception, for this is most apt to illustrate a concern for evidence . . . and for presence . . . (*Husserl*, pp. 181–82).

By abutting these two "phenomenologies" Ricoeur not only reintroduces the problem of understanding and sensibility meeting in a "transcendental imagination" but begins the weighting of his dialectic in favor of the "infinite" or transcendental side of the dialectic.

This weighting becomes more evident when one notes that Ricoeur imposes a categorial scheme throughout which is a revision of the Kantian categories of quality. Transforming the original triad of reality, negation, and limitation into *originating affirmation* (infinitude), *existential difference* (finitude), and *human mediation* (the "third" limited term), Ricoeur's dialectic becomes one in which "The originating affirmation *becomes* man only by going through the existential negation that we called perspective, character, and vital feeling" (*FM*, p. 201).

Polemically, the use of this triad is directed against existentialism's use of finitist interpretations of man. "I doubt that the central concept of philosophical anthropology is finitude, it is rather the triad finitude-infinitude-intermediary." [7] But functionally the dialectic to be resolved in a "third term" is the "deduction" of a concept which opens a field for description as a fragile synthesis. "Let us try to disengage those specific categories of human limitation by initiating a kind of 'transcendental deduction,' that is, a justification of concepts through their power of making a certain domain of objectivity possible" (*FM*, pp. 205–6).

What must be noted is that, although the order to be followed in the text of *Fallible Man* always begins with the finite pole prior to moving to an implied infinite, the categorial schema

7. *Ibid.*

itself is clearly weighted *transcendentally*. It is always the infinite focus of the dialectic which is privileged. The dialectic as
a "deduction" is the measured limitation of transcendence.

In its Husserlian context transcendence becomes "idealistic."
"In transcending the world 'a-regional' consciousness includes
it and all other regions as well" (*Husserl*, p. 27). But the Kantian
interpretation limits transcendence to an intentionality without
total fulfillment. This initial and general limitation now is exceeded by the second and dialectical limitation, which is the
placing of progressive limits upon the originating affirmation or
infinite focus of each of the regions of human activity to be
explored. The dialectic of infinite-finite is described as a disproportion which makes man fragile or *fallible*. "This global
disproportion consists in a certain non-coincidence of man within
himself. . . . He is intermediate within himself, within his
selves" (*FM*, p. 4). Thus the non-coincidence of finite and infinite
limited in a third term is generated by the crossing of Husserlian
phenomenology with the Kantian philosophy of limits. It has as
its role the display of fallibility as the fragile totality of human
structural existence.

In the over-all plan fragility, fallibility, remains a structural
concept. It is the "possibility of evil: it indicates the region and
the structure of reality, which, through its point of least resistance offers a 'locus' to evil" (*FM*, p. 219). But this phenomenology of fallibility stops short of the entry into the experiences
of evil and thus falls short of an explicit hermeneutic. *Fallible
Man* as a second reading of the will is transitional. It is desig-
nated as a removal of brackets of the initial abstractions placed
upon the eidetic—but it is not to be a study of existential significations. "Now to take away the abstraction, or to remove the
parentheses, is not to draw the consequences or apply the conclusions of pure description. It is to disclose a new thematic
structure . . ." (*FM*, p. xvii). That new theme is the dialectic
of finite and infinite as a phenomenal fallibility. The process of
removing the brackets in such a way as to disclose human existence as fallible, without at the same time claiming that this
structural characterization is fully ontological, is indicative of
Ricoeur's reluctance to do existential philosophy as a structural
philosophy.

And, again, a Kantian schema is imposed to limit the analysis of *Fallible Man* to this preliminary role. The gradual removal of brackets in preparation for the exposition of existential
significations occurs in a pattern adapted from the three *Cri-*

tiques. The three cycles of knowing, willing, and feeling constitute the successive areas in which fallibility is to be located. But it is important to note that each cycle is based upon the *transcendental synthesis.* The Kantian schema is more than a mere outline. Ricoeur deliberately uses the transcendental synthesis as the model to which the subsequent synthesis of willing and feeling is to be approximated.

The imposition of a Kantian schema poses a problem. It would seem that by accepting an already established model for the transcendental synthesis, that is, the Kantian schema of understanding-sensibility-transcendental imagination, the question as to whether Ricoeur is doing phenomenology at all might be raised. This problem becomes more apparent when the second step is taken. Once the analysis of objectifying consciousness is performed, the following analyses of willing and feeling are to be patterned upon the model established in the transcendental synthesis. But, when these analyses are undertaken, differences emerge which threaten to overthrow the original model of a Kantian transcendental form. This becomes especially apparent in the case of the affective synthesis which appears closer to an existential phenomenology than Ricoeur might desire.

In spite of this problem, the essential strategy of Ricoeur's use of Kant remains in keeping with his understanding of phenomenology as a transcendental philosophy. Ricoeur holds that phenomenology always must be *first* a move away from immediacy.

All transcendental or reflective philosophy begins by "problematizing" the immediate, claims Ricoeur. The "move away" from immediacy, whether in the technical form of *epoché* or, as in *Fallible Man,* by the use of Kantian limits to phenomenology, is the condition which makes philosophy reflective. "Phenomenology becomes strict when the status of the appearing of things . . . becomes problematical. . . . In this strict sense the question of being, the ontological question, is excluded in advance from phenomenology, either provisionally or definitively" (*Husserl,* p. 202). In *Fallible Man* the move away is first addressed to intentionality itself. The transcendental synthesis "problematizes" phenomenology.

It is this motivation which lies behind the application of Kantian limits to Husserlian phenomenology and to the subsequent use of approximations of the wholistic areas of will and feeling to objectifying consciousness. The questions of will and feeling are already ontological questions in relation to human existence, and the use of a reduced transcendental (in the Kantian sense) pattern to which these areas are to be approximated imposes a limit. To get at the totality of will as a fragile synthesis, it must be first problematized and the immediacy of the lifeworld overcome.

> The order of philosophy is not a recapitulation of life, existence, or praxis, or however it might be stated. The totality that each of us is and in which we live and act becomes a *problem* only for a philosophy which has made itself aloof from it by asking another question, by giving another foundation to subjectivity, that of the "pure" things. . . . That is why transcendental reflection, though coming late in the movement of totality, must come first in the specifically philosophic order. For this reflection makes the question of the totality philosophic by making it problematic (*FM*, p. 74).

Thus for another time Ricoeur, at the very place that a movement from transcendental to existential phenomenology might be possible in a movement from transcendental consciousness to will, draws back. The lifeworld is to be approached by degrees and the brackets slowly withdrawn. "A philosophy which begins in the transcendental mode not only shows the totality as a problem but also shows it as a term of approximation; instead of proceeding straightway toward the totality it approaches it by degrees" (*FM*, p. 74).

Ricoeur moves from the "abstract" synthesis of objectifying consciousness toward the concrete totality of will and feeling as an ideal limit. In his Kantian sense he claims that "the idea of totality [is] a task, . . . a directive idea in the Kantian sense . . . a demand for totalization" (*FM*, p. 75), but a demand which is not to be fulfilled directly.

Will and affectivity are to be understood upon the base of the transcendental synthesis interpreted through the Kantian framework. The subsequent approximation of will and affectivity to knowledge is to follow the pattern of: the triadic dialectic of an infinity or original affirmation which is negated or passed through finitude or existential difference to the third limit term understood as human mediation. But since the original "problematization" of objectifying consciousness is an admitted reduction of existence to knowing, the problem of approximations becomes one of a gradual substitution of wholes for parts. This procedure threatens to break the original pattern. The end result is to envision the lifeworld as a limit-idea and its understanding as an intention which is never thoroughly fulfilled.

The aim of *Fallible Man* is to understand the structures of the will as a totality, but its achievement is not to be taken as a fundamental ontology. *Fallible Man* remains on the side of a structural phenomenology, and its task is to do a "phenomenology of fallibility" as *the* fundamental possibility of human will.

THE TRANSCENDENTAL SYNTHESIS

THE TRANSCENDENTAL SYNTHESIS is an analysis of knowing taken as objectifying consciousness. The very fact that this synthesis becomes the model to which the analyses of will and affectivity are to be approximated gives it a privileged value. But once the Kantian framework and interpretation of limits are understood the more technical use of phenomenology returns within these limits. Ricoeur joins a Husserlian description (noematic-noetic) to the Kantian outline. Knowing or objectifying consciousness is to be understood via the object as it appears. "What is first displayed, what appears is things, living beings, persons in the world" (*FM*, p. 29). Only in this case the dialectical demands of the Kantian framework will call for two separate analyses of that appearance, one as the finitude of knowing and the other as the infinitude of knowing.

The finite pole of the dialectic is revealed simply enough in a description of *perspective*. A schematic outline of perspective locates the finitude of objectifying knowledge in the recognition that the object appears only in a series of profiles (noematically) which reflectively establish the subject as a point of view (noetically).

> In what does the finitude of receiving consist? It consists in the perspectival limitation of perception. It causes every view of . . . to be a *point of view* on. . . . But this characteristic of the point of view, inherent in every viewing, is not directly noticed by me but realized reflectively (*FM*, p. 32).

The reflective turn discovers perspective by "deducing" the origin of the subject's point of view from or via the object's appearances. "Thus by a regressive route whose starting point was the characteristics of the percept, we elucidate the finitude proper to receptivity. This peculiar finitude is identified with the notion of point of view of perspective" (*FM*, p. 35).[8] Perspective as finitude is understood progressively as (a) the subject's *opening* to the world or field of objects, (b) the *here* or concrete position from which the field is perceived, and (c) the originating *motion* which allows objects to appear from different sides and which points to the *body* as the condition for perspective. The dialectic of finite and infinite now overlaps the previous dialectic of voluntary and involuntary.

The finitude of perspective is situated by bodily finitude, and once again the body is at one terminus of the reflective movement. "It is always *upon* the world and beginning from the manifestation of the world as perceived . . . that I apprehend the openness of my body, mediator of intentional consciousness" (*FM*, p. 32).

Fallible Man here rejoins the unresolved problems of *Freedom and Nature*. The phenomenology of perspective, bound to the body, makes explicit what was implicit in the distinctions between the subjective and objective universes of discourse. Not only are there two possible readings of the field of objects (as anonymous objects or as containing other conscious subjects) which may be read from two directions (from the voluntary across the body into the world and vice versa), but there are also two distinct regions which both meet at the object.

> Let us first notice that by beginning with the object and not the body, by moving from the percept [the perceived] to the perceiving, we do not risk being referred from the thing in the world to another thing in the world, which would be the body-object such as psycho-physiology observes it from the outside and scientifically knows it. This body-object is still a perceived. And it is necessary to disengage it by a special procedure because its function of mediation causes it to pass over itself and lose itself in the perceived there where the various operations of perceiving crash together, so to speak, and become identified with what is perceived (*FM*, p. 33).

The two regions are established as distinct because they are constituted differently. The object-to-object field is constituted by being *perceived*. The reflection of the subject *from* the object as

---

8. Several translators have rendered *perçu* as "the percept." In my opinion this is unfortunate since *percept* has a technical meaning within the context of sense-data theories and hence a possible confusion is raised in relation to the phenomenological sense of the perceived as a noematic correlate.

a region is constituted by going from the perceived to the *perceiving*. But the object (as perceived) is common to both regions.

The body which is both "object" and "subject" could have been clarified at this point by noting how the subject may gain alternating views of his body as object perceived ("I see my hand") while at the same time experiencing his body reflectively, thus attempting to account for the alternation of object and subject on the basis of perspective. But Ricoeur does not take this direction to its conclusion. A perceptualist resolution overlooks the "infinity" which all perspectives presuppose.

Ricoeur's answer to how man may take alternating views of himself is to be found in the infinity which *transcends* all perspectives. If perspective is recognizable as finite, the ability to apprehend this finitude already presupposes a different quality of experience.

> The very existence of a discourse on finitude should suffice to establish that the idea of perspective may be the most abstract of all the ideas about man and that it in no way attests the triumph of a concrete philosophy over the so-called abstract views of critical reflection. The very act of declaring man finite discloses a fundamental feature of this finitude: it is finite man *himself* who speaks of his *own* finitude. A statement on finitude testifies that this finitude knows itself and expresses itself. Thus it is of the nature of human finitude that it can experience itself only on the condition that there be a "view on" finitude, a dominating look which has already begun to transgress this finitude. (*FM*, pp. 37–38).[9]

This transcendence, originating affirmation and thus first in the dialectic, is only secondarily limited by bodily perspective.

But transcendence, too, must be reflected through the appearance of the object, and a second analysis is called for. Phenomenological accounts of perception indicate that while an object is perceived from a side, and thus seen from a point of view, all the other sides are meant or *signified*. The transcendence of finite perspective is implicit from the object. The (literally) unseen side is signified (intended) in what is seen. A "judgment" or meaning is given for the thing itself. The thing-as-signified has as its reflective pole the intention to signify. This transgression is the intention to signify. Through it I bring myself before a sense which will never be perceived anywhere by

9. Ricoeur uses *transgression* in a way similar to the uses of *transcendence* by other existential phenomenologists.

anyone, which is not a superior point of view . . . but an inversion into the universal of all point[s] of view" (*FM*, p. 41). The "judgment" as the intention to signify recaptures the crossing of the Kantian theme which guides the deduction.

The general (or empty) intention to signify is then further located in the *power of speech*. "If I now note that to signify is to intend, the transgression of the point of view is nothing else than speech as the possibility of expressing, and of expressing the point of view itself" (*FM*, p. 41). Human transcendence is the intention to signify and is the power of speech. "I am not merely a situated onlooker, but a being who intends and expresses. . . . As soon as I speak I speak of things in their absence and in terms of their non-perceived sides" (*FM*, p. 41).

This power of speech, taken first in its ability to *express absence*, is a stronger indication within *Fallible Man* of Ricoeur's shift of phenomenology toward its subsequent affirmation that "man is language." The signification in absence is the sign and "in the sign dwells the transcendence of the logos of man" (*FM*, p. 43).

The weighting of transcendence over finitude as an originating infinity ultimately implies a weighting of language over perception:

> This transcendence of signification over perception, of speaking over perspective, is what makes the reflection on point of view as such possible; I am not immersed in the world to such an extent that I lose the aloofness of signifying, of intending, aloofness that is the principle of speech (*FM*, p. 48).

In the movement *from* infinity *to* limitation it must not be forgotten that finitude is the dialectical limitation to transcendence. The intention to signify as the transcendence of man is the basic intention which is not fulfilled.

Its essence lies in the limited intentionality of expressing absence. To speak of things in their absence or to locate signification in the non-present side of things is to view transcendence as an intentionality without fulfillment. But it also gives a privilege to that class of expressions which indicate this transcending capacity.

> This transcendence of *saying* is attested by its excess in relation to fulfillment. Without being paradoxical we may say that the *least fulfilled expressions are the most instructive* in this connection and that the height of signification is that of the one which in principle cannot be fulfilled, the absurd signification. I am the

power of absurd significations. This single power attests that I do not exhaust myself in an intentionality of fulfilled presence . . . by its nature of being impossible to fulfill, the absurd signification only reveals the property that all meaning has of exceeding every present perceptive fulfillment: I say more than I see when I signify (FM, pp. 43–44).

Perspective, the limit of bodily existence, is the finitude of knowing. But the originating affirmation of knowing is the power of signification. These co-intentionalities which meet in the object are the finite and infinite disproportion of transcendental consciousness. The identification of the first with perception and the second with speech is Ricoeur's reintroduction of the Kantian problem of understanding and sensibility.

In discovering the breach between the finite and infinite [our reflection] has also uncovered the "disproportion" between the verb which gives expression to being and truth at the risk of falling into error, and . . . the passive look which is riveted to appearance and perspective. This "disproportion" is . . . the duality of the understanding and sensibility in Kantian terms (FM, p. 57).

But the disproportion which is possible by reflectively problematizing the appearance of the object cannot overcome the first phenomenological fact that the object appears as a unitary whole. Thus the "synthesis" which unites the limitation of perspective and the excess of signification is given before it is problematized, and the synthesis in a transcendental imagination is somewhat anticlimactic.

What is the thing? It is the unity which is already realized in the correlate of speech and point of view: it is the synthesis as effected outside. That synthesis inasmuch as it is in a correlate, bears the name of objectivity. Indeed, objectivity is nothing other than the indivisible unity of an appearance and an ability to express; the thing shows itself and can be expressed (FM, p. 58).

The thing is a unitary appearance united reflectively in the "transcendental imagination."

After going behind phenomenology, the Kantian detour returns to what is first. Objectifying consciousness intends the thing—this is the project of objectivity. It is exhausted in this project. It is an intentionality by which consciousness is constituted (in Husserlian terms) but an intentionality which is without fulfillment, since the thing always exceeds its appearances (again in Kantian terms).

The limitation of this reflection appears directly along with its strength: the synthesis that it reveals and inspects will only be a synthesis in the object . . . a synthesis which is merely intentional. . . . Undoubtedly we will be able to call this power of synthesis "consciousness" as Kant did, and speak of the synthesis *as* "consciousness" (*FM,* p. 28).

It remains limited to an intention which projects objectivity, but it remains short both of self-consciousness and of the totality which is existence. "The synthesis . . . between understanding and sensibility [or in our terminology, between meaning and appearance, between speaking and looking] is *consciousness* but it is not self-consciousness" (*FM,* p. 70). Such a consciousness is a reduced form, a pattern. "The 'I' of I think is merely the form of a world for anyone. It is consciousness in general, that is a pure and simple project of the object" (*FM,* p. 70). This form, however, sets the pattern to which are approximated the totalities of will and affectivity.

THE PRACTICAL SYNTHESIS

THE KANTIAN PATTERN of knowing consciousness is now considered established, and the task Ricoeur sets for himself is that of approximating will and affectivity to this pattern. As a general strategy this task might well be seen as one which continues the perceptualist model of phenomenology. The initial form of intentionality was one which arose from the analysis of the knowing subject's experience of things (the project of objectivity). But, as the variations which arise from the approximating process show, a basic problem also arises. The knowing consciousness is but a part or a bare form of the existent person, whereas will and affectivity, claims Ricoeur, are totalities. It is questionable that by beginning with a partial form one can ever thoroughly approximate a totality to it.

Nevertheless, the basic triadic pattern of the transcendental synthesis is imposed upon the analysis of the will, and the Kantian framework is paralleled to the form of knowing consciousness. In this case the exposition will follow the final, rather than the apparent, order of the dialectic: (a) The infinite field of "word" is paralleled in the case of the will by the infinite field of all possible human motivations. This field, termed *humanity* by Ricoeur, is the infinite or transcending side of willing in its general aim toward happiness.

My field of motivation is open to the whole range of the human. . . . "Nothing human is foreign to me." I am capable of every virtue and every vice; no sign of the human is radically incomprehensible, no language radically untranslatable. . . . My humanity is my essential community with all that is human outside myself; that community makes every man my like. (*FM*, p. 93).

One should note here that the use of infinity is ambiguous and that in the cases of both "will" and "affectivity" infinity often is equated with totality, whereas in the case of "word" it was used to mean a general openness. Ricoeur admits that "the very word infinite is more expressive than meaningful. It does not and could not denote a concept of reason, for it is rather indefinite. . ." (*FM*, p. 21). In fact, were it not for the need to dialectically pair finitude with infinity, it might be more accurate to understand infinity as merely the indefinite. The indefinite field of possible human motivations is the open field of possibilities for the will.

(b) But this totality of possibilities is merely intentional, since its "infinity" is factually limited by the finitude of the will which Ricoeur locates in the concept of character. "My character is not the opposite of that humanity; my character is that humanity seen from somewhere. . . . Character is the narrowness of the 'whole soul' whose humanity is openness" (*FM*, pp. 93–94). Character as a totality is paired with point of view, and the limit of the will is approximated to the limit of perspective.

(c) The duality of infinite and finite is mediated in a project, which in the case of the will is termed the *idea of the person*. The project of the person approximates the project of objectivity. Person, however, is an ideality stated in Ricoeur's Kantian framework as a reassertion of the end-in-itself.

In the form of the person, I intend a synthesis of a new kind: that of an end of my action which would be, at the same time, an existence. An end, consequently a goal to which all the means and calculations of means are subordinate; or in other words, an end in itself . . . (*FM*, p. 109).

In this general form the approximations establish the basic Kantian framework within which specific phenomenological descriptions occur. Once the approximations are noted a return to the phenomenological analysis of experience can be made, again from each side of the dialectic. At the infinite pole Ricoeur indicates a phenomenology of desire. The will "intends" or desires totality, which is revealed through the presence of the field, humanity. "The idea of a complete volition and the destination of reason hollow an infinite depth in my desire . . . which dwells in the human will and in this way becomes the source of the most extreme 'disproportion': that which preys on human *action* and strains it between the finitude of character and the infinitude of happiness" (*FM*, p. 103).

The indication for such a totality of happiness is located in what Ricoeur terms feelings of immensity and narrowness:

> Just as I receive indications of my perceptual narrowness—if only through being at variance with others—I also receive signs of my destination to happiness. These are privileged experiences, precious moments in which I receive the assurance that I am on the right path. Suddenly the horizon is clear, unlimited possibilities open up before me the feeling of the "immense" then replies dialectically to the feeling of the "narrow" (*FM*, p. 104).

The movement is one from the "infinity" of originating affirmation which is limited by the narrowness of character. In relation to humanity as total possibilities, the person is always a finite actualization.

The parallelism, however, is not perfect, and the approximation of such existential functions as will to knowledge shows variations which reintroduce the concept of absolute necessity. Perceptually the finitude of bodily perspective is relative to motion, and the subject may change the position from which the object is seen.

> But if I can change my position, I cannot change my character. *There is no movement by which I could change the zero origin of my total field of motivation.* . . . In this way I attain the idea of an immobile source, in the literal sense, perspective, in the sense that I cannot "enter" it nor could I "leave" it. It is in this sense that my character is the radically non-chosen origin of all my choices (*FM*, p. 95).

The themes of *Freedom and Nature* are again met with in the finite focus of character. The non-chosen origin of character is the absolute involuntary which is not the result of taking a position. The location of character as a zero origin in an approximation to the "space" of perspective may also be extended temporally as the non-chosen limit indicated in birth.

> My birth designates the primary fact that my existence is itself a fact. . . . My birth therefore is nothing other than my character; to say that I was born is merely to point to my character as

that which I find. My birth betokens the "having been," the mark of the past which clings to the state of existing. My birth is the already-thereness of my character (*FM*, p. 96).

Necessity is not outside the self; it is the origin, the limitation which is the finitude of the subject.

In this new dialectic the finitude and necessity implied in character are the narrowing of a vaster totality. Character is the limitation upon the infinite demand for happiness revealed in the unrealizable field of possible motivations. Character as finitude once and for all limits the intentionality of the will to a lack of fulfillment. The "immensity" of the desire for happiness passes through the "narrowness" of character, and this disproportion is the dialectic which institutes human limitation. "Man is the Joy of the Yes in the sadness of the finite" (*FM*, p. 215).

The synthesis or mediation of this disproportion is the constitution of the *person,* the project of person.

> This project is what I call humanity, not in the collective sense of all men but the human quality of man, not an exhaustive enumeration of human beings but the comprehensive significance of the human element which is capable of guiding and regulating an enumeration of human beings.
> Humanity is the person's personality, just as objectivity was the thing's thingness; it is the mode on which every empirical appearance of what we call a human being should be patterned (*FM*, p. 107).

It is not accidental that the term humanity reappears in Ricoeur's description of the project of the will. As a field term humanity was the indefinite totality of possibilities; as the project of a person humanity is an ideality seen as an ideal limit in the fundamental possibilities. Ricoeur has repeated his understanding of structure both as limited by a border of indefiniteness and as expressed in an ideality. The totality of human possibilities constitutes the field of the limit, but the highest possible realization of that field constitutes the ideality. The idea of person is a limit idea in that sense. It, too, finds its Kantian limitation in being an intention without fulfillment.

> The person is still a projected synthesis which seizes itself in the representation of a task, of an ideal of what the person should be. The Self is aimed at rather than experiences. . . . This self is still a projected self, as the thing was the project of we called "consciousness." Self-consciousness is, like the consciousness of the thing, an intentional consciousness (*FM*, pp. 106, 110).

The person as unfulfilled intention remains a task rather than an achievement, but this implies that the totality itself must remain unachieved. The approximation of the will to knowing retains this limitation.

THE AFFECTIVE SYNTHESIS

AFFECTIVITY poses a special problem in the series of approximations to the primary transcendental pattern. Not only is there no clearly structured parallelism, but in the analysis Ricoeur comes closer to doing an orthodox phenomenology than in the previous cycles. The phenomenology of affectivity threatens the Kantian outline.

Ricoeur sees affectivity as the inverse side of objectifying consciousness. It is that mode of human subjectivity which interiorizes knowing. "Indeed, the significance of feeling appears in the reciprocal genesis of knowing and feeling . . . feeling and knowing 'explain each other'" (*FM*, p. 126). Affectivity, traditionally a delicate problem for philosophy, is amenable to a phenomenologically modeled description as an intentional behavior. Ricoeur notes this and seeks to understand affectivity as a type of consciousness of. . . .

But in the analysis Ricoeur notices immediately that there is a dual reference implied by affectivity, a reference which might be said to be immediately reflective.

But it is a very strange intentionality which on the one hand designates qualities felt *on* things, *on* persons, *on* the world and on the other hand manifests and reveals the way in which the self is inwardly affected . . . an intention and an affection coincide in the same experience, a transcending aim and the revelation of inwardness (*FM*, p. 127).

In its noematic direction affectivity, like any form of intentionality, refers beyond itself toward the world.

Feeling, for instance love or hate, is without doubt intentional: it is a feeling of "some thing"—the lovable, the hateful. . . . For it is *on* the things elaborated by the work of objectification that feeling projects its affective correlates, its felt qualities: the lovable and the hateful, the desirable and the loathsome, the sad and the joyous; thus it seems to play the game of the object (*FM*, pp. 126–27, 134).

However, this initial reference to an object displays characteristics which Ricoeur designates as surplus and as lack. In most epistemologies it is the lack apparent in affects which is accounted for and emphasized. Affectivity lacks the autonomy proper to objectivity. Affectivity is constituted upon or around the perceptually (or imaginatively) constituted object in an "intentional correlate but without autonomy. It is the perceived and known object which endows [the object] with a center of significance, a pole of objectivity and, one might say, the substantive of reality" (*FM*, pp. 127–28). Ricoeur thus accepts a basically Husserlian perspective in relation to the affections. The perceptual object provides the core to which are "added" the affective qualities.

At the same time, however, affectivity contains a certain "surplus" in the experience of the object which the analysis must account for. There is a reflexive reference to a state of the subject in affectivity. Not only does the subject indicate that "there is an X which is . . . (lovable, hateable, etc.)," but at the same time the subject feels that love, hate, etc., the affections, reveal his own state of . . . (loving, hating, etc.). In Ricoeur's analysis this dually referenced intentionality is linked with objectifying consciousness itself.

> Here the reciprocity of feeling and knowing is very illuminating. Knowing, because it exteriorizes and poses its object in being, sets up a fundamental cleavage between the object and the subject . . . knowing constitutes the duality of subject and object. Feeling is understood, by contrast, as the manifestation of a relation to the world which constantly restores our complicity with it, our inherence and belonging in it, something more profound than all polarity and duality (*FM*, p. 129).

To recognize the dual reference of feeling as directed toward objects *and* as revealing inwardness poses a particularly difficult problem for philosophy. There is no clear and easy way to express this double-directed intentionality within the limits of the usual philosophical models of subject and object. Ricoeur pushes the blame further and indicates that at base these limits are to be found in *language*.

> We live in the subject-object duality which has structured our language, this relation can only be reached *indirectly*. . . . Since the whole of our language has been worked out in the dimension of objectivity, in which the subject and object are distinct and opposed, feeling can only be described paradoxically as the unity of

an intention and an affection, of an intention toward the world and an affection of the self (*FM*, p. 134).

If we remain within the limits of a directly structured subject-object duality, we end up falsifying the experiential nature of the dual reference of affectivity. There are two traditional errors which may follow and which should be avoided:

(a) Not finding in feeling the mode of objectivity proper to the thing, we say it is "subjective." In that case we miss its intentional dimension and falsify the connection between the objectivity of knowing and the intentionality peculiar to feeling (*FM*, p. 135).

(b) Conversely, out of a concern for doing justice to the specific intentionality of feeling, we attribute the feeling objects or quasi-objects which we shall call *values*. . . . [But] these false substantives still only point to the intentional signs of our affections (*FM*, pp. 135, 137).

Indirectly, however, these limitations may be overcome through a display of the dual reference of feeling in a specific case. The cases developed in *Fallible Man* are again under the sign of a Kantian "phenomenology" of the passions (possession, domination, and honor).

The first example, possession, is sufficient to establish the phenomenological demonstration of the dual reference of the affections. The general outline of Ricoeur's approximations move from (a) the basic model of objectifying or knowing consciousness; to (b) a series of approximations toward the life-world; and culminate in (c) the discovery of a limit idea revealed by feeling. The "surplus" of affectivity is to be modeled upon the object, and the question of the appearance of the thing takes precedence.

If our theory of feeling is valid, the feelings which gravitate around . . . having . . . ought to be correlative with a constitution of objectivity on a level other than that of the merely perceived thing. . . . The theory of the object is by no means completed in a theory of representation: the thing is not merely what others look upon (*FM*, pp. 170–71).

Beginning with the appearance of the object, the question is one of moving from a bare objectivity to the interiorization of the affections in relation to the object. The analysis of affectivity is to be approximated to objectifying consciousness.

The investigation of authentic human affectivity, therefore, must be guided by the progress of objectivity. If feeling reveals my adherence to and my inherence in aspects of the world that I no longer set over against myself as objects, it is necessary to show the new aspects of objectivity which are interiorized in the feelings of having. (*FM*, p. 171).

Objects within the field of a subject's gaze are not normally "neutral." In the case of possession the "economic object" is not restricted to the appearance of a bare object of perception. Objects appear as desirable, undesirable, interesting, uninteresting, valuable, and unvaluable. Out of the whole range of such possibilities the "economic object" as an object to be possessed appears with a recognizable set of characteristics. The object in the fully human and cultural world is "more than" a bare perceptual object. Moreover, such economic objects relate at base to human needs. Food (to be desired), clothing (to be desired), etc., are objects which are referable to the interior feelings of the subject.

Whereas the simple need is only an oriented lack, the desire for the economic object is relative to the object's availability for me. Insofar as the thing is "available" it creates the whole cycle of feelings relative to acquisition, appropriation, possession and preservation (*FM*, pp. 173–74).

The object viewed "economically," as available for a subject, is more than the object in terms of a bare or abstract perception. The object is seen as to be possessed, as valuable. But by the same stroke the dual reference is one which refers back to the feelings of the subject.

That which is properly feeling here is the interiorization of the relation to the economic thing, the reverberating of "having" in the I in the form of the "mine." The I, then, is affected by having which adheres to me and to which I adhere. Through this feeling I experience both my control over having of which I can avail myself and my dependence with regard to that which is other than myself and on which I make myself dependent (*FM*, p. 174).

To possess, within the interiorizing activity of affectivity, is to view objects in a certain way and to constitute the subject in a certain way. Possession establishes the "I." "Mine and yours, by mutually excluding each other, differentiate the I and the you through their spheres of belonging" (*FM*, p. 174). The feelings of possession are the constituting dimensions in relation to the subject which ultimately may be seen to reveal a dimension of

existence. A limit is reached which reveals a stuctural characteristic. "Thus imaginative variation encounters a limit which bears
witness to the resistance of an essence: I cannot imagine the I
without the mine or man without having" (*FM*, p. 176).

Possession is an essential structure of human existence
which is revealed through the dual intentionality of feeling. Affectivity reveals existence. It is both a transcending feature of
consciousness, referring beyond itself to the "economic object"
and an involvement of the self with the world through the "internalization" of the mine. In this sense feeling, affectivity,
breaks through the usual meaning of subject and object.

> The universal function of feeling is to bind together. It connects
> what knowledge divides; it binds me to things, to beings, to being.
> Whereas the whole movement of objectification tends to set a
> world over against me, feeling unites the intentionality, which
> throws me out of myself, to the affection through which I feel my-
> self existing. Consequently, it is always shy of or beyond the
> duality of subject and object (*FM*, pp. 200–201).

It is in this analysis of affectivity that Ricoeur comes closest both
to a phenomenology of the existential type, which begins by
viewing man in a lifeworld, and to the final circle of his Kantian
approximations.

As a totality, affectivity in its role of revealing existence
serves to "interiorize" the previous disproportion of man. Fallibility is *felt* as conflict.

> But by interiorizing all the connections of the self to the world,
> feeling gives rise to a new cleavage, of the self from the self. . . .
> The disproportion of feeling gives rise to a new mediation, that of
> the *thumos*, of the heart. . . . It seems, then, that *conflict* is a
> function of man's most primordial constitution; the object is
> synthesis; the self is conflict. The human duality outruns itself
> intentionally in the synthesis of the object and interiorizes itself
> affectively in the conflict of subjectivity (*FM*, p. 201).

Conflict internalized is the personalization of all disproportion.
But the felt fragility of existence remains structural. It is the
weakest point of man's existence—but it remains short of accounting for Fault itself. Although fallibility is the possibility
for the entrance of guilt and suffering, it is not a necessity that
man undergo Fault.

This conclusion to the structural phenomenology, always
limited by Ricoeur to a preliminary role, remains short of a *de-*

duction of man's actual experiences of evil and suffering. Ricoeur draws back from making any structural characteristics into a fundamental ontology. He opts instead to begin from a second basis and plunges into the realm of expressions of evil under the sign of Fault.

4 / From Structural Phenomenology
to Hermeneutics

FROM AN OLYMPIAN PERSPECTIVE not concerned with
method, the appearance of *The Symbolism of Evil* seems to an-
nounce a dramatic shift of approach. The "abstract" quality of
both *Freedom and Nature* and *Fallible Man* and the concern
for conditions of possible experience in relation to the will are
suddenly abandoned. Instead, a "detour" into a *mythics* concerned not with structures but with religious "confessions" of
experienced evil and suffering appears. *The Symbolism of Evil*
initiates a linguistic-historical inquiry into actual and concrete
symbols and myths of Western culture. Ricoeur begins to examine the "existential anguish" of men in history as they express themselves in metaphor and story.

In terms of Ricoeur's philosophical anthropology, of course,
this is the movement from the possibility of Fault to its actuality
in the fullness of human experience. But Fault is never to be
approached head-on. Ricoeur continues to deny that it is a
structural characteristic of human existence which can be
merely described phenomenologically. Its actuality contains
more subtle implications than can be had from the model of a
"system." Instead, the meaning of Fault is to be observed from
the side, obliquely as it were, through its most poignant expressions.

These Ricoeur finds in the symbols and myths which express
and attempt to account for human evil and suffering. These
prephilosophical expressions contain a suggestive richness of
material which entices thought in its full critical form. *The
Symbolism of Evil* begins the turn to hermeneutics in the full
sense of interpretation and a concern for language—here sym-

[81]

bolic and mythical language. *The Symbolism of Evil* continues Ricoeur's self-conscious concerns with method and begins to elaborate more completely what is involved with a hermeneutic phenomenology. This theory of symbol and myth is then applied to the major types of symbolic and mythological understandings of evil.

The disjunction between a structural phenomenology concerned with structures of experience and a hermeneutic phenomenology concerned with expression has been heightened in this exposition by deliberately leaving the anticipations of explicit hermeneutics underdeveloped to this point. Now, however, the hermeneutic turn must be seen in its full impact. *The Symbolism of Evil* announces a series of major exchanges in this shift: (a) The whole realm of *neutrality* which imposed brackets upon Fault is exchanged for the realm of human existence under the dramatic signs of suffering and evil. (b) The *abstraction* of the structural field of fundamental possibilities is exchanged for the concrete field of expressions of the religious confessions of evil. And (c) the method of transcendental examinations within the limits of Ricoeur's versions of *epochē* is exchanged for a hermeneutic examination of texts and symbolic language. *The Symbolism of Evil* appears as a methodological and thematic "leap" from abstract structural phenomenology to an existential or concrete *mythics*.

There is a shift, a hermeneutic turn, which is deliberate. But the shift may be understood in several ways. The shift in both theme and method is the culmination of a movement toward hermeneutic phenomenology which has been the implicit developmental aim from the beginning. It becomes overt in *The Symbolism of Evil*. But a first impression of abruptness is useful in pointing up the separation of this hermeneutic "third way" from Husserlian phenomenology.

To this point Ricoeur has been notably reluctant to enter the realm of "existential significations" and thus enter into what could be a philosophy of existence. But the inner logic of all his structural phenomenology pointed to an ultimate need for dealing with just those significations. Once the brackets in the concept of fallibility were removed, further postponement could not be further justified. Thus the shift from a structural phenomenology to hermeneutics occurs at just the point at which Ricoeur could have moved into an existential phenomenology.

This he does not do, although the hermeneutic turn is perhaps confused with its existential parallel because *the theme of Ricoeur's hermeneutic is "existential" while the method is not.* The exchanges in *The Symbolism of Evil* are marked by an almost Kierkegaardian concern with guilt, anguish, and alienation. The realm of Fault takes as a theme the question of evil, which always poses a major problem for philosophical comprehension. This theme serves as an extreme test case for the powers of philosophical reflection. The method in this reflection, however, is to be one which interprets *expressions* rather than turning to a direct analysis of *experience*.

Ricoeur's double criticism of existential phenomenology discloses his reason for turning away from a structural model at this point. On one side, continuing his reluctance to move too quickly into a discussion of existence in its full sense, Ricoeur argues:

> In dealing with a problem, if we go straight to the "existential project," to the "movement of existence" to which all authentically human conduct leads, then we risk missing the special character of the problem and blurring the outline of different functions within a sort of indistinct existential monism . . . (*Husserl*, p. 215).

Furthermore, this too-quick move to totality retains a structural model in its "monism." The existential method of analysis of alienation, error, and the whole realm of Fault is thus led to locate guilt ontologically in finitude: "Philosophy tends to reduce the event of guilt to a structure homogenous with other structures of the voluntary and the involuntary . . . [this is] a temptation which seems inherent in a philosophical treatment of the notion of guilt" (*Husserl*, p. 230).

The reluctance to move directly into existential deductions is clear enough. But the turn to a linguistic model which may develop these same themes in its own way remains to be explored. Hermeneutics presupposes that a "text" or an "expression" has something to say which in turn can be interpreted or resaid in another way. This notion, which recalls two classical meanings of hermeneutics, a "translating" technique for making obscure expressions clearer and an exegesis which exposes the hidden meaning of a text, relies first upon its object, the text. In this case hermeneutics is a "reading" or a "listening" to what is said. Thus a new field of inquiry is outlined, the field of expressions, a "language."

Ricoeur's entry into this field is at first limited in *The Symbolism of Evil* to the third reading of the will. Only a selected type of expression is to be investigated, that which is symbolic or analogical;[1] and of this type Ricoeur interprets only one group of examples, those which deal with the symbols and myths of evil. The narrowness of examples in a potentially broad field keeps the theme of *The Symbolism of Evil* in line with the previous need to explicate existential significations—through expressions. The symbolic language of the confessions of evil is the field for understanding Fault as the existential situation of man.

This narrow door into hermeneutics does have some retarding effect upon its fully theoretical development. But it also opens to wider methodological considerations. In this light the apparent initial abruptness of the hermeneutic turn serves to obscure rather than clarify the movement of hermeneutics, particularly in its movement from a transcendental base. There is also a more gradual transition from structure to symbolic language, which ameliorates the turn. The question of a *mythics* is already a problem in the margins of Ricoeur's structural phenomenology.

On the structural side, the "essences" of the will, the leading concept of fundamental possibilities, were seen to have two senses which might be understood as "top" and "bottom" limits. At the "top" a fundamental possibility was an ideality which portrayed the maximum possible realization of a will within its human limits. At the "bottom" the fundamental possibility shaded off into an obscure border open only to partial clarification through phenomenological means. It is important to note that the transition from structure to symbol occurs at both the "top" and "bottom" fringes of the fundamental possibilities.

The final cycle of limit concepts in *Freedom and Nature* displays this opening to the symbolic at both the "top" and the "bottom" of fundamental possibilities. For Ricoeur all will is structurally a reciprocity of the voluntary and the involuntary. It is both an initiation of activity and a reception of capacities and limits. In the cycle of decision this reciprocity is taken to mean that *all decision is motivated*. The "top" or ideality of such a structure is the imagination of "a perfectly enlightened freedom," a wish to be "motivated in an exhaustive, transparent, absolutely rational way" (*FN*, pp. 484–85). This is a *dream of in-*

1. Symbols and myths are closely related indirect expressions. However, it is important to note that strictly speaking only symbols are considered as primitive in *The Symbolism of Evil*.

nocence which occurs in the ideality margin of human possibilities.

The same type of imagination can occur in relation to voluntary motion, which is always capacitated and limited by the body-organ. The desire for the ideality of motion is for "an incarnate freedom as man's freedom, but one whose body would be absolutely docile: a *gracious* freedom whose bodily spontaneity would be allied with the initiative which moves it without resistance" (*FN*, p. 485). These dreams of innocence are the imaginative variations which already border on both structure and myth.

But Ricoeur insists that "innocence is not accessible to any *description*, even an empirical one, but rather to a concrete mythical approach" (*FN*, pp. 25–26; italics added). The description is impossible only in the sense that the ideality is never actually experienced—*innocence is merely intended but not fulfilled*. Description is impossible only in the existential sense. All actual decision undergoes some effort. The dream of innocence which occurs at the "top" of a fundamental possibility is an *imaginative* variation. It is thus within the limits of a transcendental consideration, but not within the realm of an existential phenomenology. "It might be said, in the style of the Husserlian eidetics, that innocence is the imaginative variation that makes the essence of the primordial constitution stand out, in making it appear on another existential modality" (*FM*, p. 222). This new intention without fulfillment sees in the imaginative variation a play which indirectly illuminates the very structures of the will.

The indirectness of an imaginative variation occurs by providing an imaginary experience rather than an experience which could be called "existential" or realizable in immediate experience.

> Subjectively, the myth of innocence reveals a fundamental nature which, however, is constituted solely by the force of the concepts introduced. It is the *courage* of the possible. At the same time it provides that *imaginary* experience [which] . . . in Husserlian terms . . . serves as the springboard for the knowledge of human structures (*FN*, p. 28).

In Ricoeur's terms this imaginative variation is clearly located in the transcendental or infinite aspect of subjectivity.

This same idealization, possible at the "top" limit of fundamental possibilities, is also possible in relation to structures as a totality. The dream of innocence may occur as the ideality of fallibility:

> The imagination of innocence is nothing but the representation of a human life that would realize all its fundamental possibilities without any discrepancy between its primordial destination and its historical manifestation. Innocence would be fallibility without fault (*FM*, p. 221).

This dream which occurs at the "top" of fundamental possibilities is *expressed* in the imaginative form of symbol and myth, and the structural limit has at least one common border with the world of myth.

Innocence does not complete the countermapping of the symbolic or imaginative expression and structural characteristic, because at the "bottom" or obscurity border of fundamental possibilities a second transition occurs. It is the third and asymmetrical limit of *consent* which introduces the reverse side of all the dreams of innocence. The dream of consent intends "not [to] have the particularity of a character . . . [but rather to] reduce its contingence fully to its initiative. . . . We have in mind a freedom which would be no longer receptive . . . a freedom which would be itself by definition" (*FN*, pp. 484–85). Such a freedom would no longer be human since it exceeds the reciprocity, and thus the reverse side of the dream of innocence is a refusal of a bound freedom, a refusal of necessity.

This "bottom" border of fundamental possibilities, always inexact in the obscurity of bodily existence, does not present the all too clear conceptual definition of an absolute necessity which calls for an all too clear response: *acquiescence*. Nor is there here any greater possibility for (an existential) *description* than in the case of innocence. At the border of the opacity of bodily existence a series of variations becomes possible. These variations, which are all indirect recognitions of necessity, *interpret* in quasi-mythical terms the situation of man faced with this necessity.

The dream of innocence, at the obscurity border of consent, has a reverse side in the refusal of necessity.

> In effect *what* we refuse, is always, in the last analysis, the limitation of character, the shadows of the unconscious, and the contingence of life. I cannot tolerate being only that partial consciousness limited by all its obscurity and discovering its brute existence. . . . The initial movement of refusal is the wish for

totality in which I repudiate the constrictions of character (*FN*, p. 463).

This interpretative movement of thought, intentional but impossible of fulfillment, is a movement which is installed in philosophy itself as a speculative direction.

> Must we go even farther and admit that all idealism is Promethean and conceals a secret rejection of the human condition? . . . The philosophical Prometheus wants to be free of shadow. This philosophical titanism is not aware of itself as refusal: this is either its lie or its illusion (*FN*, p. 464).

Refusal of condition, however, implies a recognition of that which is refused, and each variation upon the limit of absolute necessity points to some form of precomprehension of necessity (*FN*, p. 464).[2]

The variations which occur at this lower border of freedom and necessity in principle are not limited to refusal. A mixed consent which divides necessity into a part refusal and part consent is also possible, and Ricoeur sees this possibility to be that of Stoicism. Its refusal is a refusal of the body. "Stoicism does not suspect that my body has precisely the unexpected significance of being neither judgment nor thing, but life in me without me: ignored as the flesh of the Cogito, it is pushed back among indifferent things" (*FN*, p. 469). Nevertheless the Stoic exile of the body into the world of objects is also a partial acceptance of necessity in its ideal of the contemplation of Logos. "What saves Stoicism on every page is that on the other hand it gives necessity the splendor which it initially deprecates. . . . Contemplation, admiration are the *detour* of consent" (*FN*, pp. 470, 472).

A third variation in a romantic identification of the self and Nature is seen by Ricoeur in Orphism. Here the admiration of the Stoics is pushed to a limit in the absorption of the self into Nature:

> Borne by the chant of Orpheus, consent to necessity annuls itself as an act and becomes joined to its primitive opposite, the spell of objectivity from which the power of refusal wrested it. It is no

2. This precomprehension applies to the understanding of human conflict and "misery" as well and is described by Ricoeur in *Fallible Man* as a *pathétique*. I shall not deal here with precomprehension, other than to indicate that it serves a role similar to that of precomprehension in the existential philosophies.

accident that Orphism tends to a nature worship in which the unique status of the Cogito evaporates in the cycle of the mineral and the animal (*FN*, p. 476).

Finally, there is another form of partial consent which is Ricoeur's own chosen variation—*eschatological* consent: "Who can say *yes* to the end, without reservations? Suffering and evil, respected in their own shocking mystery, protected against degradation into a problem, lie in our way . . . perhaps no one can follow consent to the end" (*FN*, pp. 479–80). The eschatological consent Ricoeur chooses seizes upon *hope* as a *symbolic* but partial consent.

> Hope says, the world is not the *final* home of freedom; I consent as much as possible, but hope to be delivered of the terrible and at the end of time to enjoy a new body and a new nature granted to freedom. . . . A Franciscan knowledge of necessity: I am "with" necessity "among" creatures (*FN*, pp. 480–81).

Each of these variations which occur at the borders of structural concepts is an imaginative projection which intersects with the mythical. Apart from an initial anticipation of an intimacy between myth and speculative thought, the fact that these variations are seated in an imagination which remains short of fulfillment in no way implies a negative valuation of myth. To the contrary, the imaginative variations are accorded an important status in Ricoeur's philosophical anthropology as the dramatic forms which precisely give man his understanding of himself and his situation. The symbolic has an existential function.

> The imagination has a function of projection and exploration in regard to that which is still possible to man. It is *par excellence* the institution and the constitution of the humanly possible. It is in imagining his potentialities that man exercises prophecy with respect to his own existence. . . . it is in the midst of dreams of innocence and reconciliation that hope works the very dough of the human.[3]

This imagination coalesces in the myth with its symbolic and indirect language. The symbolic expression is a "work" which arises in the imagination as the transcending activity of man.

---

3. Paul Ricoeur, "The Image of God and the Epic of Man," trans. George Gringas, *Cross Currents* (Winter, 1961), p. 49.

Mythos means word; the imagination, insofar as it is a mythopoetic function, is also the seat of a profound laboring which controls the decisive changes in our vision of the world. Every real conversion is first a revolution on the level of our directive images. By changing his imagination, man changes his existence.[4]

Mythos, the imagination, the intention to signify is the point at which Ricoeur's existential theme and hermeneutic method meet. It is the initial excursion into "language" in hermeneutic phenomenology.

Hermeneutics is the specific way in which Ricoeur opens up the problem of a philosophy of language. The last broad identification of language in its imaginative, and hence transcending, function brings the understanding of hermeneutics full circle to its broadest classical meaning. Recalling that the second part of Aristotle's treatise on logic is titled *Peri Hermeneias*, which today would be *On Interpretation* or *Hermeneutics*, Ricoeur points out, "I believe it is very important to see that in classical Greece—and for Aristotle himself—not only is the word well known, but that it has as its major signification this total meaning: All language insofar as it says interprets. It is an interpretation at one and the same time of a reality and of the one who speaks about this reality." [5] Interpretation in its broadest sense is the question of language itself.

The potential breadth of the hermeneutic question makes Ricoeur's narrow entry problematic by contrast. The taking up of archaic symbols and myths, "confession" (*l'aveu*) or the ritual-emotive recital of evil, seems too particular to create a general phenomenological hermeneutics. Yet this entry into expression, better understandable in relation to the question of the will than of a theory of hermeneutics, also poses the main questions Ricoeur wishes to raise in the philosophy of language.

The use of symbols and myths as the primitives of language places Ricoeur's approach to language in extreme contrast to much of the contemporary philosophy of language. In the dominant traditions of the Anglo-American philosophy of language the first movement is usually one which seeks the simplest unit of the language and works from the bottom upward. In this respect the concerns with formalization, with the "logic" of sim-

4. *Ibid.*
5. Paul Ricoeur, "Foi et langage, Bultmann-Ebeling" *Foi-Education*, XXXVII, no. 81 (October–December, 1967), p. 18.

ple statements, and even, in ordinary language philosophy, with the complexities of ordinary utterances, stand at the opposite pole of the language continuum. The choice of the already complex and, moreover, *opaque* and *equivocal* expression as the "primitives" of hermeneutics is a radically different choice.

But it is also a choice in keeping with the basic phenomenological strategy of Ricoeur's thought. To begin with the *fullness of language,* a phrase which serves several important functions in Ricoeur's use, is to begin from the top downward. The first aspect of a *phenomenological* hermeneutics presupposes the phenomenological inversion of all linguistic formalism and atomism. There is a polemic note in the announcement of such a program:

> In the very same age in which our language is becoming more precise, more univocal, more technical, better suited to those integral formalizations that are called precisely "symbolic" logic . . . it is in this age of discourse that we wish to recharge language, start again from the *fullness* of language. . . . The same age develops the possibility of emptying language and the possibility of filling it anew. . . . Beyond the wastelands of critical thought we seek to be challenged anew.[6]

The polemic by which Ricoeur affirms his own starting point in contrast to that of Anglo-American language philosophy is also used to distinguish his approach from certain aspects of Husserlian thought. In a seeming repudiation of the Husserlian search for a radical or presuppositionless point of departure, Ricoeur again asserts the need to begin with the fullness of language.

> In contrast to philosophies concerned with starting points, a meditation on symbols starts from the fullness of language and of meaning already there; it begins from within language which has already taken place and in which everything in a certain sense has already been said; it wants to be thought, not presuppositionless, but in and with all its presuppositions. Its first problem is not how to get started, but, from the midst of speech, to recollect itself.[7]

This seeming rejection of the Husserlian starting point, however, is not so much a rejection of a basic phenomenological

6. Paul Ricoeur, "The Hermeneutics of Symbols and Philosophical Reflection," trans. Denis Savage, *International Philosophical Quarterly,* II, no. 2 (May, 1962), 192–93.
7. *Ibid.,* p. 192.

pattern as it is a repetition of Ricoeur's rejection of an idealistic interpretation of that model. A presuppositionless philosophy is but another of the many guises by which the subject "makes circle with itself." This temptation must be limited. The turn to language, Ricoeur argues, already places a limiting function upon the subject. Language is essentially non-private. To think language with its presuppositions is to begin in an intersubjective world, since a main, if not the first, presupposition of language is a world of speaking subjects. The symbol, that privileged place within the whole of language which is to be Ricoeur's starting point, "gives reason to think that the *Cogito* is within being, and not vice versa." [8]

But if the idealism is limited, the methodological direction remains clearly dominated by phenomenology in its culminating drive toward a lifeworld. That this is the case may be shown in a preliminary way by paralleling the Husserlian and Ricoeurian directions. In the Husserlian sense phenomenology is to get "back to the things themselves." The theory of evidence weights only that which is given in intuition ("immediate" experience). To secure this evidence the whole of the *epoché* and phenomenological reductions were developed to remove all factors which obscured the *fullness of experience*. The aim was to arrive at a *pretheoretical experience* of the world.

Without any basic distortion to the Husserlian aim, this process may also be seen as a particular type of interpretation, a *regressive* analysis which removes layer by layer a series of secondary presuppositions or beliefs. The suspension of the natural attitude and of beliefs contained in the sciences regarding existence is part of this removal of secondary or tertiary interpretations. The function of the phenomenological reduction is then a type of "demythologization" which successively reveals the naïvetés and errors involved in the theoretical constructs which cover over the fullness of experience. If one is to begin anew with that fullness—in the final Husserlian case the fullness of the perceptual or representative world—such a reduction of presuppositions, but not of experience, is necessary.

In Ricoeur's adaptation of this regressive process the field is changed. *It is now language, expression, rather than the realm of direct experience which becomes the field of inquiry.*

8. Paul Ricoeur, *The Symbolism of Evil*, trans. Emerson Buchanan (New York: Harper & Row, 1967), p. 356. (Hereafter cited as *SE*.)

The search for the *fullness of language* must be seen to be the Ricoeurian parallel to the Husserlian search for the fullness of experience. The quest becomes one which seeks the "pretheoretical" equivalent in language for the pretheoretical perceptual or representative experience. Once this set of substitutions is made, the process repeats the regression to primitivity implied in all phenomenological reductions.

This may be seen to be the pattern in Ricoeur's approach to the symbol. The hermeneutics of symbols has as its aim the location and description of the basic type(s) of expression, a *prephilosophical expression(s)*. Hermeneutics will be the successive removal of the secondary and tertiary interpretations which cover over the primitivity of the symbol. To uncover the symbol in its primitive suggestiveness is to locate the fullness of language. "This recourse to the archaic, the nocturnal, and the oneiric . . . is also an approach to the *birthplace of language*" [italics added].[9]

The primacy of the symbol in language is equivalent to the primacy of perception in immediate experience—hermeneutics shifts its focus to the linguistic field, but it retains a basic phenomenological strategy. In its first sense hermeneutics is a vast phenomenological reduction of the linguistic field. In this first sense hermeneutics as phenomenology establishes the *analytic* for the subsequent development of a theory of symbol and myth. But an analytic in Ricoeur's use is always surpassed by a *dialectic* which constitutes the second movement of the hermeneutics.

The dialectic, now carried over into hermeneutics, continues the play of weighted focus against which are counterpoised the series of opposed foci. In *The Symbolism of Evil* and in the development of the cycle of myths a second set of substitutions occurs which duplicates the dynamics of Ricoeur's structural phenomenology. The substitution is the exchange of the realm of *nature* or structures for the realm of *evil* (as expressed). The Fault, viewed indirectly through its expressions in symbol and myth, discloses a new set of contraries which parallel the universes of discourse that characterized *Freedom and Nature*.

The dynamics of the hermeneutic dialectic remain more disguised than did the play of subjective and objective universes of discourse—but Ricoeur's choice of myths and the explanatory basis within them arranges the new dialectic in a pattern

9. Ricoeur, "Hermeneutics of Symbols," p. 192.

which repeats the weighting of a "subjective" focus against which the "objective" foci are to be played. In his typology of myths, centered in *The Symbolism of Evil* upon the theme of the "origin of evil," a "subjective" myth which understands the origin of evil in the use of freedom is weighted over a series of "objective" myths which explain evil by recourse to a non-human origin.

> This dynamics is animated by a deep-seated opposition: on one side are the myths that take the origin of evil back to a catastrophe or primordial conflict prior to man; on the other, the myths that take the origin back to man. . . . The world of myths is thus polarized between two tendencies: one takes evil back beyond the human; the other concentrates it in an evil choice from which stems the pain of being man.[10]

The choice Ricoeur makes weights the "subjective" focus.

This choice is to look at evil first from the perspective of what Ricoeur variously calls "the ethical view of the world" and the "anthropological" view. "To try to understand evil by freedom is a grave decision. It is the decision to enter into the problem of evil by the strait gate of human reality. . . . [it] expresses the choice of a center of perspective . . . to understand evil by freedom is itself an undertaking of freedom" (*FM*, pp. xxiv–xxv). On the theoretical and methodological plane this is clearly the reaffirmation of the transcendental perspective which characterized all the previous weightings of Ricoeur's dialectics.

It further follows in the hermeneutic dialectic that the originally weighted transcendental focus is limited by the counter-foci. The two myth types, the "subjective" now termed *reflective* in its tendency and the "objective" termed *speculative* in its tendency, are mutually demythologized and limited in the play. The reflective tendency is that direction which progressively demythologizes and removes the exteriority of evil from the speculative myths—but only to a point:

> From one point of view this *recovery* of the symbolics of evil by philosophical reflection indeed tends toward an ethical vision of the world in the Hegelian sense of the term. But on the other hand, the more clearly we perceive the requirements and implications of that ethical vision of the world, the more inescapable seems the impossibility of encompassing the whole problematic of man and

10. *Ibid.*, pp. 198–99.

evil itself within an ethical vision of the world (*FM*, pp. xxiii–xxiv).

The limit it meets is a resistant and irreducible reminder in the "objective" myths and in the speculative tendency which goes with them. "Reflective thought, in its turn, is at battle with speculative thought. Speculative thought wants to save what an ethical vision of evil tends to eliminate. It not only wants to save it, but to show its necessity." [11] The parallelism goes further. In effect *The Symbolism of Evil* is the hermeneutic counterpart of *Freedom and Nature*. One finds a new "diagnostic" arising in *The Symbolism of Evil* but its internal dialectic also remains inconclusive. Only when hermeneutics is limited in a way similar to the "Kantian" limitation of structural phenomenology will it be considered adequate.

11. *Ibid.*, p. 205.

5 / Hermeneutic Phenomenology: *The Symbolism of Evil*

THE FIRST thorough and explicit exercise in hermeneutic phenomenology begins with *The Symbolism of Evil*. Experience is to be read *through* expression—in this case, through the expressions of anguish found in the "confessions" of evil which span the development of Western man's consciousness from very archaic times to the present. Ricoeur's entrance into the field of expression is one which begins with the complex and equivocal analogies found in these confessions.

At base lie the symbols, primitive metaphors in which evil is understood to be "like" a defilement, "like" a broken relationship, "like" a self-induced punishment. Even these metaphors have their structures, their implications, their latent "systems." Higher on the scale, but still retaining the suggestive concreteness of the symbols, are myths. Myths elaborate and expand the possibilities of symbols. Ricoeur deals with four basic types of myths which in some degree illustrate exhaustively the basic possibilities of an interpretation of evil.

Nor is the matter left at the level of a "statics" of symbols and myths, at the level of a typology. In a second step Ricoeur develops the "dynamics" of symbols and myths. The tensions, transformations, and transpositions of symbols and myths are shown in such a way that a broad "logic" of myths begins to emerge. It is through this exercise that the outline of a hermeneutic phenomenology clearly shows its concern and applicability to the philosophy of culture. But prior to dealing with the actual themes announced in the *mythics,* a closer view of Ricoeur's method and the implications of the shift from structural to hermeneutic phenomenology is called for.

[95]

In the shift to a hermeneutics, there is a theoretical demand which ultimately threatens to overthrow some of the basic presuppositions of a structural phenomenology. This demand arises in the exchange of fields of investigation. An understanding of the subject remains the aim of Ricoeur's third reading of the will. "I wager that I shall have a better understanding of man and the bond between the being of man and the being of all beings if I follow the *indication* of symbolic thought" (*SE*, p. 355). The *experience* of the subject remains the focal point for that understanding, but in this context it is the experience of Fault. A hermeneutics creates a "first" and "second" order of indirectness for the understanding of experience. The "first" order of indirectness concerns the relation of experience to expression, and the "second" order of indirectness concerns the possibility of interpreting expressions through hermeneutics. Although in the usual technical sense hermeneutics only involves a problem of the second order, in Ricoeur's case interpretation refers back to the problem of experience from the order of interpretation. But some preliminary problems of method are posed at the first level.

At the first level the question of a relation between expression and prelinguistic experience arises. All structural phenomenology, whether in its Husserlian or existential guise, presupposes this nexus of prelinguistic experience. The first order of indirectness is established when the field of expression is chosen. Experience is to be understood through its expression. In this situation language becomes a *mediating* function. The movement, never thoroughly clarified, is from prelinguistic experience to expression. In the selected context of the confessions of suffering and evil the two poles of the experience-expression relation are described as being *counterparts*.

> This language of confession is the counterpart of the triple character of the experience it brings to light: blindness, equivocalness, scandalousness.
> The experience . . . is a blind experience, still embedded in the matrix of emotion, fear, anguish. It is this emotional note that gives rise to objectification in discourse; the confession expresses, pushes to the outside, the emotion which without it would be shut up in itself as an impression in the soul (*SE*, p. 7).

The relation of experience-expression as a counterpart functions in the exchange of experiential structures for the linguistic field. In Ricoeur's structural phenomenology emotions, particularly those which would reveal Fault, are always regarded as obscure. Now, on the linguistic plane, what is felt or lived as obscure is expressed as *equivocal*. "The preferred language of the fault appears to be indirect and based on imagery . . . The feeling involved is not only blind in virtue of being emotional; it is also equivocal, laden with a multiplicity of meanings" (*SE*, pp. 8–9).

If the distinction between prelinguistic experience and expression is to be maintained, the result is that an isomorphism must exist in the experience-expression counterpart. The symbolic expression functions in the field of language as the emotions function in the field of experience. This isomorphism is thus an approximation to a natural theory of expressive language. "A characteristic of the symbol is never to be completely arbitrary. It is not empty, there is always a rudiment of a natural relation between the signifying and the signified . . ."[1] The isomorphism in effect establishes a first circle at the level of the counterpart relation. The inquiry into the symbolic or opaque expression is the linguistic equivalent of inquiry into blind experience.

In Ricoeur's use of this circle the ultimate significance involves the constitution of the consciousness of self. "The consciousness of self seems to constitute itself at its lowest level by means of symbolism . . ." (*SE*, p. 9). In principle this is to hold that the constitution of the self may be read from the constitution of language.

But if at the first level expression is the counterpart of experience which is "read through" it, then expression must already have occurred for a hermeneutics to be possible at all. Language already given becomes necessary for hermeneutic phenomenology. "Have we really reached, under the name of experience, an immediate datum? Not at all. What is experienced as defilement, as sin, as guilt, requires the mediation of a specific language, the language of symbols. Without the help of that language, the experience would remain mute, obscure, and shut up in its implicit contradictions" (*SE*, p. 161). This requirement continues Ricoeur's previous understanding of phenomenology as a reflective discipline. All experience is arrived at reflectively rather than directly. The linguistically implied

1. Paul Ricoeur, "Herméneutique et réflexion," *Archivio de filosofia*, XXXII, nos. 1–2 (1962), 22.

model of hermeneutics merely substitutes a field of expression as the field which reflects experience.

The structural phenomenology reflects the subject by means of what may now be called *the object world*. In the late Husserlian phenomenology and in existential phenomenology the object world is primarily a "perceptual" one. Ricoeur's modification, in which the "project" and the "pragma" are directed toward the object world, continues this tradition by modeling the reading of the will upon the pattern of objectifying consciousness. But in a hermeneutic phenomenology the object world is exchanged for a language world. The world of expression is now the "object" correlate which is used to reflect the subject. This change of field presumably carries significations not found in the previous use of an object world.

There are several notable characteristics of a language world which immediately change some variables in the phenomenological context. In the first place expressions are the expressions *of* a subject. A language world is already a subjective (an intersubjective) world. If experience is what is aimed at, now reflected through expressions, hermeneutic phenomenology must begin where those experiences have already been expressed. Secondly, although man is now presupposed at both poles of the noematic and noetic correlates, he is to be understood in two different ways. In express*ed* language the subject is presupposed reflexively. But in an analysis of express*ing*, "to say" becomes one aspect of total human intentionality. A phenomenology of language and a phenomenology of speech do not have the same project. Finally, the second order of indirectness which constitutes the hermeneutic circle occurs entirely within the world of language. The linguistically implied model of hermeneutics hopes that the field of expressions may reflect subjectivity in its cultural setting better than an object world. The second order of indirectness is the order of culture and history in relation to man's self-interpretations. A hermeneutic phenomenology thus has a philosophy of culture rather than the implied question of nature or psychology which underlies structural phenomenology.

The first circle of experience-expression is surpassed by the second circle, which constitutes the uniquely hermeneutic problem. The second circle is the expression-interpretation relation within the confines of the language world. The movement from the first to the second circle is by means of expression which belongs to both regions. This movement from the experience-expression relation to the expression-interpretation relation, however, retains its reference to the relation of experience-expression, but it is to be read reflectively from the second order of expression-interpretation. Experience, assumed now to have already been brought into expression, allows the thematization of expression as a study of *man as language:*

> The enterprise should be a hopeless one if symbols were radically alien to philosophical discourse. But symbols are already in the element of speech. We have sufficiently said that they rescue feeling and even fear from silence and confusion; in virtue of them, man remains language through and through. That is not the most important thing: there exists nowhere a symbolic language without hermeneutics . . . what is already discourse, even if incoherent, is brought into coherent discourse by hermeneutics (*SE,* p. 350).

The functional parallelism between Ricoeur's structural and hermeneutic phenomenologies continues within the second circle. Incarnate existence, considered opaque at the reflective extremity of the body and in affectivity, has its counterpart opacity in symbolic expressions. The opaque expression becomes the paradigmatic case for inquiry which, in the linguistic circle, "is why language is needed a second time to elucidate the subterranean crisis of the consciousness of fault" (*SE,* p. 8). Once experience is considered to be reflected in the expression and thereby functionally established, the hermeneutic problem may be stated more precisely. The "circle" at the second or hermeneutic level is the expression-interpretation relation. "The knot where the symbol gives and criticism interprets—appears in hermeneutics as a circle. The circle can be stated bluntly: 'We must understand in order to believe, but we must believe in order to understand'" (*SE,* p. 351). The first movement of Ricoeur's hermeneutics proper is the inquiry into the field of expression by means of interpretation. This inquiry remains recognizably phenomenological in its outline.

In the first instance the field of symbolic language must be investigated descriptively, rather than by means of explanations which go behind the symbol. "I am convinced we must think not *behind* the symbols, but starting from the symbols *according* to the symbols." [2] This respect for the symbol's "appearance" is formulated in an aphorism derived from Kant:

2. Paul Ricoeur, "The Hermeneutics of Symbols and Philosophical Reflection," trans. Denis Savage, *International Philosophical Quarterly,* II, no. 2 (May, 1962), 203.

the symbol invites or gives rise to thought (le symbole donne à penser). The symbol is to be repeated in an exercise of "sympathetic imagination."

Ricoeur has stated the initial phenomenological respect for the appearance or descriptive characteristics of the symbol in terms of "belief." In the hermeneutic context this is to presuppose that the symbol or expression has something to say and that what it has to say must first be heard or understood. This first "listening" or repetition of the symbol in belief is the first application of a hermeneutic *epochē*. Belief inside the hermeneutic circle is a phenomenological belief which has already suspended the "first naïveté" of immediacy. "We must believe in order to understand; never, in fact, does the interpreter get near to what his text says unless he lives in the *aura* of the meaning he is inquiring after" (*SE*, p. 351). To live in the *aura* of meaning is not the same thing as a natural belief at all. It is to believe in the "reduced" sense of employing an imaginative variation. Belief in its phenomenological context is an exercise in reduction. "The philosopher adopts provisionally the motivations and intentions of the believing soul. He does not 'feel' them in their first naïveté; he 're-feels' them in a neutralized mode, in the mode of 'as if.' It is in this sense that phenomenology is a re-enactment in sympathetic imagination" (*SE*, p. 19). This is to say that the starting point of Ricoeur's hermeneutics is critical in a phenomenological sense from the outset. The symbolic field must be problematized so as to exclude immediacy. "In every way, something has been lost, irremediably lost: immediacy of belief" (*SE*, p. 351). Interpretation stands aloof from the prereflective and prephilosophical immediate belief in the symbol.

As imaginative variation the hermeneutic belief is a "second naïveté." Its first step away from the immediacy of signification has as its purpose the displaying and isolating of the intentionality of the symbol. But the neutral or disengaged meaning of interpretation as a second belief includes a second criticism. The symbolic expressions Ricoeur proposes to examine are *archaic*. This choice both complicates and facilitates the problem of hermeneutic reduction.

The complication arises in the need to *recover* the intentionality of the expression which may be obscured by the historical gap between its time and the present. The facilitation lies in the problem of suspending a first naïveté of belief. The very archaic nature of the symbols and myths involved prevents any literal immediacy of belief. The modern *Weltanschauung* has already separated myth and history; myth remains "mere" myth. Both the complication and the facilitation employ a second meaning for criticism. In a specific recollection of his earlier use of the *diagnostic* Ricoeur accepts the basic insights—within the descriptive limits of phenomenological hermeneutics—of the modern tools of scientific and historical criticism. "What is peculiar to modern hermeneutics is that it remains in line with critical thought. But its critical function does not turn away from its appropriative function: I would say, rather, that it makes it more authentic and more perfect" (*SE*, p. 350).

In the revival of the diagnostic, which now uses historical and scientific criticism, the dialectical aspect is restricted. In effect, the second or scientific criticism is taken into reduction itself. "For us, moderns, a myth is *only* a myth because we can no longer connect that time with the time of history as we write it, employing the critical method, nor can we connect mythical places with our geographical space" (*SE*, p. 5). Within its phenomenologically absorbed role this use of objective criticism serves to demythologize the literal or explanatory role of myth. The "science" and the "history" of the myth are exploded: "The myth can no longer be an explanation; to exclude its etiological function is the theme of all necessary demythologization" (*SE*, p. 5).

The criticism of the historical sciences destroys the literal dimension of myth. But the diagnostic acceptance of such criticism is in return a limiting of any remaining scientific naturalism. The implication of much objective criticism is that a primitive explanation is all there is to myth. Such an interpretation confuses the etiological function of myth with the specifically symbolic—or existential—function. "This 'crisis,' this decision, after which myth and history are dissociated, may signify the loss of the mythical dimension . . . we are tempted to give ourselves up to the radical demythization of all our thinking" (*SE*, pp. 161–62). A phenomenological hermeneutics stops short of this rejection and takes a different and restorative direction.

The initial suspension of the myth's literal function is necessary; but with its rejection the myth may also be seen as an imaginative expression which is its symbolic dimension.

> . . . In losing its explanatory pretension the myth reveals its exploratory significance and its contribution to understanding, which we shall later call its symbolic function—that is to say, its

power of discovering and revealing the bond between man and what he considers sacred. Paradoxical as it may seem, the myth, when it is thus demythologized through contact with scientific history, is elevated to the dignity of a symbol as a dimension of modern thought (*SE*, p. 5).

To remove the explanatory function of myth is to remove its implied "natural attitude" without devaluing myth as such. The diagnostic acceptance of second criticism re-enforces Ricoeur's use of phenomenological brackets. The removal of the literal significance of myth is the beginning of the process of uncovering the "thing itself," the symbolic "word."

This diagnostically re-enforced phenomenology involves a series of reductions of interpretation layers (of which the naïve literal histories and cosmologies are the first) which cover over the symbolic significance of myth. "My working hypothesis is that criticism of the pseudo-rational is fatal not to myth, but to gnosis" (*SE*, p.164). The mythological dimension in its reduced sense is seen to be a concrete fantasy variation which remains similar in its function to the Husserlian variations used in a structural phenomenology. But in this case the aim is existential exploration. The imaginative "word" which displays aspects of existence in symbolic expressions opens up understandings which are not directly possible. The philosophical hope of Ricoeur's hermeneutics is to "elevate the symbols to the rank of existential concepts" (*SE*, p. 357).

But such an existential exploration in the realm of symbol remains under the limits of Ricoeur's Kantian impositions. The investigation is seen as a wager modeled upon a transcendental deduction: "We shall propose a type of 'interpretation' that is not a 'translation'; let us say, to be brief, that the very process of the discovery of the field of experience *opened up* by the myth can constitute an *existential verification* comparable to the transcendental deduction of the categories of the understanding" (*SE*, p. 164 n). Under the Kantian limit the whole of symbolic intentionality is seen as limited. The aim of the imaginative symbol is an "intuition of a cosmic whole, from which man is not separated, and this undivided plenitude, anterior to the division into the supernatural and human . . . [is] not *given*, but simply *aimed* at. It is only in intention that the myth restores some wholeness" (*SE*, p. 167). The imaginative variations of symbols are intentions without fulfillments—that is what gives them symbolic quality.

Myth or symbol as an imaginative "word" is the place within language from which Ricoeur seeks to understand man's self-understanding. With symbolic language man understands and is understood through his expressions. In this context man as language is man interpreting and expressing himself and his cultural history in myth and symbol. The "psychology" of structural phenomenology is surpassed by the "history" of hermeneutic phenomenology.

SYMBOLIC EXPRESSION

ONCE THE HERMENEUTICAL STANDPOINT is established, Ricoeur's theory of symbolic expression shows two basic and complementary movements. The first is analytic or *eidetic* in its aim and outlines the formal dimensions and structure of the symbol with its peculiar intentionality. The second is dynamic and places what may be called symbol systems into a pattern which displays an evolution of meanings and relations of transposition and development.

Although for analytical as well as strategic reasons Ricoeur differentiates between symbol as primitive and myth as a first order spontaneous hermeneutics, it remains clear that both symbol and myth share the basic structural intentionality of symbolic expression. *Primitive symbols* stand at the base of this philosophy of language. Ricoeur says: "I shall always understand by symbol . . . in a . . . primitive sense, *analogical meanings* which are spontaneously formed and immediately significant, such as defilement, analogue of stain; sin, analogue of deviation; guilt, analogue of accusation" (*SE*, p. 18). Although myth adds a temporal and character dimension to a narrative, it retains the analogical structure of symbols. "I shall regard myths as a species of symbols, as symbols developed in the form of narrations and articulated in a time and a space that cannot be co-ordinated with the time and space of history and geography according to the critical method" (*SE*, p. 18).

In both cases the structural characteristic which gives symbolic expression its particular role in language is its analogical or metaphorical *double intentionality.* The bottom and basic level of this intentionality is literal and derived from ordinary experience. ". . . The symbol of evil is constituted by starting from something which has a first-level meaning and is borrowed from the experience of nature—man's contact and orientation in space." [3] Its analogical or *symbolic intentionality* arises in and from its literal base. "The literal and obvious meaning, therefore, points beyond itself to something which is *like* stain, *like* a deviation, *like* a burden" (*SE*, p. 194). It is the symbolic intentionality which plays the existential role in an imaginative representation of man and his relationship to what he considers sacred.

In relation to the field of all possible expressions the choice of analogical expressions serves a theoretical function as well. The double-layered intentionality makes the symbol *complex*. Ricoeur begins with the complex rather than the simple in accordance with the phenomenological demand that a whole may only subsequently be analyzed into its parts. Ricoeur can later claim that the symbol contains or includes simpler characteristics. A symbol is also a sign. "They are expressions that communicate a meaning; this meaning is declared in an intention of signifying which has speech for its vehicle" (*SE*, p. 14). The conventionality which constitutes signs may stand within the symbolic construction—but the symbol is qualified in that it always remains short of total arbitrariness.

Double-intentionality, however, is both the structural source of the symbol's power and its puzzle; it surpasses the conventionally significant. "Symbolic signs are opaque, because the first literal, obvious meaning itself points analogically to a second meaning which is not given otherwise than in it. . . . This opacity constitutes the depth of the symbol, which . . . is inexhaustible" (*SE,* p. 15).

The opacity occurs in a non-dominatable relationship between the first and second levels of the analogy. The "spontaneity" of the symbol is its fullness:

> Analogy is a nonconclusive reasoning that proceeds through a fourth proportional term (A is to B as C is to D). But in symbol I cannot objectivize the analogous relation that binds the second meaning to the first. By living in the first meaning I am drawn by it beyond itself: the symbolic meaning is constituted in and through the literal meaning, which brings about the analogy by giving the analogue. Unlike a comparison that we *look at* from the outside, symbol is the very movement of the primary meaning that makes us share in the latent meaning and thereby assimilates us to the symbolized, without our being able intellectually to dominate the similarity. This is the sense in which the symbol "gives"; it

3. *Ibid.,* pp. 193–94.

gives because it is a primary intentionality that gives a second meaning.[4]

This relationship, neither arbitrary, since it depends upon a "likeness" between the two sides of the intentionality, nor reducible without destroying the symbolic significance, is one justification for giving the symbol its place as an originary fullness of language in Ricoeur's hermeneutics.

The multi-leveled meaning of the symbol gives it a linguistic role "like" that of the multidimensioned aspects of the lifeworld in an existential phenomenology. The "birthplace of language" is already the potential whole rather than the logically reduced. This places the symbol, in Ricoeur's sense, at an inverse position to the strictly formal:

> Not only does it belong to a kind of thinking that is bound to its contents, and therefore not formalized, but the intimate bond between its first and second intentions and the impossibility of presenting the symbolic meaning to oneself otherwise than by the actual operation of analogy make of the symbolic language a language essentially *bound*, bound to its content and, through its primary content, to its secondary content (*SE*, p. 17).

In addition to the structural characteristic of double intentionality, the symbol, in Ricoeur's highly selected sense, must carry a second characteristic. The symbol in its paradigmatic sense is also *undifferentiated* in its prephilosophical dimensions. Archaic or primitive symbols provide an "objective" understanding of evil. This is to say that the symbol locates and "reads" its symbolic significance as having a location in the totality of being. At the most archaic level in symbolic expression this is the cosmological dimension of the symbol. The symbol also includes a "subjective" reference as a response to evil recognizable in affects or feelings. This is the psychic or *oneiric* dimension of the symbol. Each symbol finally is an expression which dramatizes these understandings in an image. This is the *poetic* dimension of the symbol. In its religious setting these expressions form a "system" of representing and ritually dealing with evil.

These distinctions, drawn from the undifferentiated primitive symbol, serve to initiate a phenomenological genesis in description of the symbol. In this movement evil is first read *upon* the world:

4. *Ibid.*, p. 194.

Man first reads the sacred *on* the world, *on* some elements or aspects of the world. . . . First of all, then, it is the sun, the moon, the waters—that is to say, cosmic realities—that are symbols. . . . For these realities to be a symbol is to gather together at one point a mass of significations which, before giving rise to thought, give rise to speech (*SE*, pp. 10–11).

Phenomenologically, this is to say that, just as naïve experience is first directed toward the world, so in naïve or prephilosophical language the significations are first read upon the world.

In the primitive symbol the cosmic aspect is accompanied by its psychic response. In the prephilosophical state the symbol remains undifferentiated in both the cosmic and psychic moments. Thus, in its oneiric sense, the dream and the fantasy may also signify the sacred. "To manifest the 'sacred' *on* the 'cosmos' and to manifest it *in* the 'psyche' are the same thing" (*SE*, p. 12).

But in both cases it is the image which coalesces the analogues of the symbol. The poetic is the intentionality of symbolic expression itself. "Unlike the other two modalities of symbols, hierophanic and oneiric, the poetic symbol shows us expressivity in its nascent state" (*SE*, pp. 13–14). The poetic is the "birthplace of language" which gives the symbol its form and possibility of development. Thus, by virtue of both its structural complexity and its undifferentiated multiple dimensions, the symbol provides the fullness of language which Ricoeur uses as the field and base for hermeneutics.

Once the type of symbol to be examined is thus defined, a question of selection is implied. Ricoeur chooses to examine symbols which lie only within the broad history of the West. In a self-conscious way he attempts to justify this choice. The justification serves to establish the point of view or perspective which defines the relations between the symbols and the philosopher. The choice is also an affirmation of a philosophical origin.

My field of investigation is oriented, and because it is oriented it is limited. By what is it oriented? Not only by my own situation in the universe of symbols, but paradoxically, by the historical, geographical, cultural origin of the philosophical question itself.

Our philosophy is Greek by birth. Its intention and its pretension of universality are "situated.". . . The fact that the Greek question is situated at the beginning orients the human space of religions which is open to philosophical investigation (*SE*, pp. 19–20).

The acceptance and recognition of a "point of view" from which the field of symbols may be "viewed" allows a characterization of intersymbol relations without pretension.

The situating of a point of view establishes a set of field relations concerning the myth and symbol themes. But the point of view is in effect a double one. The vast multiplicity of cultural symbols is related to what Ricoeur has called philosophical consciousness, which in turn revolves around reflectivity. The first set of relations, those of proximity and distance, are situated according to their relative distances from philosophical consciousness. The whole field of myths is one which displays only a partial distance from this consciousness, since only those myths which are at the origins of Western thought are selected, and of these the Hebrew and Greek myths remain closer than the others. However, for reasons to be noted below, the doubling of the point of view occurs in Ricoeur's identification of the Adamic myth as the reflective myth. Depth relations are historico-temporal and functionally are more important for the regressive nature of Ricoeur's dynamics. At bottom Ricoeur seeks the most archaic recoverable theme: "There are themes of the religious consciousness that appear to us today . . . in the 'thickness' and the transparency of our present motivations. . . . It is impossible to overestimate the importance of the stratified structure of the consciousness of the fault" (*SE*, p. 21). Lateral relations are essentially crosscultural relations within a given historical stratum. Hebrew-Assyrian or Greek-Egyptian intercultural relations are examples. Retroactive relations refer to renewals and discoveries in the past which add to the knowledge of the symbol. In each of these historical-cultural relations the diagnostic which utilizes the information of the historical, archeological, and literary tools is necessary.

Once the situation and setting from which symbols are to be interpreted is established, it becomes possible to expose the structural and the dynamic characteristics at the same time. The "deduction" of a symbol evolution in Ricoeur's use is both *historical* and *phenomenological*. Two points, however, are essential to this exposition. First, the apparent order which traces the movement of evil from exteriority to interiority or from "objectivity" to "subjectivity" is possible only from the already functionally assumed position of Ricoeur's phenomenology. The movement is one which initiates what is to become the Hegelian moment of that phenomenology. Second, the development of the symbol from its archaic possibilities has already been noted to contain or to be isomorphic with the constitution of the self. The historico-phenomenological evolution of symbol is also a history of the subject. "Consciousness is not the first reality that we can know, but the last. It is necessary for us to arrive at consciousness, not to begin with it." [5] The structure and history of consciousness is "like" the structure and history of the symbol.

Ricoeur classifies symbols from the past to the present according to three broad types: symbols of defilement, symbols of sin, symbols of guilt. Each has a recognizable intentionality but is linked with the others by an implied historical movement.

1. The analogue of evil as defilement or stain is the most archaic of the symbol systems. "Dread of the impure and rites of purification are in the background of all our feelings and all our behavior relating to fault" (SE, p. 25). It is a symbolism which represents evil as "like" a stain. "What resists reflection is the idea of a quasi-material something that infects as a sort of filth, that harms by invisible properties, and that nevertheless works in the manner of a force in the field of our undividedly psychic and corporeal existence" (SE, pp. 25–26). This concept of evil, nearly universal in the archaic cultures of man, is the most distant to philosophical consciousness.

Its order of understanding is undifferentiated—in relation to philosophical consciousness. "The ethical order of doing ill has not been distinguished from the cosmo-biological order of faring ill . . . punishment falls on man in the guise of misfortune and transforms all possible sufferings, all diseases, all death, all failure into a sign of defilement" (SE, p. 27). In its cosmological moment the analogues of defilement are represented as infectious contacts, touch, or proximity to a quasi-material force. Its weighting is toward an externality of evil which is incurred by proximity.

Its psychic moment is a pre-ethical or undifferentiated fear. "Ethics is mingled with the physics of suffering, while suffering is surcharged with ethical meanings" (SE, p. 31). Evil as the quasi-material is to be feared and avoided. The actions of man are those which flee the contact with stain. "If you wish to avoid a painful . . . childbirth, to protect yourself against a calamity . . . observe the practices for eliminating or exorcizing defilement" (SE, p. 31).

The ritual performances which coalesce the means of dealing with the evil stain are those which systematize the interdic-

5. Ricoeur, "Herméneutique et réflexion," p. 25.

tions (do not touch dead bodies, menstruating women, etc.) and magically use ritual purifications to ameliorate the forces of evil. The *poetic* moment of defilement is already an expression in word and ritual action. "It is the rite that exhibits the symbolism of defilement; and just as the rite supresses symbolically, defilement infects symbolically . . . hence, defilement, insofar as it is the 'object' of this ritual suppression, is itself a *symbol* of evil" (*SE*, p. 35). But at its own level the poetic moment is not at first conscious of itself; rather, consciousness is constituted in the symbol which gives it its quality. It is in its potentiality for becoming self-conscious that the symbolic expression leads to its transformation into another type of symbol.

The symbolism of defilement, narrow in its intentionality of the quasi-material, is broad in its potential for transfomation. The analogue is *repeatable* in ever varying elaborations. But in being repeated the basic intentionality may also change.

2. The analogues of sin symbolism are the first order of transformation from defilement to ethics. It is precisely in the "objectification" of the experience of evil, in its ritual-poetic expression, that Ricoeur sees the possibility for such a transformation. The symbol system is a system which *defines* the pure and the impure. "Now it insinuates itself into the experience itself as an instrument by which the defiled self becomes conscious of itself. . . . Dread expressed in words is no longer simply a cry, but an avowal. In short, it is by being refracted in words that dread reveals an ethical rather than a physical aim" (*SE*, pp. 41–42). In other words, the transcendental "infinity" of the language intention, even though not self-conscious, already disrupts any total immediacy between man and his situation of suffering evil. The development and progressive coming to consciousness of the possibilities of this symbolic transcendence over evil are the "future" of the symbol.

In and through the expression and ritualization of defilement the system of pure-impure becomes an order. In turn the ordering of experience provides the opening for a set of expectations, a balancing of pains in a vengeance system and a hope for the absence or disappearance of fear. From this basis the symbols of stain are open to an ethicization. The symbolism of sin transforms the pure into the holy and purity into piety. The analogues of sin are bipolar and revolve around the relational notion of man-before-god. "Polarly opposed to the god before whom he stands, the penitent becomes conscious of his sin as a dimension of his existence and no longer only as a reality which haunts him" (*SE*, p. 48). This begins the movement toward reflection.

The analogues of sin begin the anthropologization of the experience of evil. The symbolic context is one which represents "the fundamental situation of a man who finds himself implicated in the initiative taken by someone who . . . is essentially turned toward man; a god in the image of a man . . . but above all a god concerned about man; a god who is anthrotropic . . ." (*SE*, p. 51). The before-god elevates the symbolism of evil into an anthropomorphic rather than a quasi-materialistic context. In the case of the Hebrew paradigm in *The Symbolism of Evil* this bipolarity of sin symbolism revolves around the notion of a contract, the Israelite covenant. The covenant or contract between God and his people is made and broken. Sin is the breaking of the contract; piety is the keeping of faith with the contract. But even in the emergence of Hebrew monotheism a certain "realism" remains. The cosmic moment of sin symbolism retains analogues of *position*. Man is for God or against Him; God is present or absent. Evil is a visitation of the wrath of God, a punishment for being against God.

The psychic moment of sin is also an elevation and a transformation of fear. "In rising from the consciousness of defilement to the consciousness of sin, fear and anguish did not disappear; rather, they changed their quality" (*SE*, p. 63). The psychic response is now "fear of God" and is ethicized. Dread is the dread of the wrath of God expressed in the images of presence and absence, of God removing his face or showing it in anger. Sin anthropomorphizes dread in a relational direction.

The ritual-imaginative notion of repentance retains the language of positionality. To repent is to "return," to again stand in the presence of God. The contract is re-established by the "position" of Israel. The Exile also provides a series of analogues for the experience of evil under the sign of sin. The rupture of being before-God is expressed as "wandering," being "lost," and as "exiled."

In the ethical context of sin symbolism, however, the language of defilement continues to appear. The psalmist and the penitent continue to speak of being "cleansed" (of sin)—but the whole sense of stain has been transformed. To be cleansed now means that the subject's existence has been changed and does not primarily refer to a means of escaping a quasi-physical evil. The cleansing becomes a *sign* for the good faith of the penitent. One incurs evil "because" one has broken faith with the contract, not because of an evil force. The transformation of defilement—still viewed in and through sin symbols—reverses the positivity of evil. To incur evil is to "break" the contract, to seek vanity in a false god, or to negate the covenant.

An iconoclastic relationship exists between the "higher" symbolism of sin and the "lower" defilement symbolism. Sin "demythologizes" stain. The result of taking the language of defilement into the symbolism of sin is that stain loses its original meaning. Its basic realism is transferred into a purely symbolic quality and stands for the now dominant analogue of a contract which has been broken. The sinner is under the sign of evil not because it has come upon him but because he has turned to an evil way. Sin begins the subjectivization of the experience of evil.

3. Guilt and its symbolism complete this subjectivization of the experience of evil. The analogues of "burden," "punishment," and "weight" of guilt become basically *subjective*. The metaphors have lost their basic positivity to the degree that it is the *feeling* of guilt which is the distinguishing characteristic. With guilt it is "I who . . ." which assumes the central importance in both the subjectivization and individualization of the experience of evil.

The transition from sin to guilt is observable in the movement from the contract. The "law," and with it a whole series of juridical analogues, creates the notion of guilt with its internalization of an accusation. The penitent is guilty before the law of a god or before authority. But the guilt is guilt primarily in relation to consciousness and individualization. "The second conquest, contemporary with the individualization of fault, is the idea that guilt has *degrees*. Whereas sin is a qualitative situation—it is or it is not—guilt designates an intensive quality, capable of more and less" (*SE*, p. 107). The subject is guilty in accordance with his conscious or "voluntary" activity. The "I who . . ." is responsible for evil to the degree of his conscious involvement.

To be freed of the "burden" or "sentence" of guilt is to be "pardoned" or "forgiven." The internalization of the experience of evil sees in the act of will the order and origin of evil. But with this subjectivization there is a limit. The limit for the symbol of guilt in its emphasis upon individual responsibility forms the possibility for the notion of absolute condemnation. The sense of alienation in which the individual may feel "damned" is its most intense possibility. As such, guilt is the *experience limit* for the cycle of primary symbols.

The final individualization and self-consciousness of the experience of evil under the concept of guilt results in a paradox. With guilt the self becomes its own tribunal—it has autonomy—but at the same time it is in a state of self-conscious alienation to the highest degree. With guilt the full circle of the self with itself is completed. Its autonomy may become alienation, of which the experience limit is *despair*. For despair is not only the consciousness of being enslaved; it is the consciousness of sin without promise.

The previous orders of symbolism are repeated in the symbolism of guilt. Guilt may be expressed in an obsessional or compulsive washing of hands—understood as neurotic or "psychological." Guilt incurred through the offense of the other or an infraction of the law of God may also occur in the guilt system. But guilt "demythologizes" these symbols. The experience of evil is now self-conscious. "The consciousness of guilt constitutes a veritable revolution in the experience of evil: that which is primary is no longer the reality of defilement . . . but the evil use of liberty, felt as an internal diminution of the value of the self" (*SE*, p. 102). With guilt the voluntary, the conscious, becomes the focus for the experience of evil. "It is not by accident that in many languages the same word designates moral consciousness (*conscience morale*), and psychological and reflective consciousness; guilt expresses above all the promotion of 'conscience' as supreme" (*SE*, p. 104).

At the end of the historico-phenomenological analysis of symbols and their development it is clear that the movement has been one which began by reading evil upon the world in a primitive "realism," but which progressively interiorizes this understanding until at its other extreme evil is read in the subject in terms of an ethical "idealism." In Ricoeur's understanding the reflective direction of symbol history ends in subjectivity. The progressive *telos* of symbol history repeats and absorbs the lower forms of symbol systems into higher forms.

There is a *circular* relation among all the symbols: The last bring out the meaning of the preceding ones, but the first lend to the last all their power of symbolization.

It is possible to show this by going through the whole series in the opposite direction. It is remarkable, indeed, that guilt turns to its own account the symbolic language in which the experiences of defilement and sin took shape (*SE*, p. 152).

This Hegelian movement is both a problem and a gain for Ricoeur's theory of symbols.

The gain occurs in understanding the "demythologization" of the lower-level symbols within the context of a new system. The iconoclasm of guilt towards stain and sin is a denaturalization of the "realism" of those symbols. This movement allows the symbol to become a *pure symbol*. In phenomenological terms the pure symbol is a reduced symbol.

In the reinterpretation of the symbols of defilement and sin under the subjectivized symbol of guilt, something "like" a reduction occurs. It is at this point that a symbol gives rise to thought. The subjectivization of symbols is what makes the symbol available—indirectly—for philosophic reflection; it is the counterpart of the first Copernican revolution of subjectivity. The primary symbol may only become *pure* when it has been subjectivized. "I would even venture to say that defilement becomes a pure symbol when it no longer suggests a real stain at all, but only signifies the servile will. The symbolic sense of defilement is complete only at the end of all its repeated appearances" (*SE*, pp. 154–55).

A pure symbol, in turn, is suggestive of a *concept*. "The concept toward which the whole series of the primary symbols of evil tends may be called the *servile will*." But as a concept this final donation of the symbol results in a paradox. "But that concept is not directly accessible; if one tries to give it an object, the object destroys itself, for it short-circuits the idea of will" (*SE*, p. 151). The notion of a *bound will* cannot be thought directly. The power of the symbol is to have thought the concept *indirectly*:

> Guilt cannot, in fact, *express* itself except in the indirect language of "captivity" and "infection," inherited from the two prior stages. Thus both symbols are transposed "inward" to express a freedom that enslaves itself, affects itself, and infects itself by its own choice. . . . Why this recourse to the prior symbolism? Because the paradox of a captive free will—the paradox of a *servile will*—is insupportable for thought (*SE*, p. 152).

This indirectness, suggestive of the dialectic of Ricoeur's structural phenomenology, is not only caused by the impossibility of giving an object to the concept of a servile will. It is also based in the impossibility of a total reduction. The "self-enslaved" will of the paradox is the pure symbol's circle of the self with itself. The paradox becomes the task of escaping from the "idealism" of the guilt symbols. A completely self-conscious experience of evil is impossible. This self-enclosed circle must be limited.

> The task of the philosopher guided by symbols would be to break out of the enchanted enclosure of consciousness of oneself, to end the prerogative of self-reflection. . . . The second naïveté [of hermeneutical philosophy] would be a second Copernican revolution: the being which posits itself in the *Cogito* has still to discover that the very act by which it abstracts itself from the whole does not cease to share in the being that challenges it in every symbol (*SE*, p. 356).

The pure symbol is limited in its conceptualization, and the paradox of servile will is a Kantian limit idea which "consists in justifying a concept by showing that it makes possible the construction of a domain of objectivity . . ." (*SE*, p. 355).

In Ricoeur's philosophy limits are derived dialectically. The moment and movement of symbols are taken up into a larger context in myths which situate and develop symbols in a drama of evil. The ascent to a typology of myths expands the understanding of the world of symbolic expression. The analytic of myths may be dealt with schematically, since it is the dialectic of myths which responds to the problem of the symbol's "idealism."

THE DRAMA OF MYTH

THE PRIMARY SYMBOLS remain primitive in Ricoeur's hermeneutics. Myths, he indicates, are already a first-order spontaneous hermeneutics of symbols. However, this first order of interpretation remains on the other side of philosophical consciousness in the order of expressive and indirect language. The myth is a ritual-dramatic form which portrays in imagery and drama a situation of man before the sacred. To the basic structural characteristics of symbols must be added the development of a narrative which characterizes myth: (a) The myth is set in a fantasy history which symbolically includes all mankind in a concrete universality of a primordial man. All individuals are summed up in the hero, the titan, the first man, and human experience is portrayed through this central figure or figures. ". . . in the myth the human type is recapitulated . . ."

(*SE*, pp. 162–63). (b) The myth is a movement and is given a *temporal orientation* in which the origin and destiny of experience is imaginatively portrayed. "The myth confers upon experience an orientation, a character, a tension. Experience is no longer reduced to a present experience . . ." (*SE*, p. 163). (c) The dynamic of the myth is considered by Ricoeur as an *ontological exploration*, the portrayal of an imagined original state across which (*transparait*) the current existential state of man is viewed. The transition from original to actual is made in the narrative of the myth.

The narrative form as a dramatic structure "is neither secondary nor accidental, but primitive and essential" (*SE*, p. 170). The existential exploration occurs in and through the concrete images of the myth. "It is a narration precisely because there is no deduction, no logical transition, between the fundamental reality of man and his present existence. . . . the myth has a way of revealing things that is not reducible to any translation from a language in cipher to a clear language" (*SE*, p. 163).

In fact, by taking the notion of a narrative drama somewhat more literally and rigidly than does Ricoeur, the typology which he develops can be shown with some simplicity. While this device excludes the subtlety of Ricoeur's analysis and omits discussion of many of the transitional myths, it can bring the hermeneutic dialectic of "subjectivity" and "objectivity" into clearer light. It is the ensemble of myths which finally establishes the limits for Ricoeur's understanding of Fault. The *characters* in myth are gods and men, the sacred and the primordial situation of man. The *plot* of the drama is a movement from an original state which depicts an origin of evil and moves or points to an elimination or amelioration of evil in a fantasy history. Through the depiction of the character and the plot, the understanding of man vis-à-vis Fault is uncovered in a finite series of myth types. In short, Ricoeur's understanding of myth is that it is an expressive and existential portrayal of man's understanding of himself.

Ricoeur divides Western myths into four basic types: (1) the *drama of creation*, most archaic of the myths, a theogony which has its paradigm in the Babylonian mythology; (2) the *tragic myths*, whose paradigm is to be found in Greek tragedy, and which stand as the most extreme form of originating evil in a wicked or blind god; (3) the "philosophical myth" of the *exiled soul*, a myth which creates the only dualism of body and soul;

and (4) the *eschatological* or anthropological myth of biblical history, which is taken as a central myth.

The first three myth types belong to the broader classification of speculative myths which locate the origin of evil in a state or situation prior to man. Only the last or anthropological myth originates evil with man through an act of conscious will. The dialectic of myths reopens Ricoeur's play of "objective" or external and "subjective" or conscious polarities.

Although between these main types there are a series of transitional types which show with great fineness of analysis the many historical transpositions that have occurred between times and cultures, it is necessary to exclude them from discussion. By applying the notions of character and plot the intentionality of each myth may be portrayed.

1. The drama of creation begins without characters. The primordial state is *chaos;* then the gods come into being. "The first noteworthy trait exhibited by this creation-myth is that, before recounting the genesis of the world, it recounts the genesis of the divine; the birth of the present world order and the appearance of man, such as he exists now, are the last act of a drama that concerns the generation of the gods" (*SE,* pp. 175–76). The undifferentiated and unordered state of chaos is prior to the differentiation into good and evil and the order of the cosmos. The opening act of the drama is the coming-into-being of order and the gods. "This first trait leads to a second: if the divine came into being, then chaos is anterior to order and the principle of evil is primordial, coextensive with the generation of the divine" (*SE,* p. 177).

It is this characteristic of the anteriority of evil which places the drama of creation among the speculative myths. "Man is not the origin of evil; man finds evil and continues it . . . evil is as old as the oldest of beings . . . evil is the past of being" (*SE,* p. 178). It is the creative act itself which forms the transition from chaos to order. But the creative act is first an act of violence. In the Babylonian form (with echoes to be found in the Greek myths of the Titans) the present order is brought into being through the slaying of the oldest gods. "Thus the creative act, which distinguishes, separates, measures, and puts in order, is inseparable from the criminal act that puts an end to the life of the oldest gods, inseparable from a deicide inherent in the divine" (*SE,* p. 180).

In its ritual form of a New Year's festival the repetition of the drama each year repeats and renews the creation of the

cosmos in dramatized form. The drama of creation sees its future, or better its renewal, in terms of the annual re-establish-
ment of order. Man must identify himself with the future of
being, with the gods who establish the order. The only hope for
the elimination of evil lies in the repetition of the creative act
itself. "There is no history of salvation distinct from the drama
of creation" (SE, p. 191). There is an essential ambiguity between good and evil in such a myth. Violence and creation, thus
destruction and creation, belong to the same actions.[6]

2. The ambiguity of good and evil is continued in more
radical form in the tragic myths. But its division has a direction
toward a theology which Ricoeur regards as "unthinkable." The
characters, already present as gods and men, stand in opposition to one another. At its height the drama arises in the idea of
a wicked god or a blind fate. "It may be said that the divine
malevolence has two poles, an impersonal one in moira and a
personal one in the will of Zeus" (SE, p. 217). Tragic theology
radicalizes the previous ambiguity of the myths of chaos by shifting the ambiguity toward the diabolical. "The non-distinction
between the divine and the diabolical is the implicit theme of the
tragic theology and anthropology" (SE, p. 214). The gods intend
evil toward man, who is doomed by them. Thus, the tragic myth
also belongs to the speculative class of myths which originate
evil prior to man—man finds himself doomed in an evil situation.

The plot of tragedy, in Ricoeur's terms, "does not appear until
the theme of predestination to evil—to call it by its name—
comes up against the theme of heroic greatness; fate must first
feel the resistance of freedom, rebound . . . from the hardness
of the hero, and finally crush him, before the pre-eminently
tragic emotion—φόβος—can be born" (SE, p. 218). The drama
occurs in the opposition of freedom to fate or the will of the
gods, in the delay before inevitable doom.

The hero, primordial man, is victim but also is to be ad-
mired.[7] The implication is that man has an ambiguous innocence before the gods. But this innocence is not complete, and
the tragic myths echo the ambiguity of the dramas of creation.
In the example of Prometheus Bound the central character, re-

6. Ricoeur sees this myth as an anticipation of themes worked
out in later German mysticism with its emphasis upon the becoming
and growth of divinity.

7. Ricoeur rejects the temptation to locate a sin for the hero in
the concept of hubris, a later moralizing tendency in Greek thought.

garded as prefiguring primordial man rather than as a god equal to Zeus, is a guilty-innocent. The theft of fire is a gift to man; the same act is both crime and benefit. "Prometheus is the benefactor of mankind; he is the humanity of man; he suffers because he has loved the human race too much. Even if his autonomy is also his fault . . ." (SE, p. 223).

The ambiguity of creation-violence is repeated in the tragic myths, but the innocence of Prometheus is only retrospectively related to his guilt. "The tragedy of Prometheus begins with unjust suffering. Nevertheless, by a retrograde motion, it makes contact with the original germ of the drama . . . the benefaction was a theft. Prometheus was initially a guilty innocent" (SE, p. 225). His suffering in the current existential state is given a background—but his actual state is the resistance of freedom to the divine doom. "The freedom of Prometheus is a freedom of defiance and not of participation." (SE, p. 224). His grandeur lies in his refusal of the blind or wicked decree.

The dramatic resolution of tragedy poses a difficult problem, given its force in a predestination to doom. The "unthinkable" theology of tragedy is hard to maintain. Thus, in the tragic tradition itself, there are several drifts away from the tragic. In the first case there is a suggestion that even the gods may change with time, "which wears out the claws and teeth of the wrath of men and gods." (SE, p. 227). This implies a change in the tragic characterization of the gods which drives this myth type back toward its archaic root. Zeus, in the end, is not wicked; the tyrant becomes just—a god "becomes." But this is precisely the theme found at the divine pole of the creation myth. "Thus it is that the 'epic' that saves 'tragedy' by delivering it from the 'tragic'; the 'wicked god' is reabsorbed in the suffering of the divine . . . (SE, p. 228). Such a resolution pays the price of destroying the tragic dialectic itself.

Tragic deliverance in its authentic sense remains bound to the spectacle. It is through pathos that tragedy attains an aesthetic deliverance. "The tragic vision, when it remains true to its 'type,' excludes any other deliverance than 'sympathy,' than tragic 'pity'—that is to say, an impotent emotion of participation in the misfortunes of the hero, a sort of weeping with him and purifying the tears by the beauty of the song" (SE, p. 227). Deliverance transforms the participant without changing his doom. Tragedy opens "the law of suffering for the sake of understanding" (SE, p. 229).

The spectacle of the drama is the poetic dramatization of the existential understanding of a culture. One source of Greek humanism is to be found in the ritual drama of tragedy which aesthetically establishes the tragic compassion for man.

3. The third myth also makes its appearance in Greek soil but is marginal to both the previous two types and to the eschatological myth discussed below. It is the myth of the exiled soul. Its importance cannot be questioned—it is the most "philosophical" of the myth types, and when transposed into an amalgam with the anthropological myth of the Bible, it plays an important role in Western man's understanding of himself.

What constitutes the uniqueness of this myth is its *dualism of body and soul,* a dualism lacking in each of the other types.

> It tells how the "soul," divine in its origin, became human—how the "body," a stranger to the soul and bad in many ways, falls to the lot of the soul—how the mixture of the soul and body is the event that inaugurates the humanity of man and makes man the place of forgetting, the place where the primordial difference between soul and body is abolished. Divine as to his soul, earthly as to his body, man is the forgetting of the difference . . . (*SE,* p. 280).

In fact the myth itself must be largely reconstructed from philosophical sources, thus accounting for a certain lack of concrete features. Its roots lie in a pattern reminiscent of both Eastern thought and the archaic theogonies in which life and death are but two sides of an eternal circle. But its intentionality remains: to develop the soul in order to eventually escape the imprisonment in the body which is doomed.

There is a theogonic origin to the Orphic myth. The Orphic myth adopts a Greek version of the myths of creation. Through a long series of geneses man is eventually produced as a mixture of the divine (soul) and the earthly (body). In its derivation of the source of suffering in the dark roots of a theogony prior to man's present state, the myth of an exiled soul remains speculative in its tendency.

But if the characters of this drama are not clear, its plot and mode of deliverance are. Man is divided in his essential being. In his present existence he forgets this essential state and thus remains bound to the body. The drama moves first toward a "fall" into the earthly, then toward a process of recovery; the soul is both punished and educated. Trapped in the prison of bodily existence, the soul is in conflict with the passions and seeks an eternal repose united again with its divine origins.

The philosophic modification of this myth is one which systematizes a *deliverance through knowledge.* "Now the act in which man perceives himself as soul, or, better, makes himself the same as his soul and other than his body . . . this purifying act *par excellence* is knowledge" (*SE*, p. 300).[8] *Know thyself* is a ritual word which "invents" the dualism and which roots all knowledge in the direction of freeing the soul from its bodily prison.

4. The Adamic or anthropological myth, according to Ricoeur's interpretation, belongs to a different type from the three previous myths in its radical introduction of a new intentionality. It situates the origin of evil not prior to man but in the bad use of freedom by man himself. Ricoeur "reads" the Adamic myth twice, however. In effect, the first reading of the Adamic myth makes the typological intentionality clear; the second reading is possible through Ricoeur's dialectic of myths.

The characterization of the dramatis personae of the anthropological myth immediately separates it from the intentions of the speculative myths. "The etiological myth of Adam is the most extreme attempt to separate the origin of evil from the origin of the good; its intention is to set up a *radical* origin of evil distinct from the more *primordial* origin of the goodness of things" (*SE*, p. 233). The biblical God is holy and innocent, and biblical man is finite and innocent. Creation begins as an essential good at both the divine and human poles. Moreover, man, although he is the "first man," "relates the origin of evil to an *ancestor* of the human race as it is now whose condition is homogenous with ours" (*SE*, p. 233). It is this characteristic which makes the Adamic myth properly anthropological.

The plot is the movement from a primordial innocence to an existential deviation. Man deviates from his originally good destination through an act of will. "The Adamic myth is a myth of 'deviation,' or 'going astray,' rather than a myth of the 'fall' " (*SE*, p. 233). The deviation occurs in the first reading of the myth as the action of this first man. "It tends to concentrate all the evil of history in a single man, in a single act—in short, in a unique event" (*SE*, p. 243). Evil comes to be *through* man as a radical and absurd *event*. By accepting a temptation Adam ini-

8. Note that the body of the ancients is not that of later "Cartesian" dualism but is the symbolization of certain types of desire or passion which are felt. The body is not yet an "object."

tiates evil, which then becomes the condition of all men throughout actual history. Evil is *historical,* not structural.

The first reading of the Adamic myth announces what Ricoeur calls the ethical vision of the world in radical form. Evil originates in an act of will—the subject is responsible for and takes upon himself radical evil as *bad will.* God remains innocent; man, through his deviation, corrupts the universe.

In its biblical setting, this myth sees evil as a historical end. Deliverance is *eschatological.* Biblical history becomes the history of rectification and the hope for deliverance. And although there are a series of modifications and variants, the "return" to innocence is to be through a human figure. The People or the Remnant are to be delivered through a Messiah or the Son of Man. The myth sees deliverance as a restoration of condemned freedom to its uncondemned state.

These four myth types form the basic units for a series of cross relations which Ricoeur inserts into his version of dialectic.

MYTH AND THE DIALECTIC

THE DIALECTIC of hermeneutic phenomenology elevates the problem of *objectivity* to a new level. The oppositions of the myths are a repetition of the "subjective" and "objective" modes of thought as means of accounting for the experience of evil. The *reflective* myth begins with man and locates its account of evil in an *act* of will; the *speculative* myths locate their accounts of evil in a *state* of being and thus make of evil that which precedes man. This is the functional reciprocity of *The Symbolism of Evil.*

The dialectical moment of the hermeneutics of myth commences with an affirmation by which Ricoeur *weights* one myth with a central role—the anthropological myth of Adam. An eidetic of symbols and myths is surpassed in a dialectic.

The transition to philosophical hermeneutics was begun when we passed from the statics to the dynamics of the mythical symbols. The world of symbols is not a tranquil and reconciled world; every symbol is iconoclastic in comparison with some other symbol, just as every symbol, left to itself, tends to thicken, to become solidified in an idolatry. . . . I entered that circle as soon as I admitted that I read the ensemble of the myths from a certain point of view, that the mythical space was for me an oriented space, and that my perspective was the pre-eminence of the Jewish confession of sins. . . . By that adoption of one myth, the appropriation of all of them became possible, at least up to a certain point (*SE,* p. 354).

This new weighting remains consistent with all of Ricoeur's choices. In Ricoeur's interpretation the anthropological myth is the "subjective" or reflective myth which begins radically with the subject. The dialectic is a play of that central myth against a set of counterfoci provided by the speculative myths which begin evil "objectively" outside or prior to man. The new reciprocity which underlies this dialectic is the *reciprocity of evil as act and state.* The stakes of the dialectic are also consistent with Ricoeur's previous choices. Can a reflective myth "absorb" all speculation? The answer may be anticipated in a qualified "no." The speculative myths *limit* the reflective myth through the dialectic. The implied "idealism" of the subjective myth is limited by the inability to totally absorb the problem of evil prior to man. It is the dynamics of the myths which effectually make the second reading of the Adamic myth possible as a limiting of the first and ethical vision of the world.

In each case the speculative myths originate evil in a source anterior to man—in what may be called philosophically *a category of being.* The Adamic myth reverses its radical first intentionality by making evil primarily an *event of history*—the dominant aim of ethical monotheism seeks to preserve the innocence of God and the essential goodness of finitude. This aim of the Adamic myth also corresponds to a functional aim of Ricoeur's hermeneutic phenomenology. Fault is not to be located in structures of the will alone. The will seduces itself, and its captivity is a self-induced captivity—to a point. But the question posed by the dialectic of myths is "to what point?". How is the implied "idealism" of the reflective myth to be limited? Thus the problem of objectivity as a dialectical limit reappears in hermeneutics.

The dialectic of myths, by using the Adamic myth as a weighted focus, establishes a set of limits to these two divergent intentionalities. These limits are anticipated and clarified in what Ricoeur calls the second reading of the Adamic myth, the deviation as a transition. By placing the relations between the myths in a correspondence with this second reading, the dialectical limits are more easily shown. Thus again the four myth types are related—now, however, in a dynamic reading.

1. The myth of creation from chaos is, in its Babylonian version, clearly close to the Adamic myth in time and culture, though not necessarily in type. In its historical setting the creation story of Genesis is clearly iconoclastic toward its Babylonian neighbor. In its polemical theological dimension the Hebrew God is portrayed as a God of power who has no need to struggle with chaos. He creates through his word—he speaks and it is so—there is no violence involved in bringing the world into its form. The scornfulness toward other gods in this assertion of Yahweh's power is matched by his essential goodness, which is carried over into the Creation itself. The world, finitude, is originally good, and man is destined to a good, if finite, fulfillment.

The status of man in the innocent Creation also implies a "superiority" of Adamic man over his Babylonian counterpart. In the Babylonian myth of chaos man is a result of an act of violence and is destined to be merely a servant of the gods whom he is to feed. In the biblical Creation man has his own destiny as the lord of this earth over which he is to have dominion. The Hebrew "demythologization" of the myth of chaos contains an intentionality radically counter to the intentionality of its earlier forms. Its direction removes the origin of evil from a category of being and places evil in a history. The ethical view of the world makes evil the act of a subject.

The dialectic however, is concerned with the mutual situating and limiting of the cycle of myths. Can the *reflection* implied in the Adamic myth be considered a complete conquest over the darkness of *speculative* chaos? Can the status of evil be completely reduced to a deviation of will? Ricoeur's second reading of the Adamic myth responds to this question negatively. The Jewish anthropological myth itself contains a vestige of its Babylonian antecedent. The serpent who tempts the primal pair is reminiscent of the monsters of chaos. "The Yahwist appears to have kept the serpent intentionally; the only monster who survived from the theogonic myths, the chthonic animal, has *not* been demythologized" (*SE*, p. 255). It is the case, however, that the serpent in the Genesis account is *merely* a creature and thus finite rather than divine. The vestige remains secondary to the primary intention of the myth as ethical.

In Ricoeur's second reading of the Adamic account the instant of the Fall is retold as a transition. The serpent poses a secondary problem for the Adamic initiation of evil. To the *initiation* of evil in an act of will is added a discovery of evil *already there,* revealed through the serpent's seductivity. Evil cannot be totally reduced to an act of will if another evil has preceded it. There is a positivity to the evil discovered that exceeds its initiation. The curse which is visited upon Adam outweighs the single act of disobedience. The "objectivity" or externality of evil, though begun or yielded to in will, cannot be reduced to mere will.

The underlying theme of all the speculative myths is that evil already existed, prior to man, in a "category of being." As the prefiguration of evil discovered in the non-human, the serpent enigmatically creates a "subterranean liaison" between the Adamic myth and the speculative myths.

2. But it is the tragic myths which bring out the logic of the dialectic in relation to the irreducibility of non-human evil.

In terms of a typology the tragic myth stands as the polar opposite to the ethical myth of Adam. The moralizing tendency which is iconoclastic toward tragedy is not absent from Greek thought (the gods must be moral, hence the fault of the hero is *hubris*) but is clearly apparent in the biblical tradition. "The Adamic myth is anti-tragic; that is clear. The fated aberration of man, the indivisibility of the guilt of the hero and the guilt of the wicked god are no longer thinkable after the twofold confession . . . of the holiness of God and the sin of man" (*SE,* p. 311).

The tragic sense of fate, a doom "exterior" to man, is an evil which is prehuman. Again the serpent poses the enigma. In Ricoeur's interpretation the serpent's temptation revolves around the notion of finite limit. What is originally a finite limit as *orientation* is called into question by the serpent in such a way that the limitation appears as an interdiction, the limit becomes *"other"* (*SE,* p. 253). The Fall of Adam is an alienation and deviation from the originally good destiny of finitude.

The tragic myths begin with the notion that the very nature of freedom implies a destiny, a fate. They are the "reverse side" of the ethical confession of sin. To choose is to be encompassed by a destiny even if unknown; it is a narrowing of existence. Finitude itself is the narrowness which is potentially tragic. To begin an evil which is then discovered as "other" *limits* the ultimate possibility of totalizing the subjective or ethical view of evil:

Here . . . is a fault no longer in an ethical sense, in the sense of a transgression of the moral law, but in an existential sense: to become oneself is to fail to realize wholeness, which nevertheless remains . . . the dream . . . which the Idea of happiness points to. Because fate belongs to freedom as the non-chosen portion of all our choices, it must be experienced as fault (*SE*, pp. 312–13).

The tragic myths, which limit the Adamic myth through the figure of the serpent, preserve the *opacity* which characterizes evil and which always signifies a limit function for Ricoeur. "They leave intact the opacity of evil and the opacity of the world 'in which such a thing is possible' " (*SE*, p. 326).

The limit, however, remains secondary to Ricoeur's continued affirmation of the subjective position. The representation of evil as "other" and as non-human, as the "source of evil for which I cannot assume responsibility, but for which I participate in every time that through me evil enters into the world . . ." (*SE*, p. 314), is not allowed to dominate the ethical confession. "It might be said that the avowal of evil as human calls forth a second-degree avowal, that of evil as non-human. Only tragedy can accept and exhibit it in a spectacle, for no coherent discourse can include that Other" (*SE*, p. 314).

The mutual limits of the dialectic "save" rather than destroy the Adamic myth. In Ricoeur's sense, the tendency of the Adamic myth, left to itself, is to a sterile moralism, a condemnation of man. This idolatry of the ethical view of the world is limited by the tragic view, which continues to reaffirm the fateful and un-chosen dimension of freedom. Man cannot be responsible for the unchosen and thus cannot be condemned in a total fashion. The *compassion* for the tragic hero "saves" the *moralism* of Adamic anthropology.

3. The myth of the exiled soul poses a special problem for the dialectic. The dualism of body and soul in the myth of Adam contrasts with the monism of all of the other myths which treat man as a totality. Yet despite the typological difference, historical transpositions brought the myth of Adam and the myth of the exiled soul into an intermingled amalgam. Ricoeur sees the basis for this transposition in the use the two myths make of the externality of evil as a seduction scheme.

In the Adamic myth the external figure is the serpent who seduces the original pair first through Eve's frailty and then through Adam's. In the myth of the exiled soul the intentionality is quite different—it is the body which is understood as external and the source of a seduction into evil. "The Orphic myth develops the aspect of the apparent externality of the seduction and tries to make it coincide with the 'body,' understood as the unique root of all that is involuntary" (*SE*, p. 331). In the two cases the nature of the external seduction is at first different: the serpent of the Adamic myth is non-human; the exiled soul takes the externality of the body into the *mixture* which is man.

At this level a countermovement of approximation is already possible. In the Orphic myth the conflict is internalized by making the body a *symbol-body*. Experience is understood as an internal conflict between (bodily) desires and the aim of the soul for repose. "For the body itself is not only the literal body, so to speak, but also a symbolic body. It is the seat of everything that happens in me without my doing. Now seduction is also in me without my doing; and so it is not so astonishing that the quasi-externality of the involuntary motions of the body could serve as a schema of externality (*SE*, p. 332).

From the Adamic side a second movement originated even prior to the Hebrew-Greek intercultural mixture of symbol systems. As sin symbolism began to develop in the direction of guilt, a progressive internalization of deviation can be detected. The suite of biblical expressions lays the basis in the biblical tradition itself. The "exile" of Adam and Eve from the garden and the historical Exodus as a "wandering in the wilderness" are potentially capable of internalization as "inner exiles." Nor is biblical language without a certain symbolism concerning the body. The "heart of stone," the "lewdness of the adulterer like the rut of beasts," (*SE*, p. 332), suggest the symbol-body even though in the context of sin symbolism the metaphor is being used in a reference which revolves around a change of will.

But by the time of the prophets the positional absoluteness of sin against God is also understood in terms of feelings of guilt. "Step by step, the Biblical theme of sin tends toward a quasi-dualism, accredited by the inner experience of cleavage and alienation" (*SE*, p. 333). Once experience is understood as inner conflict the approximation of the conflict of the exiled soul to the conflict of deviation is possible.

Finally, in the late Hebrew and early Christian era the invasion of body-soul dualism makes its full appearance in biblical language. In particular the Pauline treatment of sin and the law in the language of "spirit" and "flesh" allows the amalgamation to occur—in spite of the repeated Pauline emphasis on the "resurrection of the body" and the literalizing of Adam which seeks to preserve the monism of the Hebraic concept of man. The result is that the myth of Adam gains a different and a stronger significance in the Pauline account—Ricoeur notes that the Adamic myth plays a much less important role in Old Testament use than in the New Testament.

> Adam will be less and less the symbol of the humanity of man; his innocence will become a fantastic innocence, accompanied by knowledge, bliss, and immortality, whether by nature or as super-added gift; at the same time, his fault, instead of being a case of "going astray" will become truly a "fall," an existential down-grading, a descent from the height of a superior and actually superhuman status; . . . consequently, Adam's fall will no longer be very different from the fall of the souls in Plato's *Phaedrus*, where the soul, already incarnate, falls into an earthly body (*SE*, pp. 334–35).

Ricoeur notes that it is a two-way movement that eventuates in the amalgamation. The philosophizing of the myth of the exiled soul, particularly in the Platonic context, is one which drives the Orphic myth closer to an ethical interpretation. The Platonic unification of desire as two sides of a single aim of man in effect demythologizes the stronger dualism of the early myth. The Platonic use of the myth "represents an inflection of the symbolism of the 'evil body' in the direction of the theme of 'evil choice' " (*SE*, p. 344).

In later Western history the myth of Adam and the myth of the exiled soul intertwine in a mixture of ethical and existential themes concerning the experience of evil. The one who experiences evil is seduced by that "other" which is already there (the Devil), but the victim himself must initiate the act. Once initiated, however, bad choice binds the subject to a fate which binds the will itself.

Thus here, as in all the terminations of the myth cycle, the paradox of a servile will is again resighted. The myths arrive at a limit which was already recognized as a final irreducibility in the primitive symbols. The will is act and state; evil is initiated and discovered.

Symbol and Limits

At the end of Ricoeur's analysis, myths are seen to be variants upon the schemas of evil originally suggested by the symbols. The symbols remain the enigmatic *invariants* which provide the basic intentionalities for subsequent interpretations. *The symbol is the invariant.*

The invariance of the symbol, however, serves more than one purpose in this hermeneutics. In its first aspect the invariance is that of the "fullness of language" which functions clearly at the end as the whole from which all parts are derived.

Symptomatically, this may be seen from the very beginning or bottom of the symbol series. "Several times we have alluded to the symbolic richness of the oldest of the symbols of evil, the symbol of defilement. Defilement is always more than a stain, and so it can signify analogically all the degrees of the experience of evil, even to the most elaborate concept of the servile will" (*SE*, p. 336). The puzzle around which the whole multiple intentionality of defilement revolves is the "objectivity" of evil. And although as a *pure symbol* this "objectivity" has been phenomenologically reduced, the naïve interpretation as a quasi-material evil literally incurred through touch is demythologized. The intentionality of an "objectivity" remains.

Ricoeur sees three aspects to the intentionality of defilement as a pure and irreducible symbol: (a) Its "objectivity" is "the schema of 'positiveness': evil is not nothing; it is not a simple lack, a simple absence of order; it is the power of darkness; it is posited; in this sense it is something to be 'taken away'" (*SE*, p. 155). (b) Positivity is also "externality." "Evil comes to a man as the 'outside' of freedom, as the other than itself in which freedom is taken captive. . . . This is the schema of seduction; it signifies that evil, although it is something that is brought about, is already there, enticing" (*SE*, p. 155). And (c) its "infection" is that of the self-infected will. "The ultimate symbol of the servile will, of the bad choice that binds itself . . . signifies that seduction *from the outside* is ultimately an affection of the self by the self . . . by which the act of binding oneself is transformed into the state of being bound" (*SE*, p. 156). Each of these schemas revolves around the "objectivity" of evil in the sense that it is never thoroughly reducible to a pure act of will. This is the case with "infection" as much as with the schemas of "positiveness" and "externality," since a servile will is one which cannot free itself.

But what may be seen in the stratification of the schemas is that a two-way reading is possible. One may begin with positivity and move toward a self-affection; or one may begin with a self-affection and regress toward positivity. The speculative myths move in the first direction; the reflective myth meets its limit in the second direction. Directions of reading, already anticipated in the diagnostic of structural phenomenology, are given a Hegelian tendency in Ricoeur's hermeneutics. The two directions are progressive-regressive readings which reach a clearer development only in *Freud and Philosophy*, which will be discussed at length in the following chapter.

Secondly, the symbol as invariant makes all subsequent interpretation a variant. Such is the case with myth as the first-order spontaneous hermeneutics of symbol. Myth is already interpretation.

The myth takes the schema and provides it with its orientation, its "explanation," but it also remains a second-order interpretation. In the case of the exiled soul the external-seduction schema is primitive; the identification of the externality with body is secondary: "The body in its turn, can serve as a symbol for a symbol; it . . . is on the border between the inner and the outer . . . that is why 'explanation' of evil by the body always presupposes a degree of symbolic transposition of the body" (*SE*, p. 336). It is the symbol which reveals originary experience.

The symbol is finally the third term which, on Ricoeur's methodological grounds, is that which unites the double circles of hermeneutic phenomenology. The symbol reveals experience through expression; the myth interprets the expression which the symbol gives. The hermeneutic problem at this level then becomes one of finding an interpretation which is adequate to the invariance of the symbol. The experience of evil must be interpreted across the expression in such a way as to retain the primary intentionalities of the symbol.

A candidate for just such an interpretation is seen by Ricoeur in the Augustinian concept of original sin—but bereft of its gnostic tendencies. Original sin as a *functional concept*, a reflection upon myths and symbols, seeks to preserve the irreducible paradox of the symbols. The "biologizing" tendency of the Augustinian idea is an attempt to preserve the existential side of the experience of evil as already there, while the emphasis upon the act of will seeks to preserve the subjectivity of the Adamic tradition.

Hence the intention of the pseudo-concept of original sin is this: to incorporate into the description of the bad will . . . the theme of a quasi-nature of evil. *The concept's irreplaceable function is therefore to integrate the schema of heritage with that of contingence.* . . . The quasi-nature is in the will itself; evil is a kind of involuntary, no longer over against it, but in it—and there you have the concept of the servile will.[9]

The previous reciprocity of voluntary and involuntary on the level of Fault becomes the reciprocity of *state* and *act*. To experience evil is both to initiate and to receive evil. The limiting of a reciprocity of evil between act and state allows the dialectic between "subjectivity" and "objectivity" to stand. "The inscrutable for us consists precisely in this, that evil, which always begins *by* freedom, is already there *for* freedom: it is act *and* habit, arising *and* antecedence"[10] *The Symbolism of Evil* is a hermeneutic repetition of the dialectic and the indirect method of *Freedom and Nature*. A field of structures is changed for a field of expression.

9. Ricoeur, "The Hermeneutics of Symbols," p. 211.
10. *Ibid.*, p. 213.

6 / Toward the Philosophy of Language
Freud and Philosophy: An Essay on Interpretation

FIVE YEARS AFTER the publication of the first hermeneutic exercise in *The Symbolism of Evil*, Ricoeur published a
long and involved study of Freud which "grew" out of the Terry
lectures at Yale. The Freud book seemed to have broken the continuity of the philosophy of will that Ricoeur had outlined and
promised in his previous books. But in fact, *Freud and Philosophy* continues the investigation into the problems of method and
the question of hermeneutics which his earlier work had begun.
The Freud study further sharpens the hermeneutic tool.

In *The Symbolism of Evil* Ricoeur noted that the structure of
symbols was multilayered and that symbols, in their archaic
contexts, had at least three dimensions. The symbols of evil
read evil *on* the cosmos, *in* the psyche, and expressed their meaning in terms of *poesis*, the creative word. *Freud and Philosophy*
continues the interrogation of symbolic meanings. In *The Symbolism of Evil* the primary explication of the symbols and myths
of evil dealt with the "cosmic" aspects of symbolic discourse.
Ricoeur elaborated the prephilosophical world-view contained
in the various types of myths. The expressivity of myths was a
word structure through which the man of the myth understood
his relationship with Being. Ricoeur's seeming digression into
Freud, however, raises to primacy the "psychic" side of symbol
structures. The wanting-to-say of desire, understood in Freud as
a pervasive sexuality, is addressed. How does the unconscious
become expressed? the unsaid become said? It is another side of
the function of symbols that is investigated here. This, of course,
leaves still a third level unaccounted for, the level of the third

term, *poesis* itself. That is the subject for a "poetics of the will," a step that remains Ricoeur's own yet-to-be-said.

But at the same time that Ricoeur continues his quest for understanding the nature of symbolism, he reopens his dialectical version of philosophy with yet another counterfocus—the figure of Freud. *Freud and Philosophy*, however, is more than a mere study of Freud.

In summary *Freud and Philosophy* has two basic aspects. The first is a thorough, fastidious, and sometimes tedious philosophical reinterpretation of Freud and his intellectual journey. Ricoeur traces the movement from Freud's earlier more mechanistic, "scientific" psychology to the later and broader interests in culture and creativity. In tracing and analyzing this development Ricoeur begins to bring out certain relationships between language and the theory of the unconscious.

It is this concern which underlies the second aspect of *Freud and Philosophy*. The role and significance of the unconscious is tied to a problem of interpretation—psychoanalysis in its attempt to deal with symbolic and indirect language is one type of interpretation. Thus, before and after the "Analytic" upon Freud, Ricoeur adds sections which deal directly with his concern for hermeneutics. The introductory "Problematic" surveys the varied field of hermeneutics and finds that psychoanalysis occupies a particularly interesting position of opposition to phenomenology. This opposition is rooted in the Freudian "suspicion" concerning consciousness.

Ricoeur never allows oppositions to remain merely that; thus after rereading Freud he adds another long section, a "Dialectic," which attempts to show hidden relationships between the Freudian form of interpretation and phenomenology as it is broadly conceived. In fact, there are *two* figures in the dialectic with Freud—Husserl and *Hegel*. It is in this movement that Ricoeur's own concerns with the symbol and the subject return to full form. In effect, Freud performs a limiting and radicalizing function in relation to phenomenology, a function which limits the pretension of the "transcendental illusion" Ricoeur fears. But in turn Freud is counterbalanced by a "new phenomenology" which emerges under the sign of Hegel. Through a detour via Freud Ricoeur claims an advance in the understanding of the enigmas of symbolic language. The detour is one which expands Ricoeur's own understanding of hermeneutic phenomenology.

THE PROBLEMATIC: THE QUESTION OF LANGUAGE

THE FRENCH TITLE, *De L'Interprétation*, alludes to Aristotle's treatise, and Ricoeur proposes a vaster exercise concerning the philosophy of language than was shown in *The Symbolism of Evil*. With *Freud and Philosophy* Ricoeur enters a more theoretical phase of the concern with language.

Today we are in search of a comprehensive philosophy of language to account for the multiple functions of the human act of signifying and for their interrelationships. How can language be put to such diverse uses as mathematics and myth, physics and art? It is no accident that we ask ourselves this question today. We have at our disposal a symbolic logic, and exegetical science, an anthropology, and a psychoanalysis and, perhaps for the first time, we are able to encompass in a single question the problem of the unification of human discourse. The very progress of the aforementioned disparate disciplines has both revealed and intensified the dismemberment of that discourse. Today the unity of human language poses a problem (*INT*, pp. 3–4).

But the French subtitle, *Essai sur Freud*, indicates further that the entry into language will be another of Ricoeur's detours.

The question of a philosophy of language is to be posed via the Freudian psychoanalysis of language. This choice may appear odd, particularly if Freud is taken on his own ground. It would seem that Freud's naturalism—or more strongly his biologism—and his discounting of the role of consciousness would not only stand contrary to the positions of phenomenology but would have been one of the first positions to have fallen under a Husserlian critique. But this is a mere seeming in Ricoeur's case, because after an agonizing and intricate analysis of Freud the detour is one which serves a basically non-Freudian purpose. Ricoeur wishes to recover from Freud a hermeneutics which may be posed as a radical counterfocus to a reflective and phenomenological procedure. His aim is ultimately a radicalized "new phenomenology."

Thus the "Analytic" of *Freud and Philosophy* repeats Ricoeur's reflective "demythologizations" in order to see Freud's development increasingly hermeneutical. It is Freud the hermeneut and psychoanalysis as the set of rules for interpretation which remain the center of interest. Through this denaturalizing of Freud Ricoeur concludes that the "analytic experience bears a much greater resemblance to historical understanding than to natural explanation" (*INT*, p. 374).

This detour by way of Freud, however, reopens the same questions which were dealt with in *The Symbolism of Evil*. The double relations of *experience-expression* and *expression-interpretation* which characterize Ricoeur's hermeneutics re-emerge. From the beginning psychoanalysis as hermeneutics is seen to be closer to phenomenology than an empirical science would be, because psychoanalysis in its approach to language does not *totally* discount experience. Unlike linguistics, which abstracts from subjects and makes language an "object," psychoanalysis retains a version of the experience-expression relation for consideration. The Freudian analysis discounts only a particular or immediate consciousness for a functional or therapeutic reason. But in the end psychoanalysis as hermeneutics reaffirms consciousness as that by which the hidden may become manifest in the psychoanalytic cure. What interests Ricoeur is the different way in which psychoanalysis proposes to get its interpretations.

Further, psychoanalysis remains related to Ricoeur's continued concern with the symbol as the privileged expression field from which he wishes to begin an inquiry within language. The dream text of Freudian interest is already part of the oneiric or psychic dimension of the symbol. In its Freudian context the experience which gives rise to expression is that of (sexual) desire. Ricoeur sees in Freud the development of a "semantics of desire." Such a "semantics" announces that desire will appear in terms of a structure of meanings which in turn arise at the juncture of experience and expression, but which must be deciphered to be understood. The dream is the place within experience where expression begins to occur. "By making dreams not only the first object of his investigation, but a model . . . of all disguised, substitutive, and fictive expressions of human wishing or desire, Freud invites us to look to dreams themselves for the various relations between desire and language" (*INT*, p. 5). The archaism of the dream and its associated imagery and obscurity is a "birthplace of language." It is where primitive experience comes to expression.

But the text is not the dream itself. "It is not the dream as dreamed that can be interpreted, but rather the text of the dream account. . . . It is not desires as such that are placed at the center of the analysis, but rather their language" (*INT*, pp. 5–6). Again, as in *The Symbolism of Evil*, the need for hermeneutics is where experience has already come to birth in expression and where again the counterpart of primitive experience and obscure expression is recognized. All the Freudian theorizing, including the concepts of the unconscious, the barrier between the conscious and the unconscious, and the work involved in interpretation become a functional hermeneutics upon this text. The symbol holds the puzzle for a philosophy of language. "The issue here is not the problem of evil, but the epistemology of symbolism" (*INT*, p. 14).

The choice of the symbol which stands as the third term, belonging to the relations of both experience-expression and expression-interpretation, is to open the philosophy of language to what Ricoeur calls the fullness of language. Ricoeur makes both a weak and a strong justification for this choice. In its weak sense a philosophy of language cannot be considered complete until it is able to give account of indirect expressions and symbols.

> As I see it the problem of the unity of language cannot validly be posed until a fixed status has been assigned to a group of expressions that share the peculiarity of designating an indirect meaning in and through a direct meaning and thus call for something like a deciphering, i.e., an interpretation, in the precise sense of the word. To mean something other than what is said—this is the symbolic function (*INT*, p. 12).

But the stronger claim is one which holds that "the problem of symbolism is . . . coextensive with the problem of language" (*INT*, p. 16). *The problem of the symbol equals the problem of language.*

The reason the symbol equals language is to be found in the concept of the fullness of language. Presumably, the symbol already holds this fullness within itself enigmatically. In reclaiming the concept of the fullness of language, Ricoeur treats at least two important aspects of this concept.

First, with the long traditions of Romanticism, Ricoeur continues to assert that the poetic is the "birthplace of language." In *The Symbolism of Evil* that function was limited to an investigation of the symbols of evil by which the self gave itself a language to express the blind world of suffering experience. This bringing of experience to expression reappears in *Freud and Philosophy* as the bringing to expression of opaque desire. The same indirectness and equivocity apply to the dream as applied to the symbols of evil. The symbolic expression is the place within language where primitive experience and primitive expression meet.

There is no symbolism prior to man who speaks, even though the power of symbols is rooted more deeply, in the expressiveness of the cosmos, in what desire wants to say, in the varied image-contents that men have. But in each case it is in language that the cosmos, desire, and the imaginary achieve speech. To be sure the Psalm says: "The heavens tell the glory of God." But the heavens do not speak; or rather they speak through the prophets, they speak through hymns, they speak through liturgy. There must always be a word to take up the world and turn it into hierophany. Likewise the dreamer, in his private dream, is closed to all; he begins to instruct us only when he recounts his dream. This narrative is what presents the problem, just like the hymn of the psalmist. Thus it is the poet who shows us the birth of the word, in its hidden form in the enigmas of the cosmos and of the psyche. The power of the poet is to show forth symbols at the moment when "poetry places language in a state of emergence," to quote Bachelard again, whereas ritual and myth fix symbols in their hieratic stability and dreams close them in upon the labyrinth of desires where the dreamer loses the thread of his forbidden and mutilated discourse (*INT*, p. 16).

The poetic word is the "first word" which emerges from experience. The primitives of experience and expression function isomorphically. Thus the poetic symbol holds a privilege in the totality of the hermeneutic field.

But this "first word" is enigmatic, indirect, opaque and calls for a "second word" of interpretation. "Thus a symbol is a double-meaning linguistic expression that requires an interpretation, and interpretation is a work of understanding that aims at deciphering symbols" (*INT*, p. 9).

The second sense of the symbol's fullness is structural and is located in what Ricoeur now terms the *polysemic* structure of the symbol. The symbol is multi-intentioned and, from the start, overdetermined with an excess of meanings. Its complexity of structure already contains the problem of language in its multi-dimensioned totality. To understand the symbol calls for an understanding of a full architectonic of meaning.

What gives rise to this work is an intentional structure which consists not in the relation of meaning to thing but in an architecture of meaning, in a relation of meaning to meaning, of second meaning to first meaning, regardless of whether that relation be one of analogy or not, or whether the first meaning disguises or reveals the second meaning (*INT*, p. 18).

The symbol "contains" the problem of language in both senses. In relation to the first sense the problem of the subject may again be raised—how does the symbol reflect the subject? In relation to the second sense the problem of a "logic" of the symbol is raised—how does equivocity signify? Taken together the hermeneutic problem of language may be seen as a renewal of transcendental logic. The detour by way of Freud thus also initiates more openly the Hegelian moment of Ricoeur's philosophy:

> The only radical way to justify hermeneutics is to seek in the very nature of reflective thought the principle of a *logic of double meaning*, a logic that is complex but not arbitrary, rigorous in its articulations but irreducible to the linearity of symbolic logic. This logic is no longer a formal logic, but a transcendental logic established on the level of the conditions of possibility; not the conditions of objectivity of nature, but the conditions of the appropriation of our desire to be. Thus the logic of double meanings, which is proper to hermeneutics, is of a transcendental order (*INT*, p. 48).

The movement toward a Hegelian moment in phenomenology remains in a direct line of development from *The Symbolism of Evil* in its affirmation of the primacy of the symbol. But in its expansion of theoretical interests certain modifications of emphasis may also be detected. As in *The Symbolism of Evil* the symbol remains bound to its metaphorical structural characteristics.

> Symbols are bound in a double sense: bound *to* and bound *by*. On the one hand, the sacred is *bound to* its primary, literal, sensible meanings; this is what constitutes the opacity of symbols. On the other hand, the literal meaning is *bound by* the the symbolic meaning that resides in it; this is what I have called the revealing power of symbols, which gives them their force in spite of their opacity. The revealing power of symbols opposes symbols to technical signs, which merely signify what is posited in them and which, therefore, can be emptied, formalized, and reduced to mere objects of a calculus. Symbols alone *give* what they say (*INT*, p. 31).

But the opacity and the necessary connection between a first and literal meaning and a second and symbolical meaning are now seen to be more complex than the analogues of *The Symbolism of Evil*. "I would consider rather that analogy is but one of the relations involved between a manifest and a latent meaning" (*INT*, p. 17).

Again, as in *The Symbolism of Evil*, the equivocity of the symbol is precisely that characteristic which makes it an invita-

138 / HERMENEUTIC PHENOMENOLOGY

tion to thought. "Enigma does not block understanding, but provokes it; there is something there to unfold to 'dis-implicate' in symbols. That which arouses understanding is precisely the double meaning, the intending of the second meaning in and through the first" (*INT*, p. 18). But now it is seen that the revealing power of the symbol may also be a severe dissembling, calling for a hermeneutics of doubt—such as the Freudian model may provide.

But if at its first level the very richness or overdetermination of meanings poses the hermeneutic problem, at the level of interpretation another problem exists. There are also multiple hermeneutics, and the multiple meaning of symbols is open to a series of differing interpretations. "The bond between symbol and interpretation, in which we have seen the promise of an organic connection between *mythos* and *logos*, furnishes a new motive for suspicion. Any interpretation can be revoked; no myths without exegesis, but no exegesis without contesting. The deciphering of enigmas is not a science, either in the Platonic, Hegelian, or modern sense of the word 'science'" (*INT*, pp. 41–42). Instead, there exists a series of hermeneutics, "the hermeneutic field, whose outer contours we have traced, is internally at variance with itself" (*INT*, p. 27). At this level the question is also one of an orientation among, and a confrontation between, the various types of hermeneutics. It is in this context that Ricoeur again uses the dialectic of methods which characterizes his own indirect approach.

Ricoeur notes that hermeneutics have been a problem from classical times to the present. On one side stands the Aristotelian logical model for hermeneutics which isolates a logic of univocity, but with a cost. The choice of concentration upon univocal meaning results in "the logician [leaving] the other types of discourse to rhetoric and poetics and retaining only declarative discourse, the first form of which is the affirmation that 'says something of something'" (*INT*, pp. 21–22). This choice has dominated Western logic to the present and has been radicalized in recent times by the invention of symbolic and mathematical logic. But formalization in this pattern remains too narrow for Ricoeur's concern with indirect expressions. In fact, this choice excludes from its range of interest the symbolic function which says something other than it (literally) says. A formal logic must either attempt to reduce all statements to its univocal operations or abandon indirect discourse altogether.

A second traditional model of interpretation in Western history is to be found in biblical exegesis. In this case multiple meanings and indirect discourse were dealt with in classical form through the development of four presumed levels of meaning (literal, allegorical, analogical, and symbolic) found in biblical texts. But the concern of exegesis with sacred texts was equally restrictive in its range. However, for Ricoeur's purposes this tradition did make two contributions. First, it did appreciate and develop the general theme of analogical meanings and was in principle non-reductive in its methods. And, secondly, the idea of a text of multiple significance is a worthwhile model. "The exegetical tradition affords a good starting point for our enterprise, for the notion of a text can be taken in an analogous sense" (*INT*, pp. 24–25).

One set of oppositions, then, is between a strictly reductionist view of meaning, that view of meaning which claims that the starting point for investigation is with the simplest and most direct type of signification, and the view which sees the original enigma of language as its multivocity. It is clear that Ricoeur, by choosing to address himself to those theories of language which hold to the latter, has limited his inquiry largely to those philosophies of language which are dominant on the Continent. He addresses himself to the class of hermeneutics which *begins* with the enigmas of indirect and multivocal discourse.

In more recent times, and particularly in Continental thought, the question of hermeneutics has retained a certain importance. Both Schleiermacher and Dilthey in the nineteenth century and Heidegger, Gadamer, and Bultmann today specifically deal with the problem of hermeneutics. But in a broader sense Ricoeur sees a divergence of types which again fit into a dialectical pattern. The hermeneutic field is approached at the extremes by two major types of interpretation, Ricoeur argues. A "hermeneutics of belief" is set against a "hermeneutics of suspicion."

Philosophically this latter classification is one which dialectically poses the tradition of transcendentalist philosophies of the general Cartesian orientation against the philosophies of false consciousness which arise from the Hegelian left. The hermeneutics of suspicion begins in a severe critique of consciousness in its immediacy and posits some version of a false consciousness which must be overcome through interpretation; it is part of the whole range of iconoclastic interpretations that includes those of Nietzsche, Marx, and above all, Freud. *Freud and Philosophy* takes Freud as the paradigmatic case for dealing with a theory of false consciousness and becomes a concrete confrontation between a hermeneutics of belief and a hermeneutics of suspicion.

DIALECTIC: THE WAR OF HERMENEUTICS

THE DETOUR into Freud as hermeneut in the emergent classification of two polarly opposed sets of hermeneutics reestablishes Ricoeur's general dialectic in which some version of "phenomenology" will have as its counterfocus some "antiphenomenology" through which a set of limits may be reached. In *Freud and Philosophy* the dialectic is seen to have three distinct moments which progressively revolve around the gradual change of meanings Ricoeur gives to his own understanding of phenomenology.

These three moments of the dialectic are three progressive encounters between a phenomenological and a non-phenomenological interpretation—but in the progression phenomenology changes its meaning. The first moment is one of opposition. The debate of a hermeneutics of belief with a counterhermeneutics of suspicion is an opposition of *motivation,* and in this context the model for the phenomenological pole is provided by the phenomenology of religion (including in principle the "belief" of Ricoeur's earlier study of symbols and myths in *The Symbolism of Evil*).

The second moment of the dialectic is one of *approximation.* Ricoeur in this case uses a more specific understanding of Husserl, who is approximated to Freud in the indirectness of his method. It is this second moment which most typically reveals, in a revival of diagnostic, a set of mutual limits to both Husserlian phenomenology and psychoanalysis.

But there remains a residue from the second moment of approximation, and Ricoeur's favored phenomenological focus is threatened by its counterfocus of Freudian thought. The threat, however, is the issue of false consciousness which has been equated throughout Ricoeur's philosophy with the possibility of a transcendental illusion, the "circle the self makes with itself." Phenomenology must be limited to prevent this circle, and Freud becomes the figure who symptomatically serves this function. But at the same time the reductive strategy of Freud must not be allowed to overcome the gains of transcendental philosophy. Thus there appears a figure who has subtly been a background figure in Ricoeur's understanding of phenomenology and who increasingly assumes importance in relation to the issue of the symbol and the subject: Hegel. The third and final moment of the dialectic is its Hegelian moment which in Ricoeur's use restores a radicalized understanding of the symbol and the subject.

1. *The Moment of Opposition: Belief versus Suspicion*

The oppositional moment of the dialectic occurs at what may be termed a "motivational" level. The phenomenological pole of this first opposition is identified with the phenomenology which has developed in the history of religions. The use of phenomenology in this field is one which Ricoeur sees as motivated by a "belief." The "belief" is the aim *to restore* (lost) *meaning*. But it is also clear that phenomenology in this sense was also employed in *The Symbolism of Evil*, and the "belief" is Ricoeur's.

In its hermeneutical employment the phenomenology of this moment consists first in the *descriptive* approach to the field of symbols and myths. The *epochē* which excludes explanation in order to concentrate upon the "appearance" of the object-field also presupposes an exercise in the mode of "as if." To enter the "aura" of the symbol's meaning, to "sympathetically repeat" the symbol, is necessary in isolating its referential aim. But the presupposition is that the symbol has this to offer—hermeneutics is first a listening, a "belief." Second, this presupposition is one which grants the symbol a certain "truth" from the beginning. This "truth" may be merely that of the possibility of a signifying intention which may then be classed among other types of intentionality. But it is only through the willingness to "believe" that the symbolic dimension may be so described. The truth of the symbol which it "gives" in its indirect discourse is discoverable only in this way. Third, the "belief" that the symbol has something to say and that the philosopher may learn from the symbol finally presupposes a degree of active participation on the part of the philosopher which belies the presumed disinterestedness of a transcendental consciousness. "The fully declared philosophical decision animating the intentional analysis would be a modern version of the ancient theme of reminiscence" (*INT*, p. 31). Hermeneutics in this version of restoration of (lost) meaning is motivated by the will-to-hear.

This reaffirmation of the basic stance of *The Symbolism of Evil* is a claim that the symbol seen aright has *revealing power*, a "word." But on the side of the observer this presupposition calls for a willingness to believe. The qualification, however, remains the same—the belief is already phenomenological. All "second naïveté" is already critical in the sense that a reduction is presupposed.

> The contrary of suspicion, I will say bluntly, is faith. What faith? No longer, to be sure, the first faith of the simple soul, but rather the second faith of one who has engaged in hermeneutics, faith that has undergone criticism, postcritical faith. . . . It is a rational faith, for it interprets; but it is a faith because it seeks, through interpretation of a second naïveté. Phenomenology is its instrument of hearing, of recollection, of restoration of meaning (*INT*, p. 28).[1]

If this is, on one side, to make *epochē* a kind of "faith," on the other side it is to leave open the door to an expansion of what may count for criticism. Left to the one emphasis of "belief," the revealing power of the symbol is appreciated. But the symbol is opaque and harbors a possible dissemblance. For this possibility another motivation is needed.

The countermotivations of a hermeneutics of suspicion are those which begin from a *demystification* of the symbol. A hermeneutics of suspicion takes as its aim the *removal of illusions*. Its hypothesis is one which begins with the positing of a "false consciousness" which is deceived (either by its situation or in self-deception). This positing, recognized in Ricoeur's case as a procedural decision, is equally a "motivation." It is a motivation which opposes the decision to "believe." The implied iconoclasm of a "suspicious" hermeneutics is directed against the Cartesianism of the primacy of consciousness. Second, in function the suspicion is one which further posits some version of a barrier between consciousness and its (intended) meanings. All immediacy of meaning is questioned. The hermeneutics of suspicion calls for a deciphering of what underlies the illusion or is implied behind the barrier of false consciousness. The meaning of symbolism is other than is first evident *and other* than that which consciousness may "intend." But, third, the hermeneutics of suspicion rests upon its own version of positivity. The need to overcome illusion, to surpass false consciousness, is ultimately an appeal to some principle of reality. Although not necessarily

---

1. Professor A. Schuwer has frequently argued that the relation between faith and Ricoeur's use of reduction is a key to understanding Ricoeur. I do not dispute that Ricoeur's philosophical concerns are also ultimately religious concerns. My interpretation here brutally underplays these, however, for the sake of developing Ricoeur's methodology and the emergent theme of language.

apparent from the beginning, the reality principle (different in the various instances) gives the interpretation its final coherence.

What may be surmised in the first general encounter of a phenomenological and non-phenomenological hermeneutics is that the starting points of Ricoeur's interpretation are exactly counter to one another. The methodological decision employed in each version of interpretation carries consequences concerning the outcome of understanding. Potentially the problem of the two "Copernican revolutions" is included here as well as a continued argumentation between a reflective and a speculative theory of interpretation. However, the hermeneutics of both belief and suspicion are directed to the field of expression, and both presuppose that the subject may be understood through or across this field.

They differ in that the reflective or broadly phenomenological hermeneutics of belief is largely descriptive or "ontological," while the hermeneutics of suspicion "believes" that there is a hidden substratum which is the real hidden under a set of appearances. The hermeneutics of suspicion is "metaphysical." Ricoeur is concerned here, as throughout his career, that the first approach is open to the naïveté of a transcendental illusion which too easily takes its descriptions as correct ontology while at the same time not wanting to return to the objectivist naïveté of past metaphysics.

The "Problematic" poses this opposition as the background to the study on Freud. The "Analytic" of the Freud book accomplishes that study, placing Freud as a primary figure in the class of suspicious hermeneuts.

2. *The Moment of Approximation: Phenomenology and Psychoanalysis*

The second moment of the dialectic of phenomenology with the Freudian non-phenomenology begins the reversal of sheer oppositions of "belief" and "suspicion." In a much more technical discussion Ricoeur attempts to *approximate* the reductions and perceptualist model of Husserlian phenomenology to psychoanalysis. The issue is one which centers on the problem of *indirect* methods.

The issue of indirectness is specifically raised in the comparison of the functions of phenomenological reductions as they approximate a Freudian theory of the unconscious. It is important to note that Ricoeur "demythologizes" the naturalism of

Freudian models from the outset. The dialectic of phenomenology and psychoanalysis presupposes the "Analytic" of *Freud and Philosophy* which views the theory of the unconscious as a set of interpretative rules. Ricoeur rejects any "realism" of the unconscious. Ricoeur's counterplay to denaturalize the counterfocus provided by psychoanalysis follows a pattern already set by the diagnostics of *Freedom and Nature*.

The first approximation of phenomenology to psychoanalysis lies in the general indirectness of their respective procedures. Neither is a basically introspective method in the ordinary sense. Ricoeur had earlier noted that "An introspective psychology does not hold up in the face of the Freudian or Jungian hermeneutics; whereas a reflective approach by the detour of a hermeneutics of cultural symbols, not only holds up, but opens a true debate of one hermeneutics with another." [2]

The indirectness of phenomenology is to be found in reflection, which is implicitly a type of suspicion. This suspicion is the systematized suspension of immediacy or naïve consciousness, the first goal of *epochē*. "This immediate consciousness is disposed along with the natural attitude. Thus phenomenology begins by a humiliation or wounding of the knowledge belonging to immediate consciousness" (*INT*, p. 377). The reduction, understood as a hermeneutic rule, is a theory which begins to approximate the questioning of immediate consciousness which is also the first principle of psychoanalysis.

But in the case of Husserlian phenomenology the model is one which is directed by the question of appearances, which Ricoeur argues are based on a representationalist or perceptualist framework. Any approximation to an "unconscious" must first be understood from the perceptualist model. Ricoeur argues that this is possible in the understanding of the *implicit* or *co-intended* aspect of a phenomenology of perception. An object, when intentionally referred to, is always presented as having both a front and a back—but the back or unseen side is co-intended or implicit rather than given in the same fashion as the front. The implicit is the first place in phenomenology where the "hiddenness" of an "unconscious" could be approximated. "The first unconsciousness or unawareness (*inconscience*) phenomenology reveals has to do with the implicit, the co-intended: for the model

2. Paul Ricoeur, "The Hermeneutics of Symbols and Philosophical Reflection," trans. Denis Savage, *International Philosophical Quarterly*, II, no. 2 (May, 1962), 195.

of this implicit—or better, this co-implicit—one must look to a phenomenology of perception" (*INT*, p. 378). In Ricoeur's case this approximation of an "unconscious" to co-intention is heightened by the previous use of his Kantian interpretation of perspective and word. The Kantian distinctions more clearly break apart the unity of the Husserlian understanding of intentionality than otherwise would be the case.

But if phenomenology begins by questioning the naïveté of immediate consciousness, it retains consciousness as its central theme. Phenomenology remains a transcendental philosophy and presupposes a nexus of originary experience which becomes the field for investigation.

The theme of this consciousness is intentionality. Ricoeur sees a second approximation to psychoanalysis in the use phenomenology makes of reflection in order to thematize intentionality. In his understanding of phenomenology the first turn to the object (noema) acquires an irreducible primacy. The subject is always thematized by a *re*-flection from the object, and intentionality becomes thematic only after or through the "mirror" of the object world. In a statement which places Ricoeur closer to existential phenomenology than his earlier critiques, he notes the "impossibility of total reflection, hence the impossibility of the Hegelian absolute knowledge, thus the finitude of reflection . . . are written into this primacy of the unreflected over the reflected" (*INT*, pp. 378–79). Reflection is always partial, and this is the source of the enigma and the opacity of bodily existence.

First, then, in the perception of objects Ricoeur sees an approximation of phenomenological description to a theory of the "unconscious." But following his practice of making a reflective turn, the second area in which phenomenology and psychoanalysis are to be approximated must be in the subject. Here the terminal pole of phenomenology centers upon the I-body. The post-Husserlian phenomenologies of bodily existence may be approximated to some aspects of the "unconscious." The subject-body becomes a second place at which a connection occurs.

When asked how it is possible for a meaning to exist without being conscious, the phenomenologist replies: its mode of being is that of the body, which is neither ego nor thing in the world. The phenomenologist is not saying that the Freudian unconscious is the body; he is simply saying that the mode of being of the body, neither representation in me nor thing outside of me, is the ontic model for any conceivable unconscious. This status as model stems not from the vital determination of the body, but from the ambiguity of its mode of being. A meaning that exists is a meaning caught up within a body, a meaningful behavior (*INT*, p. 382).

Thus, both at the object pole and the reflective terminus, phenomenology is open to its own version of an "unconscious."

Ricoeur argues that there is more involved in a hermeneutic turn than the mere extension of a perceptualist model to the linguistic field, because when the language field is substituted for the world of perceived objects, a reflection is possible which is the discovery of the spirit. "It must be rediscovered with Hegel that language is the being-there (*être-la*) of the mind [spirit]" (*INT*, p. 384).

Freud and Philosophy begins to make clear more of the implications of a linguistically oriented phenomenology. Ricoeur has always held that there is a difference between a phenomenology of speech and a phenomenology of language, and it is the latter which holds a certain preferential status in Ricoeur's mind. But the movement to a linguistic phenomenology cannot be made too abruptly if it is to remain in line with its origins. The movement *from* the perceptualist model must first be recognized. Under a description of what Ricoeur calls a dialectic of language, the movement from the perceptualist basis indicates what is involved with the correlated phenomenologies of speech and of language. Beginning with perception, one may speak of a dialectic of presence and absence in relation to the object which is either present or absent (or present with implied but "literally" absent aspects). In the substitution of expressions for objects the aspects of this dialectic are changed. "Man's adoption of language is in general a way of making himself absent to things by intending them with 'empty' intentions and, correlatively, of making things present through the very emptiness of signs" (*INT*, p. 384). This is the essential transcendence of work over object, the origin of a dialectic of signification.

The ascent to language, however, also changes what is noticed regarding intentionality. A phenomenology of perception rightly concentrates upon the appearance of the object—but this very concentration is one which accepts a certain naïveté concerning language. It takes for granted that the object may be expressed ("We say the world"). The struggle with language, the frequent use of metaphor or the coining of new terms, which has so noticeably marked the existential phenomenologies, is a partial functional result of this naïveté. The struggle with experience takes language for granted. The hermeneutic turn proposes to create in reverse an awareness of the non-neutrality of the language in use.

In a similar manner the now traditional emphasis of phenomenologists upon the speech act displays a similar blind area. The signifying intention which aims to "say something of something" makes *vouloir-dire* its theme. In the speech act language is a mediation—the reference always points beyond the words themselves. This attention, proper in its limits, tends to further cover over the field of language as a theme for itself.

The hermeneutic substitution of the language field for the world of objects involves a further step. By turning to the presence of the language field, the structure of that field may be noted for its own dialectic. "Language has its own way of being dialectical: each sign intends something of reality only by reason of its position in the ensemble of signs. No sign signifies through a one-to-one relation with a corresponding thing; each sign is defined by its difference from all the others . . ." (*INT*, p. 384). So considered, the language field itself becomes the "object" to be considered. And with this consideration Ricoeur opens himself to a need for encountering the linguistic disciplines.

Such an encounter is not yet to be undertaken in *Freud and Philosophy*. But what does occur is the outline of method. The language field has become the theme which serves as a reflective surface from which the subject is to be viewed. The reflective turn which correlates subjectivity with an object-correlate has language as its "object."

But, if language is noted to have its own structural characteristics which include the fact that meanings are derived both from a transcending reference *and* from the ensemble of signs, then the partiality of the bare speech act itself may be seen. To speak is to engage far more than *vouloir-dire*. "In ordinary language each sign contains an indefinite potential of meaning . . . to speak is to set up a text that functions as the context for each work" (*INT*, p. 384). Thus what is said carries a significance which essentially exceeds any merely conscious intentionality. The indefiniteness and open structure of language are such that it surpasses in its very nature any simple immediacy of knowing what is fully signified. To engage language in speech is already more than the mastery of consciousness over its meanings. But it is only reflectively that the limits of *vouloir-dire* can be discovered as partial. Analogically, there remain various factors which relate the perceptual base of phenomenology to the linguistic field. The opacity of the body and the ambiguity of the thing function in a fashion which is isometric with the opacity and partial hiddenness of meaning in language. In the movement from perception to language, "the ambiguity of 'things' becomes the model of all ambiguity of subjectivity in general and of all the forms of intentionality. . . . the question of consciousness becomes as obscure as that of the unconscious" (*INT*, pp. 385–86).[3] Moreover, the illusion possible from a concentration upon the primacy of the speech act—that consciousness may rule in a transparent fashion over its meanings—parallels the illusion that bodily existence could become perfectly transparent. "Unconsciousness" is modeled not only on the ambiguity of the thing, upon the opacity of the body, but upon the hiddenness of meaning in language.

The turn to the circles of language is also a turn to intersubjectivity. In language, "*all* our relations with the world have an intersubjective dimension" (*INT*, p. 386). The perceptualist basis of phenomenology only begins the opening to intersubjectivity in its understanding of the constitution of objectivity. An object is perceived by a subject limited to a positional perspective —but the object is in principle open to inspection by *other subjects*. Moreover, those aspects which presently may not be displayed to one subject may be precisely those aspects present to the others. The same may be said of meanings. "Every meaning ultimately has intersubjective dimensions; all 'objectivity' is intersubjective, insofar as the implicit is what another can make explicit" (*INT*, p. 386).

The application to a theory of the "unconscious" is immediate. That which is hidden or only implicit to the immediate consciousness of the operating subject may be apparent or made explicit by another. The implication is one which relates to psychoanalytic techniques—here restricted to their hermeneutic significance.[4] Psychoanalysis begins with the intersubjectivity of expression rather than arriving at it by way of a perceptual constitution. In relation to the problem of expressed desire, psychoanalysis begins immediately with the problem of intersubjectivity and implicit meaning. "The intersubjective structure of desire is the profound truth of the Freudian libido theory" (*INT*,

3. Note the shift from the primacy of consciousness affirmed in *Freedom and Nature!*
4. Herbert Spiegelberg's phenomenological workshop develops yet another direction for this purpose. By group reporting, a comparison, crosschecking, and correction in the noting and describing of phenomena are used.

p. 387). A phenomenological hermeneutics and psychoanalysis as hermeneutics approximate one another in the need to explicate the implicit.

In Ricoeur's case the aim of such an exploration into the latent and hidden meanings of language remains tied to the need to understand the subject. To understand language is in one sense to understand the subject. The subject remains the reflective terminus of the cycles of interpretation-expression and expression-experience. But this understanding is to be arrived at by detour through hermeneutics. Through the questioning of the immediacy of experience a deeper understanding of that experience is to be had. In this sense phenomenology and psychoanalysis eventually are approximate in aim:

> Phenomenological reduction and Freudian analysis are homologous in that both aim at the same thing. *The reduction is like an analysis,* for it does not aim at substituting another subject for the subject of the natural attitude . . . the subject doing the reduction is not some subject other than the natural subject, but the same; from being unrecognized it becomes recognized. In this respect the reduction is the homologue of analysis, when the latter states, "where id was, there shall ego be.". . . Both have the same aim, "the return to true discourse" (*INT*, pp. 389–90).

A dialectic of approximation, however, has two sides, and phenomenology and psychoanalysis remain only approximate. If both methods are indirect, the basis of their indirectness remains radically distinct. Ricoeur shows that the indirectness of each theory is in effect constituted by different types of reductions. The perceptual model of phenomenology remains based in a reflective procedure which thematizes *consciousness;* but the analytic procedure begins by a reduction of consciousness. Thus, what is indirect in one theory is direct in the other by an inverse set of rules.

> But this initial homology between methods is understood only at the end. Phenomenology attempts to approach the real history of desire *obliquely;* starting from a perceptual model of the unconscious, it gradually generalizes that model to embrace all lived or embodied meanings, meanings that are at the same time enacted in the element of language. Psychoanalysis plunges *directly* into the history of desire, thanks to that history's partial expression in the derealized field of transference (*INT*, pp. 389–90).

Phenomenology as a reflective discipline takes all its cues concerning consciousness from the object-correlate—*"the spectacle is at the same time the mirage of self in the mirror of things"* [italics added] (*INT*, p. 379). What is essential is to isolate the meaning of this image in Husserlian terms. Freudianism, however, while indirect in relation to consciousness is direct in relation to its theory of meaning. *"It is possible to give a direct definition of the psychism without appealing to self-consciousness"* [italics added] (*INT*, p. 379). It is this which marks Freudianism as an indirect but non-reflective method. It "brackets" precisely that which becomes the theme of the phenomenological approach. In this difference Ricoeur sees the possibility of considering psychoanalytic theory as a *countermethod*. In a diagnostic use of Freudian theory Ricoeur proposes to limit the use of phenomenology. Freud in the hermeneutic context, like Kant in the structural context, counterposes the tendency to "idealism."

It is not accidental that one recognizes here a return to the tactics of Ricoeur's diagnostic. But with *Freud and Philosophy* there emerges a significant difference in its use. In its earlier form the diagnostic was a reading technique which also employed a dialectic in relation to a countermethod of an "objectivist" type. But its use remained narrowly limited and single-edged. Although even in *Freedom and Nature*, Ricoeur admitted clearly that objectivism was not totally reducible to a phenomenological universe of discourse and retained a certain advantage in relation to the border areas of experience, he never thoroughly indicated what this irreducibility was.

Secondly, although the limits of a purely eidetic phenomenology were presumably established by encounter with an irreducible countermethod, the movement remained focused upon phenomenology. The diagnostic "de-naturalized" the objectivist method by reducing it to a "reading" function—but any countermove which would inversely "demythologize" phenomenology remained unperformed.

But with the moment of approximation this second movement is made. The "excess" by which psychoanalysis enters into areas either restricted or blind to phenomenology is interpreted as an inverse *epoché* which "demythologizes" certain aspects of the phenomenological subject. The Freudian hermeneutics of suspicion becomes the limiting means by which the transcendental illusion is to be overcome.

This is not to say that Ricoeur abandons his previous preference for phenomenology or reflective methods; it is to say that he wishes these methods chastized. The issue is the transcendental illusion of "idealism."

The "weakness" of phenomenology is not its so-called subjectivism. In taking the concrete point of view of the subject-I-am, phenomenology gains certain insights which lead to the destruction of a simple objectivism. However, in taking this point of departure and in gaining certain insights through this point of view, a temptation occurs which may lead to the absolutizing of the ego.

Phenomenology remains a thematization of *consciousness* and thus is blind to any distortion which may occur at the very origin of meaning. Phenomenology, in revealing the misconceptions of the natural attitude, opens itself to a self-deception on its own part. It is prepared to regressively push to the origins of meaning from the world of perception—but it is unprepared to understand the dissociation which occurs there and which the genius of Freudianism has revealed. "But another technique is required in order to understand the remoteness and division at the basis of the distortion and substitution that make the text of consciousness unrecognizable" (*INT*, p. 393).

To arrive at a semantics of desire which makes a distortion at the origin of meaning understandable, Freudianism develops a new "reduction," a reduction of phenomenology itself. If phenomenology directly centers itself in the ego, then psychoanalysis displaces this center in order to gain a different perspective upon the subject. "What is in question is the very subject of immediate apperception. . . . Here we have reached a sort of end point of the reduction of consciousness and, one may say, of phenomenology as well" (*INT*, pp. 425–26).

In this sense psychoanalysis serves to decenter the ego and "humiliate" it. But this "humiliation" is precisely what is needed to correct or supplement the direct phenomenological insights Freud adds to the phenomenological field:

> *In te redi*—the phrase is St. Augustine's; it is Husserl's, too, at the end of the *Cartesian Meditations;* but what is peculiar to Freud is that this instruction, this insight, must involve a "humiliation," since it has encountered a hitherto masked enemy, which Freud calls the "resistance of narcissism" (*INT*, p. 427).

From here, while it remains impossible to reduce psychoanalysis to phenomenology, it is possible to integrate within degrees its insights into a reflective philosophy. Freud achieves his perspective upon the ego by a detour around direct consciousness. This detour follows (a) the development of the theory of the unconscious and (b) the development of therapeutic relations in which one subject interprets for another. It is in this procedure that Ricoeur sees Freudianism as the development of a hermeneutics:

> [Analysis] achieves a decentering of the home of significations, a displacement of the birthplace of meaning. By this displacement, immediate consciousness finds itself dispossessed to the advantage of another agency of meaning—the transcendence of speech or the emergence of desire. This dispossession, which the Freudian systematization requires of us in its own way, is to be achieved as a kind of ascesis of reflection, the meaning and necessity of which appear only afterward, as the recompense for an unjustified risk (*INT*, p. 422).

The wager which Freud takes is initially not justified—but once in operation it is precisely what yields the insight necessary for the discovery of the distorted or hidden meanings within the language of desire. "We must really lose hold of consciousness and its pretension of ruling over meaning, in order to save reflection and its indomitable assurance" (*INT*, p. 422). This wagered detour which produces a gain in insight is *hermeneutics*. Freudian theory *functions* as a rule of interpretation which justifies the indirectness of the procedures. "It is in relation to hermeneutic rules and for another person that a given consciousness 'has' an unconscious; but this relation becomes manifest only in the dispossession of the consciousness which has that unconscious" (*INT*, p. 438).

The contribution of Freud to reflective philosophy is the development of a hermeneutic technique which yields a key to the semantics of desire. Freud *donne à penser*, and that which is given is elaborated by means of hermeneutic rules.

Reread as rules of interpretation, the theory of the unconscious relates back to the problem of the symbol. The barrier between the unconscious and consciousness which is the presumed role of repression is the rule of suspicion which makes the field of expression a theme apart from the immediate and individual consciousness. As a hermeneutic rule this suspension of conscious immediacy also makes the field of expression understandable as a field of double meaning. Immediate meaning "hides" another meaning. The symbol is a dissembling. " It is indeed another *text* that psychoanalysis deciphers, beneath the text of consciousness. Phenomenology shows that it is another text—but not that this text is *other*" (*INT*, pp. 392–93). These rules, in turn, treat the dream recital as a text. This text is of the particular indirect type Ricoeur takes as his theme for hermeneutics. The distortion of meaning posited by the dream interpretation, Ricoeur argues, calls for concepts such as those developed in the energy metaphors of Freudian naturalism. "The function of the energy metaphors is to account for the disjunction between meaning and meaning" (*INT*, p. 394).[5] The reading of the hidden meaning reveals a dimension of subjectivity which in Freudian theory is termed the "unconscious." The unconscious is a latent theory of language.

The dream text is interpreted via a theory of the unconscious. But the theory of the unconscious, now seen through a hermeneutics, is precisely the means which renders the dream text understandable as a metaphorical text. Thus, for example, the concept of repression, which in its properly Freudian context is part of the theory of the unconscious, may also be seen as an interpretative rule. Freudian "realism" functions hermeneutically. "The interpretation of repression as metaphor shows that the unconscious is related to the conscious as a particular kind of discourse to ordinary discourse" (*INT*, p. 403). The unconscious is like a language, but always a difficult and metaphorical language.

But a second set of principles is hidden in the technique of therapy itself. Here psychoanalysis finds its most distinct difference from phenomenology, exceeding it in the decentering of the Cogito. What makes psychoanalysis unique in this respect is *"treating the intersubjective relation as a technique"* (*INT*, p. 406). This is to say that all interpretation in a Freudian hermeneutics is an interpretation which begins with and exists only within the confines of a restricted and controlled intersubjective relation (between analyst and patient). It is through the interpreter that the one interpreted becomes aware of that which was hidden.

In its properly Freudian setting this technique contains three aspects: (a) the work of the analyst is to interpret the hidden and dissembling language of the analysand. Here all the methods of interpretation as an exercise in suspicion are employed, and at this level the theory of the unconscious provides the set of rules. The analyst begins directly by viewing the account of the analysand as harboring a narrowed, resistant, and barred set of

5. Ricoeur thus independently confirms a thesis also developed by Lacan. The relation of symbol to self, of course, precedes Ricoeur's *Freud and Philosophy*. It occurs in *The Symbolism of Evil* in an anticipatory fashion.

meanings which the analyst "suspects" and must get through. (b) At the same time there is work on the part of the analysand as he gradually brings forth that which is repressed. The technique in intersubjectivity presupposes a type of co-operation even in the midst of struggle. (c) Finally, through this double work of interpretation, the therapy or understanding is acted out. The dramatic repetition and recital of the trauma which "causes" the neurosis is finally brought forth and dealt with.

The theory of the unconscious (which functions as a rule which in turn reveals the dissemblance of the text) and the technique of indirection in the therapeutic relation combine as the "excess" of Freudianism which is not reducible to phenomenological reflection. Ricoeur seeks to use this "excess" to modify phenomenology. The functional reason for such a modification revolves around Ricoeur's concern with a second Copernican revolution and the need to remove the transcendental illusion.

The rebound of Freudian "excess" is to be the means to radicalize phenomenology by inverting the use of *epochē*. Thus, in the progressive dialectic of moments, the moment of approximation takes the first step toward a "new phenomenology" (*INT*, p. 462 n). *The Freudian realism (objectivism) becomes the first step in a radicalized epochē.*

If one follows Ricoeur's understanding of a general phenomenological strategy, the first demand is that whatever area is to be investigated must first be problematized, its claim to immediacy or self-evidence called into question. The "excess" of Freudian thought does precisely this for the transcendentalism of phenomenology.

The modification is one which employs a version of the hermeneutic rules which are used to decipher dissemblance. To explore indirect discourse Ricoeur now holds that it is first necessary to perform what amounts to a reduction upon the pretension of consciousness over the origin of meaning. The approximation of phenomenology to Freudianism thus brings together the needs of decentering consciousness; a methodological way of getting at the indirect; and a "humiliation" of reflective philosophy itself. "To become concrete, reflection must lose its immediate pretension to universality" (*INT*, p. 48).

But if the "excess" of Freudian indirectness may be used to "humiliate" phenomenology's transcendental illusion, does not such an opposition change the very meaning of phenomenology? Ricoeur wants to bring the Freudian "*epochē*," which first appeared as an anti-phenomenology, back into a reflective procedure. "This anti-phenomenology must now be seen by us as a phase of reflection, the moment of the divestiture of reflection. The topographical concept of the unconscious is the correlate of this zero degree of reflection . . ." (*INT*, p. 424). The change, therefore, is not one which rejects the primacy of a reflective focus but one which radicalizes that focus. Reflective procedures retain primacy, but they must be reinterpreted.

3. *Inversion: A "New" Hegelian Phenomenology*

Such a reinterpretation must transcend both the Husserlian and Freudian oppositions. Such a *new phenomenology,* would no longer be a transcendental phenomenology of consciousness but would be instead a phenomenology of spirit. This terminology is unmistakably Hegelian. The moment of opposition and the moment of approximation yield to a third moment which reinterprets Freudian thought for reflective philosophy. The "excess" of psychoanalysis must be balanced by an equal "excess" from within reflection—and the figure to provide this excess is Hegel.

Tactically, the way in which the Freudian form of analysis is to be brought back into a reflective, and thus still broadly phenomenological, philosophy is by dialectically showing how Freudianism is the *inverse* side of the Hegelian phenomenology of the spirit. *Inversion, however, implies that the two sides of the inversion belong to the same phenomenon.* At the same time this last moment of the dialectic of phenomenology and counterphenomenology is one which can return to the double theme which underlies Ricoeur's turn to language. The new phenomenology that Ricoeur calls a phenomenology of the spirit is one which revolves around the *symbol* and the *subject.* It is the phenomenology which can increasingly be expressed as the understanding of the cultural-historical constitution of the subject.

From Freud, Ricoeur claims, one learns that the subject is never what one (first) takes it to be (*INT*, p. 420). But the same lesson is already in Hegel. The respective ways toward this discovery which threatens and challenges all immediacy of consciousness proceed from two different directions. The first key to understanding the dialectic of inversion is found in relation to the problem of the subject and coming to (self) consciousness. For Ricoeur both Freudian and Hegelian theories meet in the movement of becoming (self) conscious. "Whereas Hegel links an explicit teleology of mind or spirit to an implicit archeology of life and desire, Freud links a thematized archeology of the unconscious to an unthematized teleology of the process of becoming conscious" (*INT*, p. 461).

In the Freud-Hegel inversion Ricoeur claims that all the problems which appear in Freud have already appeared in Hegel, but in an inverse order. Whereas Hegel takes the theme explicitly and proceeds directly to unfold the movement towards consciousness, Freud makes this implicit theme clear only at the end of his career. "Where Id was, there ego must become." Freud, read by way of Hegel, may be seen to "contain" the problem of becoming conscious. But Hegel has already provided the model. "*The Phenomenology of the Spirit* is an explicit teleology of the achieving of consciousness and as such contains the model of every teleology of consciousness" (*INT*, p. 461).

But contrariwise, Hegel read by way of Freud, is seen to have developed a model which also decenters immediate consciousness and which employs a detour through interpretation.

> The phenomenology of mind [spirit] engenders a new hermeneutics that shifts the center of meaning no less than psychoanalysis does. The genesis of meaning does not proceed from consciousness; rather, there dwells in consciousness a movement that mediates it and raises its certitude to truth. Here too consciousness is intelligible to itself only if it allows itself to be set off-center. Spirit or *Geist* is this movement, this dialectic of figures, which makes consciousness into "self-consciousness," into "reason," and which, with the help of the circular movement of the dialectic, finally reaffirms immediate consciousness, but in the light of the complete process of mediation (*INT*, pp. 462–63).

So it is now Hegel, too, who is being read as a hermeneut. Hegelian hermeneutics are inverse to those of Freud, but in the same class.

The inversion is also present in the order and aim of the two analyses. Freud, read by way of Hegel, displays a *regressive* hermeneutics which culminates in what Ricoeur terms an *archeology of the subject*. This is, of course, transparent in the body of Freudian theory with its drive toward the infantile and the archaic. Ricoeur notes, "For my part, I regard Freudianism as a revelation of the archaic, a manifestation of the ever prior" (*INT*, p. 440). But such a regressive direction has a zero limit, which at the bottom of the Freudian opus is found at the juncture of the unconscious and the conscious. This juncture, in terms of hermeneutics, is also the juncture between language and the prelinguistic.

This drive toward the prelinguistic limit where "language is born" places Freud closer to the existential theories of language than was seen to have been the case before. The juncture of desire and its expression in language is also the juncture of the non-said and the urge to say (*vouloir-dire*).

> The unconscious is not fundamentally language, but only a drive toward language. The "quantitative" is the mute, the nonspoken and the nonspeaking, the unnameable at the root of speech. But in order to speak this muteness, psychoanalysis has only the . . . metaphor. . . . That which, in the unconscious, is capable of speaking, that which is able to be represented, refers back to a substrate that cannot be symbolized: desire as desire (*INT*, pp. 453–54).[6]

The Freudian theory meets a limit at the same obscurity base which the existential phenomenologies find.

> If desire is the unnameable, it is turned from the very outset toward language; it wishes to be expressed; it is in potency to speech. What makes desire the limit concept at the frontier between the organic and the psychical is the fact that desire is both the nonspoken and the wish-to-speak, the unnameable and the potency to speak (*INT*, p. 457).

But in another sense, left to themselves both such regressive hermeneutics are dead ends. They arrive only at a limit. With characteristic sympathy to existentialist conclusions, but with the proviso that such limits be recognized as obscure, Ricoeur points out that

> This reduction of the act of knowing as such attests to the nonautonomy of knowledge, its rootedness in existence, the latter being understood as desire and effort. Thereby is discovered not only the unsurpassable nature of life, but the interference of desire with intentionality, upon which desire inflicts an invincible obscurity, an ineluctable partiality. Thereby, finally, is confirmed truth's character of being a task: truth remains an Idea, an infinite Idea, for a being who originates as desire and effort, or, to use Freud's language, as invincibly narcissistic libido (*INT*, p. 458).

6. In this context it is interesting to note that Freud appears closer in similarity to existential theories of language than to Hegel. The return to a "birthplace of language," to the juncture where meaning comes into being, is regressive in both Freudian and existentialist theories

The inverse direction from regressive analysis with its archeology of the subject is a progressive analysis with its unfolding of
a teleology of the subject. That is the role Hegel plays for Ricoeur
in redressing the Freudian "excess." Here the dialectic begins to
outline once more the two limits of reflection, the limit of "bottom obscurity" and the limit of "top ideality."

The understanding of archeology and teleology, of regressive
and progressive interpretations as inversions of one another,
brings Freudian and Hegelian hermeneutics into the same
sphere. The step of approximation is surpassed, and the way of
reclaiming a *Freudian interpretation* for reflective philosophy is
opened by means of Hegelian phenomenology. Furthermore both
theories are held to be theories which approach consciousness by
means of a detour. Freud detours by way of the unconscious;
Hegel detours by way of the spirit. It is less important here to
trace out the intricacies by which Ricoeur establishes all the inverse parrallelism than to indicate the results for the hermeneutic phenomenology he seeks himself. Ricoeur's dialectic is always
a technique by which one theory is read by way of another. This
dialectic, already potentially Hegelian, now adapts themes from
Hegel which begin a certain closure in relation to the symbol and
the subject.

It is instructive to take note of precisely what Ricoeur accepts
of the Hegelian style; it is this acceptance which also begins to
re-establish the weighted focus of his own method.

What is progressive about Hegelian interpretations may be
seen in the march of the figures of the spirit.

In the Hegelian phenomenology, each form or figure receives its
meaning from the subsequent one. Thus, the truth of the recognition of the master-slave relationship is stoicism; but the truth of
the stoic position is skepticism, which views the difference between
master and slave as unessential and annihilates all such distinctions. The truth of a given moment lies in the subsequent moment;
meaning always proceeds retrogressively (*INT*, p. 464).

Phenomenology in this sense, unlike both the Freudian and
Husserlian analyses, is genetic. A progressive phenomenology in
the Hegelian style is one which sees a "logic" of movement from
one stage to the next.

But by the same token, since the truth of any present moment
can never be known until it is already surpassed, a Hegelian
phenomenology cannot be considered a phenomenology of immediacy. Its own version of decentering consciousness is a de-

centering through the understanding of spirit. In the inverted forms of Hegelian and Freudian analyses there is here the agreement that the subject is never what one (first) takes it to be.

In Freud the unfolding of the spirit, the coming to self-consciousness, is the progressive counterpart to the regressive unfolding of the psyche. Hegel inverts Freud, and Ricoeur ultimately sides with Hegel. A progressive analysis of symbols and the self will have the last word in this redress of the Freudian "excess."

With this inversion it once more becomes clear that Ricoeur opts to weight the phenomenological focus more heavily. In the last analysis the self is constituted primarily in terms of progression: "The positing or emergence of the self is inseparable from its production through a progressive synthesis" (*INT*, p. 464). Thus at the end of this set of dialectical exercises the weighted focus of phenomenology—now in Hegelian guise—is restored.

If the conclusion of the dialectic of methods is that Freudian hermeneutics is not ultimately incompatible with reflective philosophy, it must be recalled that the opening question concerning *Freud and Philosophy* was one which had to do with a field of warring interpretations. Once the methodological detour is brought to a closure in the use of inversion, a return to this question may be made. The methodological dialectic already anticipates a partial answer to this question. Any two sides of an inversion meet in the phenomenon itself, and in hermeneutics that primary phenomenon is the symbol.

In Ricoeur's application of his own dialectic the hermeneutic process is first one of a detour in which one decenters (immediate) consciousness in order to get at the places of the origin of meaning. Freudian hermeneutics provides a model for this regressive aim by using a theory of the unconscious as the set of rules which provides the decentering. Its gain suggests an "archeology of reflection." But it is also necessary to recognize an antithesis to an archeology, an inverse side which is a progressive genesis of meaning through successive figures, each of which is understood from the one which follows. This model is provided by Hegelian hermeneutics which supplements the regressive direction with its own progressive and teleological direction. But since these directions are two sides of a single inversion, each is implied in the other.

These interpretations meet in a "third term," which is the symbol itself. The symbol "contains" the multiplicity. "It remains to find the *concrete* 'mixed texture' in which we see the archeology and teleology. This concrete mixed texture is *symbol"* (*INT*, p. 494). The overdetermination of the symbol, already known by Freud, contains even more than he anticipated. But only by way of the dialectical inversion is this overdetermination of meanings seen to carry multiple vectors.

Symbols carry two vectors. On the one hand, symbols repeat our childhood in all the senses, chronological and nonchronological, of that childhood. On the other hand, they explore our adult life. . . . These two functions are not external to one another; they constitute the overdetermination of authentic symbols. By probing infancy and making it live again in the oneiric mode, symbols represent the projection of our human possibilities onto the area of imagination. These authentic symbols are truly regressive-progressive; remembrance gives rise to anticipation; archaism gives rise to prophecy (*INT*, pp. 496–97).

The symbol is multiple not only in its dimensions but also in its way of revealing those dimensions. It is both a disguise and an unveiling.

True symbols are at the crossroads of the two functions which we have by turns opposed to and grounded in one another. Such symbols both disguise and reveal. While they conceal the aims of our instincts, they disclose the process of self-consciousness. Disguise, reveal; conceal, show; these two functions are no longer external to one another; they express the two sides of a single symbolic function (*INT*, p. 497).

The symbol, as a phenomenon for investigation, displays a complex and multidimensioned presence. But it also displays a structure which Ricoeur proposes to characterize in terms of a hierarchical model:

I suggest that we distinguish various levels of creativity of symbols. . . . At the lowest level we come upon sedimented symbolism: here we find various stereotyped and fragmented remains of symbols, symbols so commonplace and worn with use that they have nothing but a past. This is the level of dream-symbolism, and also of fairy tales and legends; here the work of symbolization is no longer operative. At the second level we come upon the symbols that function in everyday life; these are the symbols that are useful and are actually utilized, that have a past and a present, and that in the clockwork of a given society serve as a token for the nexus of social pacts; structural anthropology operates at this level. At a higher level come the prospective symbols; these are creations of meaning that take up the traditional symbols with their multiple significations and serve as the vehicles of new meanings. This creation of meaning reflects the living substrate of symbolism, a substrate that is not the result of social sedimentation (*INT*, p. 504–5).

If the detour of the dialectic reveals both the crossing of vectors and the multiplicity of levels to be found in symbols, it also returns to a more basic constituent of phenomenological modeling. At the end of a detour a Husserlian description emerges once again. For phenomenologists the phenomenon is almost always found to be richer than was first thought, multiple and complex in its structure, and irreducible to any simple form which would falsify its appearance. Essential as one key to a *descriptive* method is the eschewing of "explanation" in the sense of the reduction of complexity to either a single dimension or in the sense of going "behind" the phenomena. In relation to the symbol this is the usual temptation of philosophy. "The danger for the philosopher . . . is to arrive too quickly, to lose the tension, to become dissipated in the symbolic richness, in the abundance of meaning" (*INT*, p. 495). In hermeneutic terms "explanation" sees in symbols only primitive attempts at science or epiphenomenal expressions of certain abstract "drives" of human beings. Such a move "demythizes" symbols.

For Ricoeur the symbol is the concrete expression which has more than a single function. From the phenomenologist's point of view this is to say that the phenomenon displays multiple dimensions and aspects. Thus the hermeneutic model of multiple readings at which Ricoeur arrives is also thoroughly phenomenological in the best Husserlian sense. The symbol in its concrete imaginative appearance is not less than, but more than, that which is open to a merely explanatory or linear approach. Its "logic" is not univocal but has its own form. "Thus the ambiguity of symbolism is not a lack of univocity, it is rather the possibility of carrying and engendering opposed interpretations, each of which is self-consistent" (*INT*, p. 496).

The non-reducibility of the symbol is reaffirmed, but the detour taken to reach this point has shown how one may get at the various vectors which may be reflected from the symbol. Ricoeur also allows his Husserlianism to re-emerge in relation to an over-all understanding of interpretation. The relation of expression-interpretation is the relation of "word" to reflection. But reflection is essentially a type of *epochē*. The symbol, for Ricoeur, is the concrete moment of the dialectic, but it is not *immediately* known. To "hear" the word of the symbol one must first go through the detour of thought. This is the necessity of the hermeneutic circle. Ricoeur rejects all "first naïveté," and affirms a "second naïveté" of listening only after and only through criticism. The learning which occurs under *epochē* is a learning which suspends literality from the start. It is an aesthetic approach to symbols. Just as one may learn to better appreciate art through criticism, so does the philosopher of culture learn to appreciate the symbol through reflection. Without the first "word" of the symbol, no wealth; without the second word of interpretation, no understanding. The hermeneutic circle of belief and understanding remains the dual focus underlying Ricoeur's use of expression-interpretation.

> In its return to the spoken word, reflection continues to be reflection, that is, the understanding of meaning; reflection becomes hermeneutic; this is the only way in which it can become concrete and still remain reflection. The second naïveté is not the first naïveté; it is postcritical and not precritical; it is an informed naïveté (*INT*, p. 496).

This "second naïveté" functions as a phenomenological attitude. The method of a dialectical detour is a guarantee that the listening be informed in its reflection.

Ricoeur's hermeneutics is phenomenological in its form and in its aim. Just as Husserl before him fought to create a philosophy which avoided the problems of both realism and idealism in relation to more traditional epistemology and metaphysics, so Ricoeur seeks to create a philosophy of language which avoids today's major alternatives of romanticism and formalism. Against all attempts to reduce language to a univocal calculus and against all attempts to revert to prelinguistic silence, Ricoeur sees in the philosophy of the symbol a different possibility. And although this possibility is yet to be fulfilled in its totality— Ricoeur promises a poetics of the will and indicates that *Freud and Philosophy* is but a propaedeutic to a larger work on language —the emergent outline is already available in what here may be seen as the hermeneutic turn.

The hermeneutic turn is that direction which attempts to go between formalism and romanticism and to formulate a phenomenology of language which exceeds both the Husserlian and existential versions of phenomenology. The clue to this "new phenomenology" is located in the *fullness of language* which

Ricoeur sees in the symbol—the problem of the symbol equals the problem of language.

> In order to think in accord with symbols one must subject them to a dialectic; only then is it possible to set the dialectic within interpretation itself and come back to living speech. . . . This return to the immediate is not a return to silence, but rather to the spoken word, to the fullness of language. Nor is it a return to the dense enigma of initial, immediate speech, but to speech that has been instructed by the whole process of meaning. Hence this concrete reflection does not imply any concession to irrationality or effusiveness (*INT*, p. 495).

The fullness of language is not to be found in the romanticism which surrounds the drive toward prelinguistic silence. This is a limit to which both Freudian theory and the existential theories of language return. Only upon arrival at a "birthplace of language" is a limit reached.

Nor is the fullness of language to be found by reducing the symbol to sterile univocity. The whole thrust of Ricoeur's latent philosophy of language rejects this possibility. His "logic" of symbols is a multivocal or phenomenological "logic" which has as its task the unification of the multiple vectors symbols allow.

It is at this point that what is unsaid in the hermeneutic turn may be said. The way between romanticism and formalism is in aim the same as the way of Ricoeur's earlier structural phenomenology. The fullness of language is a fundamental possibility inscribed *in* and *upon* the authentic symbols of historical cultures. Hermeneutics substitutes the natural world of the body and the thing for the cultural world of the symbol and the subject, a language world. The symbols as the "living words" of culture are the historical basis from which man understands himself. The language world is the cultural lifeworld. "I propose therefore that cultural phenomena should be interpreted as the objective media in which the great enterprise of sublimation with its double value of disguise and disclosure becomes sedimented" (*INT*, p. 523).

At this point Ricoeur makes contact with his over-all aim to establish a hermeneutic philosophy of *existence*. Hermeneutically the symbol becomes the focus, the primitive, for philosophical interest. The philosopher, deliberately engaged in the battle of the various hermeneutics, seeks both to respect and understand the "word" of these symbols and to think according to their disguising-revealing richness—the symbol invites thought—but on the other hand he must maintain his insistence upon rationality and critical intelligence. " 'Symbols give rise to thought,' they are also the birth of idols. That is why the critique of idols remains the condition of the conquest of symbols" (*INT*, p. 543).

What emerges in this struggle to attain a philosophy of existence neither divorced from the "living word" of man's concrete existence nor devoid of the rigor of rational clarity, the two themes which Ricoeur has used to characterize philosophizing, is this shift in method and emphasis. Ricoeur hopes that by making the symbol the focus of interest *indirect* insight will be yielded in relation to the structures of human existence. This stands in contrast to the relative directness of most phenomenological investigations into the structures of consciousness. Hermeneutic phenomenology stands at least one remove from both Husserlian and existential phenomenologies.

This way *between* limits is formally parallel with structural phenomenology. In a fundamental pattern of Ricoeur's thought the third way utilizes the recognition of limits which are established dialectically. In structural phenomenology a fundamental possibility was seen to have both a "top" or ideality limit and a "bottom" or obscurity limit. The same use of founded limitations occurs in Ricoeur's hermeneutic phenomenology. The dialectical detour demarked those limits. Freudian regressive hermeneutics establishes the "bottom" or obscurity limit; Hegelian progressive hermeneutics begins to show an ideality limit in the concept of the creative or poetic use of archaic figures. "From now on regression and progression do not represent two truly opposed processes; they are rather the abstract terms employed to designate the two end limits of a single scale of symbolization" (*INT*, p. 522).

The tactic of inversion established the possibility of placing these limits upon the same scale. The structure of symbols, from the archaic residue which lies at the bottom obscurity border of language, ascends from its base toward its ideal possibility, the creation (poesis) of human possibilities.

It thus becomes possible to locate the oneiric and the poetic on the same symbolic scale. The production of dreams and the creation of works of art represent the two ends of the scale, according to whether the predominant emphasis in the symbolism is disguise or disclosure, distortion or revelation. By this formula I attempt to account both for the functional unity existing between dreams and creativity and for the difference in value that separates a mere product of our dreams from the lasting works that become a part of the cultural heritage of mankind. Between dreams and artistic creativity there is a functional continuity, in the sense that disguise and disclosure are operative in both of them, but in an inverse proportion (*INT*, p. 520).

The "word" of the symbol is not the last, but the first word of *Freud and Philosophy*. It is the starting point, as it was in *The Symbolism of Evil*, for Ricoeur's hermeneutic endeavor. But after symbol comes *myth*, which Ricoeur has characterized as a first spontaneous hermeneutics of symbols. The next word must be the word of the great cultural myths. But in one respect this next word lies beyond the limits of a strictly philosophical hermeneutics.

In a concluding meditation Ricoeur ponders upon the relation of hermeneutics, the "second naïveté," and his earlier persistent problem of belief, which is in a sense stronger than phenomenological belief.

To this point Ricoeur had remained within the bounds and direction of *The Symbolism of Evil*. But now he risks more. Where formerly the philosopher has studied the myth as a wager, Ricoeur is now ready to proclaim that myths, in particular the myths of the origin of evil, are privileged. Such "words" are not mere fables or fantasies but explorations in a symbolic and imaginative mode of man's very relation to Being. It is because myth condenses a richness of significations which exceeds philosophy that hermeneutics becomes a necessary task. Freud's rediscovery of mythical themes is taken as a partial confirmation of this importance of myth for man's self-understanding.

Ultimately, and at the highest level, the imagination of myth may be seen as a word addressed to man.

If there is an authentic problematic of faith, it pertains to a new dimension which I have previously described, in a different philosophical context, as a "Poetics of the Will," because it concerns the radical origin of the *I will*, i.e., the source of effectiveness of the act of willing. In the context of the present work, I describe this new dimension as a call, a kerygma, a word addressed to me (*INT*, pp. 524–25).

We approach here the limits of an exposition devoted to the elaboration of the essentially philosophic implications of Ricoeur's hermeneutics. But even if one notes that the claim that the myth is a word is addressed to man in terms of the problem of

166 / HERMENEUTIC PHENOMENOLOGY

faith, a philosophical problem remains. Any call (interpellation) needs interpretation. Rationality and faith converge in an "Anselmian" fashion:

An Anselmian type of procedure, i.e., the movement from faith to understanding, necessarily encounters a dialectic of reflection, which it attempts to use as the instrument of its expression. . . . The "hermeneutic circle" is born: to believe is to listen to the call, but to hear the call we must interpret the message. Thus we must believe in order to understand and understand in order to believe (*INT*, p. 525).

Ricoeur's hermeneutics must eventually turn to the elaboration of the *poesis,* the creative activity of mythological language which displays possibilities for human existence in history. A poetics of the will must be another chapter in hermeneutic phenomenology.

Through these questions the Freudian hermeneutics can be related to another hermeneutics, a hermeneutics that deals with the mytho-poetic function and regards myths not as fables, i.e., as stories that are false, unreal, illusory, but rather as the symbolic exploration of our relationship to beings and to Being. What carries this mytho-poetic function is another power of language, a power that is no longer the demand of desire, demand for protection, demand for providence, but a call in which I leave off all demands and listen (*INT*, p. 551).

7 / Hermeneutics and the Linguistic Disciplines: New Counterfoci

AT THIS STAGE of Ricoeur's development the final outcome of a phenomenologically based philosophy of language remains sketchy. But its outline nevertheless begins to emerge with more and more distinctness. *The Symbolism of Evil* and *Freud and Philosophy* were the first two direct exercises in hermeneutic phenomenology in which the enigmas of symbolic, polysemic expressions were held to be the key to the problems of language.

Today the equation evoked in *Freud and Philosophy*—the problem of the symbol equals the problem of language—may be restated. Ricoeur now sees that the essence of this equation lies much more broadly within language than was understood in the studies of the symbols of evil and the detour by way of Freud. This is largely the case because a new set of counterfoci has appeared in Ricoeur's confrontation with a wide series of linguistic disciplines. These counterfoci to a central phenomenological focus include structural linguistics, Chomskyan generative linguistics, and the linguistic philosophies of the Anglo-Americans. Unfortunately, to date only the encounter with structural linguistics has taken clear shape in terms of published materials.[1]

In the largest sense the setting of an operating position remains constant with Ricoeur's earlier stances. He initiates the latest set of dialectical debates from a reaffirmation of certain basic Husserlian insights; progresses, now much more openly, to

1. In the Parisian environment, the prestige of Claude Lévi-Strauss is very high. In fact, one may easily generalize that much philosophical interest today centers broadly upon structuralism and the philosophy of language.

a critique of earlier existential phenomenology; and plunges into a new set of interrogations with the linguistic disciplines. It is possible to briefly summarize the outline of this latest step toward a philosophy of language and to expose at the same time some of the contributions the linguistic disciplines have made to Ricoeur's thought.

A HUSSERLIAN MODEL OF LANGUAGE

THERE ARE two related directive concepts found in Ricoeur's interpretation of Husserl's view of language which are centrally employed in Ricoeur's own view of language. The first is that language is essentially a *mediation*, a third term, situated between two limits or borders. In a recent comparative study of Husserl and Wittgenstein, Ricoeur repeatedly claims:

> Language is therefore an intermediary between two levels. The first one, as we said, constitutes its *ideal* of logicity, its *telos:* all meanings must be able to be converted into the logos of rationality; the second one no longer constitutes an ideal, but a ground, a soil, an origin, an *Ursprung.* Language may be reached 'from above,' from its logical limit, or 'from below,' from its limit in mute and elemental experience. In itself it is a medium, a mediation, an exchange between *Telos* and Ursprung.[2]

This understanding of Husserl's view of language, accepted by Ricoeur, is clearly the same understanding of a third term which has guided Ricoeur's method throughout. The mediation between an ideality, aimed at but never reached, and an obscurity border has characterized each stage of Ricoeur's development. Today he locates this base within the Husserlian understanding of language.

As a mediation in terms of the broader philosophy of language, this concept means that language proceeds in two directions at the same time. "For [speaker and listener] language aims at something, or more exactly it has a double direction: an ideal direction (to say something) and a real reference (to say about something). In this movement, language leaps across two thresholds: the threshold of ideality of sense and, beyond this

2. Paul Ricoeur, "Husserl and Wittgenstein on Language," in *Phenomenology and Existentialism*, ed. E. N. Lee and M. Mandelbaum (Baltimore, Md.: The Johns Hopkins Press, 1967), p. 209.

sense, the threshold of reference." [3] The combination of a meaning system with directional aim, *intentionality*, cannot be missed. One may invert the usual formula and say that the intentional structure is a linguistic structure.

The first guiding concept relates intimately to a second, also derived from Ricoeur's understanding of Husserl. Language itself is a type of "phenomenological reduction"—although it may be better said that the phenomenological reduction is patterned upon a certain understanding of language. The way between limits attributes both a certain immanence and a certain transcendence to language; a located or situated distance is inherent in the power of language. Language can be neither a pure ideality (here lies the basis of Ricoeur's critiques of the linguistic disciplines) nor a simple description of the generation of meaning from prelinguistic experience (here lies the basis for Ricoeur's critiques of existential phenomenology). All language is already instituted as a breaking of any unity with natural surroundings:

> But this relation between language and prelinguistic experience is not a simple one. It implies in its turn a new polarity between two trends: the first one, symbolized by the "reduction," implies a suspension, which does not necessarily mean a retreat within an ego secluded from reality, *but the kind of break with natural surroundings which is implied in the birth of language as such* [italics added]; there is no symbolic function without the sort of mutation that affects my relation to reality without substituting a *signifying* relation for a natural involvement. Reduction, we might say, means the birth of a speaking subject. [4]

But one must add that, while language itself is already a transcending or located distance from the natural surroundings, to be a reduction in a philosophical sense implies that this distance be made as reflective as possible. The birth of language is already a potentially theoretical awareness.

> We are forever separated from life by the very function of the sign; we no longer live life but simply designate it. We signify life and are thus indefinitely withdrawn from it, in the process of *interpreting* it in a multitude of ways.

3. Paul Ricoeur, "Structure, Word, Event," trans. Robert D. Sweeny, *Philosophy Today*, XII, nos. 2–4 (Summer, 1968), 118. (Originally "La Structure-le mot-l'événement," *Esprit* [May, 1967].)
4. Ricoeur, "Husserl and Wittgenstein," p. 212.

And, above all, if language is only a mediation, an intermediary between several levels, between *Logos* and *Bios,* a critique of ordinary language is itself possible. . . . We are no longer engaged in a practical activity, but in a theoretical inquiry . . . philosophy itself is made possible by the act of reduction, which is also the birth of language.[5]

Once defined, this Husserlian stance provides the platform from which Ricoeur distinguishes his own method from that of existential phenomenology and the linguistic sciences. In spite of the fact that once engaged in the new dialectic with the linguistic disciplines Ricoeur repeats with his own emphasis some of the criticisms offered by earlier phenomenology, he wishes carefully to draw up the sides of the debate in such a way as to include rather than exclude the dominant objectivism. But to begin too soon with the subject's immersion in prelinguistic experience, as the existential theories of language are tempted to do, is equally to risk a bad subjectivism. "The prepredicative and prelinguistic structures are not given; we cannot start from them. We have rather to be *brought back* to them by means of a process that Husserl calls *Rückfragen* ('backquestioning')." [6]

The lifeworld is a *limit* toward which a previously perceptualist phenomenology aims—but for Ricoeur it remains a limit and never a given. "This so-called lived experience, for men who were born among words, will never be the naked presence of an absolute, but will remain that toward which this regressive questioning points." [7] The existential phenomenologies, correct in reraising the question of the subject and his experience, also come perilously close to taking subjectivity for a direct ontology. To do so is to exclude from the beginning a consideration of the merits of objectivist gains.

In a specific criticism of Merleau-Ponty Ricoeur claims (and indeed Merleau-Ponty would agree) that his theory of language was ill formulated. The reason is that the question arises, *"in a form which excludes any connection with modern linguistics and the semiological disciplines which have been established on a linguistic model."* [8] Merleau-Ponty, by proposing too exclusively a return to the speaking subject, places "the phenomenological

5. *Ibid.,* p. 217.
6. *Ibid.,* p. 213.
7. *Ibid.*
8. Paul Ricoeur, "New Developments in Phenomenology in France: The Phenomenology of Language," trans. P. G. Goodman, *Social Research,* XXXIV, no. 1 (Spring, 1967), 11.

attitude . . . in opposition to the objective attitude . . . the
scientist is given little place in the dialogue—indeed, he is given
none at all." [9] In this case a subjectivism is set up against an
objectivism. "The danger here is to set up a phenomenology of
speech in opposition to a science of language, at the risk of
falling again into psychologism or mentalism, from which structural linguistics has rescued us." [10]

Ricoeur's sympathies with Heidegger are a bit stronger. In a
sense it may now be said that Heidegger is perhaps the only
phenomenologically oriented philosopher to have developed a
hermeneutic phenomenology prior to Ricoeur. The "ontology of
language" which becomes Ricoeur's aim is also Heidegger's. But
again Ricoeur wishes to differentiate his own method from
Heidegger's on the basis of its indirectness and its dialectic with,
rather than an exclusion from, the linguistic disciplines. In an
article, "Existence et herméneutique," Ricoeur states the problem
as one of *grafting* the hermeneutical problem to a phenomenology. But Heidegger's way is the short way toward what Ricoeur
calls a "direct ontology of comprehension," breaking all methodological debates and driving directly toward an ontology. In
Heidegger's case, "To comprehend is no longer a mode of knowledge, but a mode of being, the mode of that being who exists in
comprehending." [11]

It is true that Ricoeur enters a reservation concerning closing
off the route of Heidegger's hermeneutical phenomenology. "For
perhaps we are always on the way toward language, although
language itself may be the way. I will not take this Heideggerian
way toward language, but let me say in conclusion that I have
not closed it, even if I have not explicitly opened it." [12] The long
way Ricoeur wishes to open in a confrontation with the linguistic
disciplines is one which follows their methods from the bottom
up. "Heidegger does not proceed according to the ascending order
that we have followed, which is a progressive order of elements
within structures, then of structures within process." [13]

Thus Heidegger, in spite of his prior graft of hermeneutics to
phenomenology, remains within the limitation of the strategy of
existential phenomenology, either to avoid encounter or to oppose

9. *Ibid.*
10. Ricoeur, "Structure, Word, Event," p. 119.
11. Paul Ricoeur, "Existence et herméneutique," *Dialogue,* IV,
no. 1 (1965), 7. (My translation—D.I.)
12. Ricoeur, "Structure, Word, Event," p. 128.
13. *Ibid.*

objectivism. "How, we ask, do we get an organon for exegesis, that is to say, an intelligibility to texts? How do we found the historical sciences faced with the natural sciences? These problems are not properly considered in a fundamental hermeneutic; and that by design: that hermeneutic is not determined to resolve them, but to dissolve them." [14]

Against this short way, cautiously or "conservatively," Ricoeur wishes a hermeneutic phenomenology which continues the debates with the sciences in the search for models and methods which are adequate to the subject matter. Relating Husserl's aim in the *Krisis* to the graft of phenomenology and hermeneutics, Ricoeur notes:

> Its relation to hermeneutics is double: on the one side it is in the last phase of phenomenology that the critique of "objectivism" is opened to its final consequences. This critique of objectivism concerns the hermeneutic problem not only indirectly because it challenges the epistemological pretension of the natural sciences to furnish the human sciences with a single valuable method. But it also relates directly because it calls the Diltheyan enterprise into question for furnishing to the cultural sciences a method which is as objective as those of the sciences of nature. [15]

The methodological battle is not yet closed.

Ricoeur returns to his own dialectical and indirect way. "The return to the spoken or living language has perhaps prevented the encounter with the linguistic fact: this confrontation requires that the return should be less direct and make a detour via the science of language." [16]

NEW COUNTERFOCI: THE LINGUISTIC DISCIPLINES

RICOEUR'S DETOURS, by now, should be well recognized. They will enter a series of debates with linguistics and linguistic analysis before issuing in even the most cautious ontology of language. In outline they will employ in ever more subtle form the diagnostics whereby Ricoeur seeks to be informed by objectivism, but never reduced to its methods. A general outline of the new dialectic has already been provided most systematically in

14. Ricoeur, "Existence et herméneutique," p. 9.
15. *Ibid.*, p. 7.
16. Ricoeur, "New Developments," pp. 13–14.

"Existence et herméneutique," which Ricoeur calls his most orderly treatment to date. Three levels of progress are envisioned:

First, at a *semantic level*, the encounter with the linguistic disciplines must be entered. This stage is already underway, particularly in the case of structural linguistics, and to some degree with both Chomskyan generative grammar and the work of linguistic analysis. Under this heading Ricoeur calls for the enumeration of the possible symbolic forms and, interestingly, sees the work of linguistic analysis performing some of this task. Once the possible forms are catalogued, he requests a criteriology of types through a revisitation of the classes of metaphors, analogies, similes, etc. He then asks for a study of the varied types of interpretations. In another sense, particularly in *Freud and Philosophy*, Ricoeur has begun this process himself. Here the recognition of the methodological construction of "filters" in interpretation must be understood because each single hermeneutics (psychoanalytic, phenomenology of religion, Marxian, etc.) employs its own set of rules which creates its "reduction."

At the higher and more philosophical level which Ricoeur calls the *reflexive level*, the new dialectic begins its move toward ontology. Here the question is one which has formed a major thrust throughout Ricoeur's work: In what way does the comprehension of signs relate to the comprehension of self? This is a hermeneutic question at the philosophical level. "In proposing to re-bind symbolic language to the comprehension of self I think the most profound view of hermeneutics may be satisfied." [17] At this level, too, the rigor of a transcendental or hermeneutic logic is called for to deal with equivocal expressions. "This logic is thus no longer a formal logic, but a transcendental logic: it is established at the level of the conditions of possibility: not the conditions of the objectivity of nature, but the conditions of the appropriation of our desire to be." [18]

But finally, reflection must be exceeded at the *existential* or ontological level, where the movement toward an ontology of language parallels Heidegger. "I would dare to say in a word: the sole philosophical interest in symbolism is that it reveals, by its structure of double-meaning, the equivocity of being. 'Being is said in multiple ways.'" [19] The symbol shows being, and language

17. Ricoeur, "Existence et herméneutique," p. 17.
18. *Ibid.*, p. 19.
19. Paul Ricoeur, "Le Problème du 'double' sens comme problème herméneutique et comme problème sémantique," *Cahiers internationeaux de symbolisme* (1967), p. 63. (My translation—D.I.)

is openness to being. But at the same time Ricoeur retains a reluctance. "So, ontology is the promised land for a philosophy which begins by language and reflection. But, like Moses, the speaking and reflecting subject can only glimpse it before dying."[20]

While it is premature to predict the outcome of this latest dialectic and its ambitious program, a preliminary critique of the linguistic sciences and several potentially momentous shifts of emphasis due directly to the linguistic sciences have already appeared. Through the re-employment of the techniques of a diagnostic, Ricoeur has commenced a criticism of structuralism. A phenomenologically grounded demystification remains in line with all Ricoeur's critiques of objectivism in which the mystique of the "object" is broken. The major effect in this case is to show how the "new empiricism" is functionally a "new idealism."

Structural linguistics, perhaps the leading method being employed by a wide range of the social sciences, has produced a workable "empirical" model which Ricoeur sees in need of a phenomenological challenge. The first step in this challenge is to break the mystique which often surrounds the initial successes of objectivist procedures. But the "new empiricism" no longer falls under the same degree of naïveté which overlapped with the common-sense aspects of a "natural attitude." Instead, the introduction of deliberate modeling processes in the sciences, recognized in part by the Husserl of the *Krisis*, makes for a thoroughly theoretical constitution of an object of study. An empirical "reduction" is a theoretical device which carefully reduces its field of study to the level of "object."

The tactic, in brief, is clear with structural linguistics: By first distinguishing between speech, the use of language by actual speakers in actual situations, and language proper, the institution of a given language as a system, structuralism begins by removing "subjective" variations from its study. The subject is "bracketed out." By further distinguishing language in a given state, synchronics, from the genetic process of change, dychronics, and by further weighting the stable structure over the process, a new linguistic "object" is made to stand still before the eyes of the investigator. Then, by considering this public object *apart* from any real references, that is, by considering it only in its systemic aspects, the object is effectively constituted as closed. Language considered as a closed system of signs and apart from

20. Ricoeur, "Existence et herméneutique," p. 25.

the uses of any concrete users removes any simply naïve subjective concerns from appearing. At least those subjective concerns which remain at the level of thinking that the sign is to be simply paired with a thing become impossible.[21]

"By constituting the linguistic object as an autonomous object, linguistics constitutes itself as a science. But at what cost?" [22] The cost can be seen in philosophic terms. The constitution of a closed, finite system of signs lacking external reference inside a semiological system is the creation of an abstract object with only *internal relations*. It is an ideal object, and since it was constituted through rigorous theoretical means the resultant precision is gained at the cost of mimicking a "new idealism." Arguments entering objections or reservations concerning such an idealized linguistic object will thus find themselves returned to an insistence upon some type of "realism." And to a degree this is the case with Ricoeur's opening phenomenological criticisms. It is strange that, given the long traditions of "empiricism" and "idealism," the transcendental philosophies now find themselves on the "realist" side.

It is not that Ricoeur objects to the methods of the linguistic sciences as such. As semiological disciplines they are valid and effect a heretofore unknown precision *within limits*. But those limits have to be established. At first and externally it appears that Ricoeur's objections return to the phenomenological insistence upon the primacy of the speaking subject. The problem with all scientifically constituted or idealized objects is that in certain ways they belie *experience*.

> Now the experience which the speaker and listener have of language come along to limit the claim to absolutize this object. The experience we have of language reveals something of its mode of being which resists this reduction. For us who speak, language is not an object but a mediation. Language is that through which, by means of which, we express ourselves and express things. To speak is the act by which the speaker overcomes the closures of the universe of signs, in the intention of saying something about something to someone; to speak is the act by which language moves beyond itself as sign toward its reference and toward its opposite. Language seeks to disappear; it seeks to die as an object.[23]

21. Ricoeur, "Structure, Word, Event," pp. 116–18.
22. *Ibid.*, p. 118.
23. *Ibid.*, p. 119.

But this objection left to itself is insufficient and remains on the level of a sheer opposition of a phenomenology of speech to a science of language.

A strong attack which would at one time situate semiology within its valid limits and open the way toward phenomenologically aided additions would be more internally directed. But to enter into such an attack means that Ricoeur must also accept certain presuppositions and certain terms of the counterfocus. Previously he has proved to be adept at this. To be informed by, but not reduced to, those methods is the diagnostic task. In terms of the long-range strategy announced in the beginning of this chapter, the insertion must first occur at the *semantic level*. This Ricoeur has done by pointing up an antinomy within the linguistic disciplines as such. The various disciplines deal, step by step, with ever larger units of language (phoneme to lexical to syntactical to sentential units). But at a certain step, which Ricoeur now designates as the step between semiotics and semantics proper, the question of speech can no longer be postponed.[24] This step is the sentence. "This is no longer the unit of a language, but of speech or of discourse. By changing the unit, one also changes function, or rather, one passes from structure to function." [25] Here the saying of language, the ultimate problems of real reference, and the extralinguistic concrete context make their entry.

Ricoeur poses the antinomy within the linguistic disciplines as one between *structure* and *event*: Discourse, in which the sentence *occurs*, is an act, transitory and time-linked. System, at the semiological level, is atemporal. Discourse entails choices of some meanings and exclusion of others. Systemic traits are constraints. Choices produce new combinations infinite in number. Structures include large but finite, numbers of units and are closed. Discourse has a reference, breaks the closure of sign, articulates a signifying intention. System regards relations as internal differences and regards only the sign within the system. Discourse also designates the subject (who speaks?) of the discourse. The subject is included in the discourse situation. Structural considerations exclude the question of the speaker.[26]

24. Ricoeur has varied somewhat in the use of the term *semantics*. For a time he has used it broadly to cover the linguistic sciences, but of late he has differentiated these into two levels, semiotic and semantic, for reasons one can see in this chapter.

25. Ricoeur, "Structure, Word, Event," p. 120.

26. *Ibid.*, pp. 120–21. Ricoeur apparently believes that the generative grammar work of Chomsky will help mediate the antinomy

It is not difficult to see how the properly semantic event-situation allows Ricoeur to return to the already emphasized concepts concerning the speaking subject, real reference, and intentionality within language. But at the same time this internal antinomy within the linguistic disciplines permits a demythologization of any semiotic *hubris*. The philosophy of language is not limited to the current state of semiotics.

A philosophy of language need not be limited to the conditions of possibility of a semiology: to account for the absence of the sign from things, the *reduction* of relations of nature and their mutation into signifying relations suffices. It is necessary in addition to satisfy conditions of possibility of discourse insofar as it is an endeavor renewed ceaselessly to express integrally the thinkable and the sayable in our experience. Reduction—or any act comparable to it by reason of its negativity—no longer suffices. Reduction is only the inverse, the negative facet, of a wanting-to-say [*vouloir dire*] which aspires to become a wanting-to-show.[27]

A diagnostic opens with a critique of each counterfocus. But in turn the dialectic is to inform the central focus. Such has already been the case in the encounter with linguistics. Semiotics, although even in the most rigorous structuralist sense the most distant from the phenomenologically oriented position, has already produced one change in Ricoeur's apprehension of the problems of language. It is a change which relates immediately to the central problem of the symbol.

The equation "the problem of the symbol equals the problem of language" was at first raised in the narrow hermeneutic context of the interpretation of expressions with multiple meanings. Polysemy remains the central linguistic problem for Ricoeur, but at the same time the findings of linguistics give polysemy a different value than previously noted.

The semiotic disciplines, at both the structural and lexical levels, have shown polysemy to be a fundamental characteristic of all language. Synchronically, each word has several meanings; diachronically, multiple meanings change and transfer meanings in time. Furthermore, this multiplicity of meanings is ruled by the extremes of "overload" (a word which is made to carry too many meanings ends by meaning nothing) and "limitation"

---

between structure and process left by the structuralists. But it remains unclear what contribution Chomsky will make to Ricoeur's thought.

27. *Ibid.*, p. 125.

(words "mean" by oppositions to other meanings). Linguistics reveals more and more precisely the mechanisms of language which govern the multiple, but finite, meanings any word may have within a given system. The description, discovery, and rules of performance are the proper domain of linguistics and can only be accepted (within their limits) by the phenomenologist.

The result, in Ricoeur's case, is perhaps the strongest example to date of a counterdemystification. The problem of the symbol, in contact with the linguistic sciences, has been itself demystified: "In this respect symbolism has nothing remarkable about it. All the words of an ordinary language have more than one signification." [28] Here falls the last vestige of a romantic view of language (often remaining behind existentialist theories of language). No single set of words is privileged to reveal the problem of language, not even primary symbols in the sense of *The Symbolism of Evil*—at least not at the structural level. Polysemy continues to contain the secrets of language, its enigmatic fullness; but *all* words possess symbolic power. The romantics may have been right—but for the wrong reasons. The symbol is privileged not because it is poetic, spontaneous, or of a particular type, but because words of that type reveal something about all language. The problem of the symbol remains equal to the problem of language, but now it is because the problem of polysemy is a *universal* problem of language.

> In receiving a determined linguistic law, the process considered receives a functional value. Polysemy is neither a pathological phenomenon in itself, nor is symbolism an ornament of language. Polysemy and symbolism belong to the constitution and functioning of *all* language.[29]

What is lost by demystification is gained in universalization over the narrower view of primary symbols.

This contribution to Ricoeur's view of language, anticipated in the inversion of multivocal over univocal views of meaning, makes univocity rather than polysemy a special problem. At the semantic level of discourse, univocity is located through the contextual situation which carefully restricts the ordinary or normative polysemy of language.

> We then understand what happens when the word returns to the discourse along with its semantic richness. All our words being

28. Ricoeur, "Le Problème du 'double,' " p. 70.
29. *Ibid.*, p. 66.

polysemic to some degree the univocity or plurivocity of our discourse is not the accomplishment of words but of contexts. In the case of univocal discourse, that is, of discourse which tolerates only one meaning, it is the task of the context to hide the semantic richness of words, to reduce it by establishing what Greimas calls an isotopie, that is, a frame of reference, a theme, an identical topic for all the words of the sentence (for example, if I develop a geometrical "theme," the word volume will be interpreted as a body in space; if the theme concerns the library, the word volume will be interpreted as designating a book).[30]

In this view the fullness of language always precedes its reduction to the isotopies of univocal discourse.

The opposite extreme, already dealt with in part by the newborn hermeneutic phenomenology, is the type of discourse which preserves a multiplicity of meanings, often by a "calculated ambiguity."

> If the context tolerates or even preserves several isotopies at the same time, we will be dealing with an actually symbolic language, which, in saying *one* thing, says something *else*. Instead of sifting out one dimension of meaning, the context allows several to pass, indeed consolidates several of them, which run together in the manner of the superimposed texts of a palimpsest. The polysemy of our words is then liberated. Thus the poem allows all the semantic values to be mutually reinforced.[31]

Poetic expression is a special case of polysemy, a case which elevates the problem to the purposefully doubled meanings of symbolic language proper.[32] Hermeneutics becomes at one level the special discipline which deals with the rules and principles of interpretation for this hypermultivocal language.

The contact with structural linguistics has already provided Ricoeur with some concepts necessary to pursue the poetics of language he spoke of earlier. The structural demystification of polysemy, however, does not mean that the mystery of language has now disappeared. Rather, its power to show reappears *through* the ordinary mechanisms of language.

30. Ricoeur, "Structure, Word, Event," p. 127.
31. *Ibid.*
32. The introduction of "calculated ambiguity" and purposeful polysemy raises the question of symbol *construction* in contrast to the spontaneity of primary symbols. This shift in emphasis has already appeared in some of Ricoeur's latest studies in symbol history. Cf. "The Father Image," *Criterion*, VIII, no. 1 (1968–69), 1–7.

It is perhaps the emergence of expressivity which constitutes the marvel of language. . . . There is no mystery in language. The most poetic, most "sacred" language operates with the same semic variables as the most banal word of the dictionary. But there is a mystery of language. It is that language says, says something, says something of being. If there is an enigma of symbolism it resides entirely at the level of manifestation where the equivocity of being becomes said in discourse.[33]

Language which wants to say (*vouloir-dire*) and to reveal meets Ricoeur's concerns beyond the confines of linguistic mechanism. But with the tools provided by the linguistic sciences the problem of the symbol now is related to the problem of the *word*.

The word, which is broader than the symbol in the technically strict sense earlier employed by Ricoeur, is that instance of language which mediates between structure and event. The structuralists have shown that the word in itself says nothing—there is no word apart from its position as a variable in the system of signs (and in the strictest sense one may even say that as an internal difference within a system one is below the full concept of a word). At the semantic level the word gains its meaning by its position within the sentence. But from another perspective, Ricoeur points out, the word is also more than the sentence. The word survives the event of the sentence. "Thus the word is, as it were, a trader between the system and the act, between the structure and the event." [34] The word in this mediating position, as a third term, is like the symbol. The mystery of language in wanting to say and wanting to show also lies at this basic level.

Other results of the encounter with the new counterfoci will doubtless emerge as the movement of Ricoeur's thought more and more thoroughly enters the question of language. It may be noted here that the concern with the linguistic disciplines is not complete. Although several articles comparing Husserl and Wittgenstein have appeared and although Ricoeur has frequently referred to the works of Austin and Strawson in his teaching, the contact and struggle with linguistic analysis is still germinal at best.[35]

It may also be noted that, in terms of the program Ricoeur has set for himself, only the semiotic and semantic levels have

33. Ricoeur, "Le Problème du 'double,'" p. 71.
34. Ricoeur, "Structure, Word, Event," p. 126.
35. During the 1967–68 academic year Ricoeur offered seminars which included work on Strawson, Frege, Austin, and Wittgenstein in addition to linguists. For a summary of this recent course work see the *Cahiers de philosophie*, nos. 2–3 (February, 1966), pp. 27–42.

received enough treatment for Ricoeur's direction to become clear. The "ontology of language," if "man is language," remains unsaid. And perhaps, given the open-ended direction of Ricoeur's dialectic, it may remain unsaid in any direct manner.[36]

But apart from the specifics which will emerge in the dialectical development of a linguistically oriented phenomenology, the grand plan unfolds. The convergence of this broadly "Hegelian" enterprise upon the poetic symbol persists. *The Symbolism of Evil*, the first direct hermeneutic exercise, dealt with the cosmic symbols—the sacred is first read upon the cosmos. And there we were promised a "poetics of the will." *Freud and Philosophy*, a second direct hermeneutic exercise, dealt in part with the psychic, oneiric symbols and promised to be a prolegomena to a broader philosophy of language. But what is first read on the cosmos and then in the subjectivity of the psyche is mediated and made manifest in the poetic symbol, the poetic word. The poetics of the will and the broad philosophy of language thus cross in the question of an ontology of language.

Hermeneutic phenomenology has not ceased but has just begun to ripen to full form. With Ricoeur one may, in a way radically different from the Anglo-Americans, speak of a linguistic turn. And through hermeneutic phenomenology one may say: *Whether or not with God, at least with man, in the beginning is the word.*

36. Since the completion of this book a new collection of essays by Ricoeur has appeared in France, *Le Conflit des interprétations: Essais d'herméneutique* (Paris: Editions du Seuil, 1969). However, most of the essays included in this volume, many of which are referred to in this chapter, have been available in other forms.

Bibliography

THE PUBLICATION of Paul Ricoeur's work, which began when he was twenty-three, has, to date, resulted in a complete bibliography of some forty pages. Fortunately for Ricoeur bibliophiles, extensive work has been done by Dirk Vansina (whose 1962 dissertation, *De Filozofie van Paul Ricoeur*, Louvain, was the first written about Ricoeur—my 1964 dissertation was, so far as I know, the second).

The first published compilation, "Bibliographie de Paul Ricoeur," appeared in the *Revue philosophique de Louvain*, vol. LX (August, 1962). And although this bibliography already filled nineteen pages, Vansina later supplemented it with a second bibliography in the *Revue*, vol. LXVI, February, 1968. The supplement picked up missing entries dating back to 1936 and continued the bibliography up to the end of 1967. I have been able to find very few references overlooked by Vansina, and most of those I have found are very minor.

Upon close examination, the complete Ricoeur bibliography turns out to contain numerous multiple entries for single articles published in different magazines and in different translations, reviews, commentaries, prefaces, and the like. Most of these items would be of little interest save to the most devoted researchers. I would point, however, to one strain of publications not listed below which is worthy of serious examination. Ricoeur has been associated with a leftist Christian group, under the influence of Emmanuel Mounier, which publishes *Esprit*. In *Esprit*, and also in *Christianisme social* and *Foi-Education*, Ricoeur has written a large number of commentaries, articles, and

[183]

discussions of contemporary social issues. These articles include studies not only of the problem of the state of Christianity in the present world, but also of the role of Marxism, university reform, political terror, and a wide variety of topics relevant for social philosophy. Ricoeur's methodologically oriented and academic philosophy is balanced by concerns about the contemporary world.

For those not able to go to France to scout out the obscure references, the important writings are almost entirely available in book form. *Histoire et vérité*, first published in 1955 and then republished in 1964 with extensive additions, contains a variety of the most important studies up to the sixties. Ricoeur's most important Husserl scholarship has now appeared in English in *Husserl: An Analysis of His Phenomenology*, published in the Northwestern University Studies in Phenomenology and Existential Philosophy. And very recently almost all the important work on hermeneutics and language has appeared in the 1969 publication of 486 pages of articles, *Le Conflit des interprétations*. Thus Part I of the bibliography would be sufficient for those primarily interested in the philosophical work of Ricoeur. I list the published books and their extant English translations, but I do not list as separate entries those articles contained in the collections. Because *Le Conflit* appeared after the completion of my manuscript, chapter footnotes often refer to articles now included in *Le Conflit*.

In Part II of the bibliography I list a series of selected publications. Section A includes a sample representation of early miscellaneous materials not included in any of the published collections. Section B contains articles bearing on the questions of language and hermeneutics that are not included in the newly published *Le Conflit des interprétations*. In some cases these entries do not appear in the Vansina bibliography, either because they were published after 1967 or because they were missed. It will be evident that the number of publications on language and hermeneutics begins to increase in the sixties and continues to grow. Finally, I have listed in Section C English translations of various Ricoeur materials. I cannot claim anything like full coverage in this category, particularly because new translations continue to appear regularly. Note that the earlier translations were largely those concerned with religious and theological matters—the first audience that Ricoeur had in the English-speaking world was largely concerned with theology.

Part III of the bibliography lists dissertations in English and secondary articles about Ricoeur in both French and English.

PART I: BOOKS

Karl Jaspers et la philosophie de l'existence. Paris: Editions du Seuil, 1947. With Mikel Dufrenne.
Gabriel Marcel et Karl Jaspers. Philosophie du mystère et philosophie du paradoxe. Paris: Temps Present, 1948.
Idées directrices pour une phénoménologie. Paris: Gallimard, 1950. Translation of E. Husserl, *Ideen zu einer reinen Phänomenologie und phänomenologischen Philosophie*, with commentary by Ricoeur.
Philosophie de la volonté. I: Le Volontaire et l'involontaire. Paris: Aubier, 1950. (English translation by Erazim Kohák. *Freedom and Nature: The Voluntary and the Involuntary.* Evanston: Ill.: Northwestern University Press, 1966.)
Histoire et vérité. Paris: Editions du Seuil, 1955. Revised with added articles, Paris: Editions du Seuil, 1964. (English translation by Charles Kelbley. *History and Truth.* Evanston, Ill.: Northwestern University Press, 1965.)
Philosophie de la volonté. Finitude et culpabilité. I: L'Homme faillible. Paris: Aubier, 1960. (English translation by Charles Kelbley. *Fallible Man.* Chicago: Henry Regnery, 1965.) II: *La Symbolique du mal.* Paris: Aubier, 1960. (English translation by Emerson Buchanan. *The Symbolism of Evil.* New York: Harper & Row, 1967.)
De L'interprétation. Essai sur Freud. Paris: Editions du Seuil, 1965. (English translation by Denis Savage. *Freud and Philosophy: An Essay on Interpretation.* New Haven, Conn.: Yale University Press, 1970.)
Husserl: An Analysis of His Phenomenology. Translated by Edward G. Ballard and Lester E. Embree. Evanston, Ill.: Northwestern University Press, 1967. A compilation of Ricoeur's important articles on Husserl and phenomenology.
Entretiens, Paul Ricoeur et Gabriel Marcel. Paris: Aubier-Montaigne, 1968. Merely an interview of Marcel conducted by his best-known student, Paul Ricoeur.
Le Conflit des interprétations. Essais d'herméneutique. Paris: Editions de Seuil, 1969.

Part ii: Articles

A. Early and Miscellaneous Articles

"Responsabilité de la pensée." *Etre*, I, no. 1 (1936–37), 4–5.
"Le Risque." *Etre*, I, no. 2 (1936–37), 9–11.
"Socialisme et christianisme." *Etre*, I, no. 4 (1936–37), 3–4.
"Necessité de Karl Marx." *Etre*, II, no. 5 (1936–37), 3–4.
"L'Attention. Etude phénoménologique de l'attention et ses connexions philosophiques." *Bulletin du cercle philosophique de l'ouest*, IV (January–March, 1940), 1–28.
"Le Renouvellement du problème de la philosophie chrétienne par les philosophies de l'existence." In *Le Problème de la philosophie chrétienne*, pp. 43–67. Paris: P.U.F., 1949.
"La Question de l'humanisme chrétien." *Foi et vie*, IL (1951), 323–30.
"Sur la phénoménologie." *Esprit*, XXI (December, 1953), 821–29.
"Sympathie et respect: Phénoménologie et éthique de la seconde personne." *Revue de métaphysique et de morale*, LIX (1954), 380–97.
"La Parole est mon royaume." *Esprit*, XXIII (February, 1955), 192–205.
"Negativité et affirmation originaire." In *Aspects de la dialectique*, pp. 101–24. Paris: Desclée de Brouwer, 1956.
"Renouveau de l'ontologie." In *Encyclopedie française*, vol. XIX, secs. 16–15 to 18–3. Paris: Larousse, 1957.
"Place de l'oeuvre d'art dans notre culture." *Foi-Education*, XXVII (January–March, 1957), 5–11.
"Le Sentiment." In *Edmund Husserl 1859–1959*, *Phenomenologica* IV, pp. 260–74. The Hague: Martinus Nijhoff, 1959.
"Du marxisme au communisme contemporain." *Christianisme social*, LXVII (1959), 151–59.
"La Place des 'humanités' dans la civilisation industrielle." *Paris-Lettres*, vol. III (August–October, 1959).
"La Sexualité: La Merveille, l'errance, l'énigme." *Esprit*, XXVIII (November, 1960), 1665–67.
"L'Humanité de l'homme." *Studium generale*, XV (1962), 309–23.
"Freud et le mouvement de la culture moderne." In *Traité de psychoanalyse*, edited by S. Nacht. Paris: P.U.F., 1965.

"La Philosophie: Sens et limites." In *Cahiers paraboles*. Weekend de philosophie (February, 1965).
"Le Conscient et l'inconscient." In *L'Inconscient*, pp. 409–22. Bibliothèque Neuro-Psychiatrique de Langue Française. Paris: Desclée de Brouwer, 1966.
"La Recherche philosophique peut-elle s'achever?" *Orientations*, special number (1966), pp. 31–44.
"La Philosophie à l'âge des sciences humaines." *Cahiers de philosophie*, no. 1 (1966), pp. 93–99.

B. *Entries concerning Language and Hermeneutics*

"The Image of God and the Epic of Man." Translated by George Gringas. *Cross Currents*, XI (Winter, 1961), pp. 38–49.
"The Hermeneutics of Symbols and Philosophical Reflection." Translated by Denis Savage. *International Philosophical Quarterly*, II, no. 2 (May, 1962), 191–218.
"Introduction au problème des signes et du langage." *Cahiers de philosophie*, no. 8 (1962–63), pp. 1–76.
"Symbolique et temporalité." *Archivio de filosofia*, XXXIII, nos. 1–2 (1963), 5–41.
"Le Conflit des herméneutiques: Epistemologie des interprétations." *Cahiers internationaux de symbolisme*, I, no. 1 (1963), 152–84.
"Réponses" (to Lévi-Strauss, etc.). *Esprit*, XXXI (November, 1963), 628–53.
"Le Symbole et le mythe." *Le Semeur*, LXI, no. 2 (1963), 47–53.
"Le Symbolisme et l'explication structurale." *Cahiers internationaux de symbolisme*, II, no. 4 (1964), 81–96.
"Le Langage de la foi." *Bulletin du centre protestant d'études*, XVI, nos. 4–5 (1964), 17–31.
"Les Problèmes du langage." *Cahiers de philosophie*, nos. 2–3 (1966), pp. 27–41.
"Problèmes du langage, Cours de M. Ricoeur." *Cahiers de philosophie*, no. 4 (1966), pp. 65–73.
"Violence et langage." *Recherches et debats: La Violence*, XVI, no. 59 (1967), 86–94.
"Demythologization et herméneutique." *Centre Européen*, Université de Nancy, Dif. 81, no. 30 (1967).
"Husserl and Wittgenstein on Language." In *Phenomenology and Existentialism*, edited by E. N. Lee and M. Mandelbaum,

188 / BIBLIOGRAPHY

pp. 207–17. Baltimore, Md.: Johns Hopkins University Press, 1967.
"New Developments in Phenomenology in France: The Phenomenology of Language." Translated by P. G. Goodman. *Social Research*, XXXIV, no. 1 (Spring, 1967), 1–30.
"Foi et langage, Bultmann-Ebeling." *Foi-Education*, XXXVII, no. 81 (October–December, 1967), 1–56.
"The Critique of Subjectivity and Cogito in the Philosophy of Heidegger." In *Heidegger and the Quest for Truth*, edited by M. Frings, pp. 62–75. Chicago: Quadrangle Press, 1968.
"Structure, Word, Event." Translated by Robert D. Sweeny. *Philosophy Today*, XII, nos. 2–4 (Summer, 1968).
"The Father Image: From Phantasy to Symbol." *Criterion*, VIII, no. 1 (Autumn, 1968–69), 1–11.
"Religion, Atheism and Faith: I. On Accusation, II. On Consolation." In *The Religious Significance of Atheism*. Vol. XVIII, pp. 57–98. Bampton Lectures. New York: Columbia University Press, 1969.

C. *Various English Translations*

"Christianity and the Meaning of History: Progress, Ambiguity, Hope." *The Journal of Religion*, XXI (1952), 242–53.
"Mass and Person" (with J. M. Domenach). *Cross Currents*, II (Winter, 1952), 59–66.
"Sartre's Lucifer and the Lord." *Yale French Studies*, no. 14 (1954–55), pp. 85–93.
"French Protestantism Today." *The Christian Century*, LXXII (1955), 1236–38.
"Associate and Neighbor." In *Love of Our Neighbor*, no. 8, pp. 149–61. London: Blackfriars Publications, 1955.
"Morality without Sin or Sin without Moralism." *Cross Currents*, V (Fall, 1955), 339–52.
"The Relation of Jasper's Philosophy to Religion." In *The Philosophy of Karl Jaspers*, edited by P. Schilpp, pp. 611–42. Library of Living Philosophers, 1957.
"Faith and Culture." *The Student World*, L (1957), 246–51.
"Ye Are the Salt of the Earth." *The Ecumenical Review*, X (1958), 264–76.
"Faith and Action." *Criterion*, vol. III (Summer, 1963).
"The Dimensions of Sexuality." *Cross Currents*, XIV (1964), 133–41.

"The Atheism of Freudian Psychoanalysis." *Concilium,* II, no. 16 (1966), 59–72.

"A Conversation." *The Bulletin of Philosophy,* I, no. 1 (January, 1966), 1–7.

"Philosophy of Will and Action." In *The Second Lexington Conference on Pure and Applied Phenomenology,* pp. 7–33. Pittsburgh: Duquesne University Press, 1967.

"The Unity of the Voluntary and the Involuntary as a Limiting Idea." In *Readings in Existential Phenomenology,* edited by N. Lawrence and D. O'Connor, pp. 93–112. Englewood Cliffs, N. J.: Prentice-Hall, 1967.

"The Antinomy of Human Reality and the Problem of Philosophical Anthropology." In *Readings in Existential Phenomenology,* edited by N. Lawrence and D. O'Connor, pp. 390–402. Englewood Cliffs, N. J.: Prentice-Hall, 1967.

PART III: SECONDARY SOURCES

A. *Dissertations in English*

Ihde, Don. "Paul Ricoeur's Phenomenological Methodology and Philosophical Anthropology." Ph.D. dissertation, Boston University, 1964.

Rasmussen, David M. "A Correlation Between Religious Language and an Understanding of Man: A Constructive Interpretation of the Thought of Paul Ricoeur." Ph.D. dissertation, University of Chicago, 1968.

Reagan, Charles E. "Freedom and Determinism: A Critical Study of Certain Aspects of this problem in the Light of the Philosophy of Paul Ricoeur." Ph.D. dissertation, University of Kansas, 1967.

Stewart, David. "Paul Ricoeur's Phenomenology of Evil." Ph.D. dissertation, Rice University, 1965.

B. *Selected Articles in French and English*

Czarneck, J. "L'Histoire et la vérité selon Paul Ricoeur." *Foi et vie,* LIII (1955), 548–55.

de Waelhens, A. "Pensée mythique et philosophie du mal," *Revue philosophique de Louvain,* LIX (1961), 171–72.

———. "La Force du langage et le langage de la force." *Revue philosophique de Louvain,* (LXIII) 1965, 591–612.

Hartmann, K. "Phenomenology, Ontology, and Metaphysics."
The Review of Metaphysics, XXII, no. 1 (September, 1968),
85–112.

Ihde, D. "Rationality and Myth." *The Journal of Thought,* II,
no. 1 (January, 1967), 10–18.

———. "The Secular City and the Existentialists." *The An-
dover Newton Quarterly,* VII, no. 4 (March, 1967), 188–89.

———. "Some Parallels between Analysis and Phenomenology." *Philosophy and Phenomenological Research,* XXVII,
no. 4 (June, 1967), 577–86.

———. "From Phénoménology to Hermeneutic," *The Journal
of Existentialism,* VII, no. 30 (Winter, 1967–68), 111–32.

Jacob, A. "Paul Ricoeur, un philosophie pratique d'inspiration
phénoménologique." *Critique,* V (1961), 360–71.

Rasmussen, D. "Ricoeur: The Anthropological Necessity of a
Special Language." *Continuum,* VII, no. 1 (Winter–Spring,
1969), 120–30.

———. "Myth, Structure and Interpretation." In *The Origin
of Cosmos and Man,* edited by M. Dhavenony. Rome: Grego-
rian University Press, 1969.

Sarano, J. "La Réciprocité du pâtie et de l'agis." *Etudes Philosophie,* X (1955), 726–29.

Stewart, D. "Paul Ricoeur and the Phenomenological Movement." *Philosophy Today* (Winter, 1968), pp. 227–35.

———. "Paul Ricoeur's Phenomenology of Evil." *International Philosophical Quarterly,* IX, no. 4 (December, 1969),
572–89.

Tilliette, X. "Réflexion et symbole: L'Enterprise philosophique
de Paul Ricoeur." *Archives philosophie,* XXIV (1961), 574–
88.

Vansina, D. "Equisse, orientation et signification de l'enterprise
philosophique de Paul Ricoeur." *Revue de métaphysique et
de morale,* LXIX (1964), 179–208.

Index